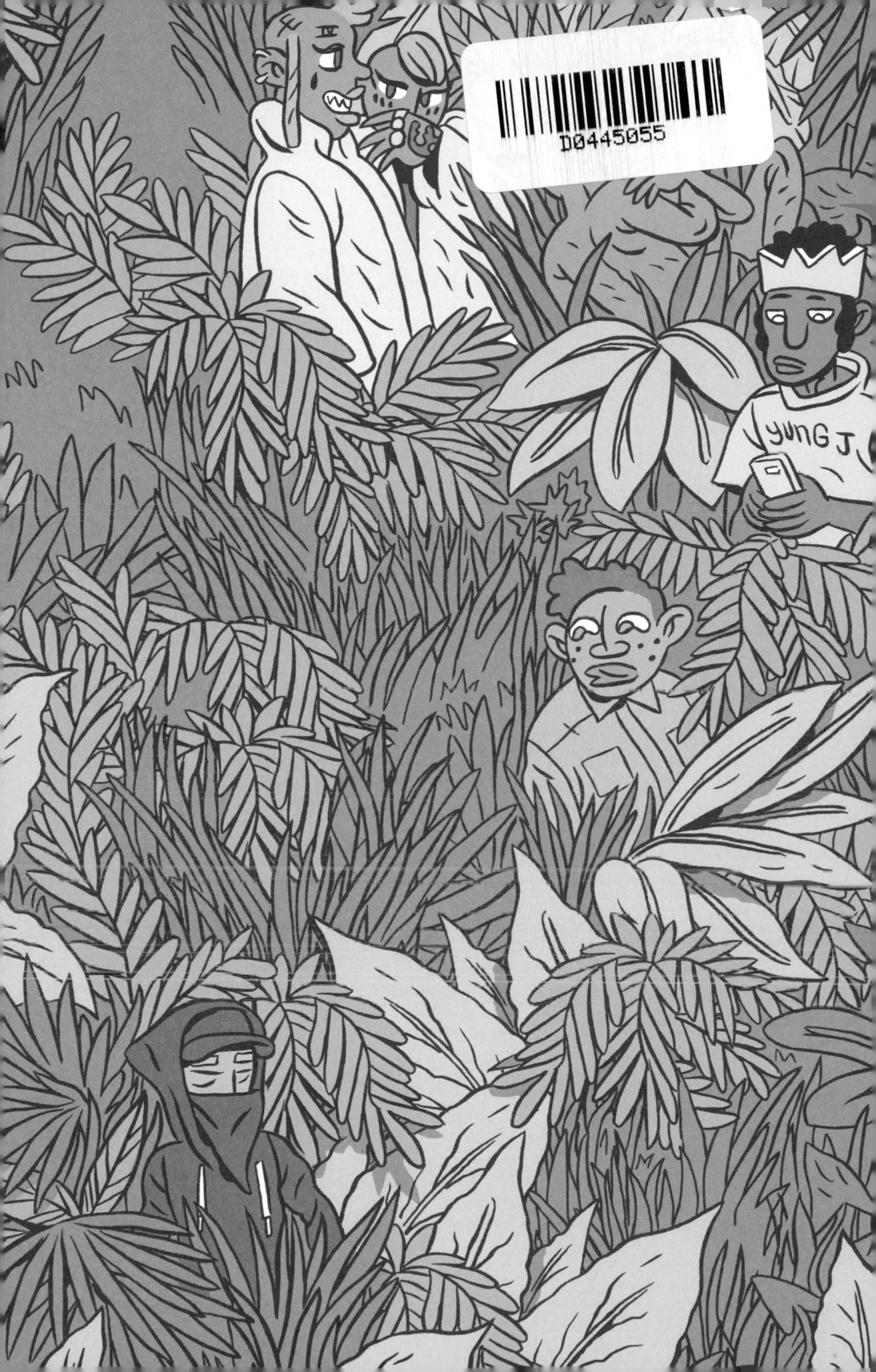
YUNG J

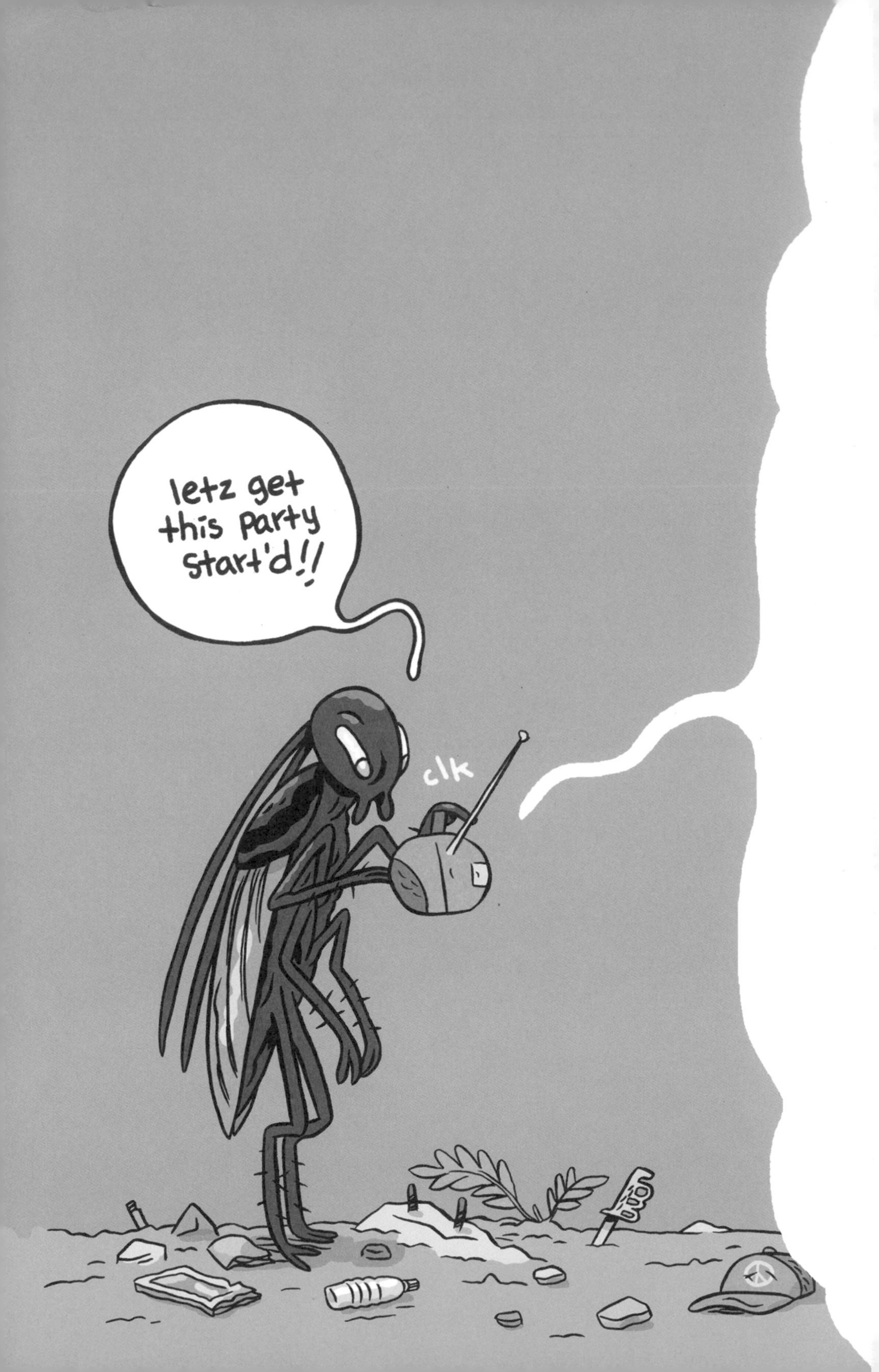
letz get this Party start'd!!
clk

Your Black Friend

and Other Strangers

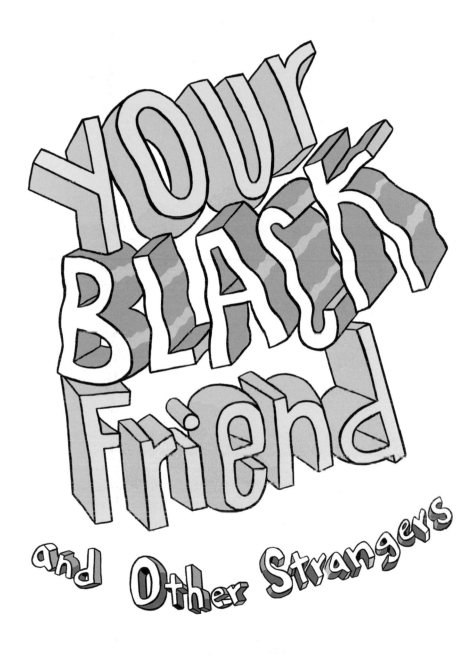

Silver Sprocket
1057 Valencia St, San Francisco, CA 94110, USA
www.silversprocket.net

Second Printing, Fall 2018

ISBN- 978-1-945509-20-9

Printed in Canada

As way of... INTRODUCTION

yvh Xvh

Like most people I feel introductions in comics serve as a series of bland glyphs to be stalled at on your way to pretty pretty pictures. Maybe I'm a troglodyte, but I'm a published troglodyte, so I dunno if that speaks to my low standards or the low standards of publishing as a whole?

Anyway, I know you picked this book up thinking you were gonna read a whole lot of wokeness from a mad inspired and inspiring melaninated revolutionary King, maybe I'd make an Angela Davis reference, talk about Egyptian hieroglyphs as some sort of jumping off point for black comics, and evoke and image of Dwayne McDuffie in a Nemes headdress and ankh. All very hotepy and therefore revisionist. I'm not really that type of SJW. While I can be credited for making all types of comics on microaggressions, gentrification, police brutality, misogyny, and sundry other types of systematic oppressions, I'm conscious of a pronounced self-satisfied mentality that people (myself included) approach these types of "political" works with. We're in an age of political edifice on the streets (and the sheets?), and because our politics fail to be dangerous to our oppressors, so does our expectations of art.

The spirit of this collection of comics is more of a reflection on ideas that span the course of four years about how to be dangerous, how to be a failure, and how to laugh in the face of a world that wants to crush us. Most of all this collection is about how to be a funny dangerous failure. And we all fail homies, it's okay. We just have to learn how to fail upward. In the 1860s there was a movement called Russian Nihilism (I'm sure they had a danker name for themselves) that was comprised of students and writers that rejected all authority. They wrote some stuff and had weird hookups, but mostly they tried to kill their King. Since they were students and writers and not assassins, they mostly just got killed. Despite dying left and right, the Russian Nihilists believed that their moment of liberation wasn't in some future utopia but in the act of defiance itself. I think there's a kind of a seemingly sisyphean but useful lesson to learned from them. There are so many periods in history when people have somehow managed to act defiantly despite overwhelming repression, and I think we should consider each of those moments successful utopias. Basically we all need to be Anarchists already, there I said it. Look I know how it sounds, but google it first. Stay off Anarchist News tho, and don't listen to Tiqqunists, they wear too much fleece. It's creepy.

The comic Your Black Friend, which is the first story in this collection, was originally xeroxed off at a copy scam in New Orleans for the Chicago Alternative Arts Expo in 2016. I made the comic while reading Frantz Fanon's Black Skin White Masks with my housemates, including Greg who's another black punk out here trying to be his best self. We recognized a language for the dysphoria we felt in the face of white supremacy in our mostly white punk scene and for the society at large. We felt like Neo seeing the Matrix's code for the first time, but you know, blacker. I made Your Black Friend because I thought it might be a mirror for other black folks feeling the same way and hopefully instructive for white people. Of course you can't plan on how a work will be received and my book about a bummed-out black anarcho-punk turned into something kids read in college classes. Sorry kids, I never meant to make homework. Your Black Friend was named on NPR's top 100 comics list, nominated for an Eisner award, and won a Dinky, Ignatz, and Broken Frontier Award in 2017. All very affirming things that contributed to your boy being able to afford some extra sides at Church's. But, I have to admit to some ambivalence about accolades, because when I reread Your Black Friend the other day, I was as frustrated and upset as I was when I made it. We live in a society that tells us what we do is who we are, and if you're a professional at being an outraged black cartoonist, that's the way they want to keep you. You'll get a check for it and some guest spots at shows and colleges if you're lucky, but it will flatten you out into a caricature of yourself. Don't let them. Don't let success bait you into warping yourself into a commodity. It's not worth it. Again, what I'm basically saying is we all need to drop everything and be Anarchists, I can't stress this enough.

There are a bunch of comics in here that are supposed to turn you into Anarchists. Most were published in other places first. It's Not About you first appeared in Irene #6. Mrsa and Billy (apologies to Mrsa) was first in Felony comics. The Vampire was printed in NOW #3 put out by Fantagraphics. Punklord and Ally I Need is Love was printed in As You Were #4 and #5 respectively. The Last Defenders was printed in Clorofilia #1 published by Kira Mardikes. Various non-fiction political essays like Take Em Down, When Trump Trumps Family, the comic about the ACLU, and Stone Mountain were first published on The Nib website. There are several comics from a series I started self-publishing in 2013 called DAYGLOAYHOLE. These comics won't make total sense to anyone other than a particular group of sweaty punks who know how to claw hammer but won't admit it, but I hope you enjoy them anyway. Goodbye was published by the good people of Silver Sprocket, long may the spider queen reign. And A Pantomime Horse #1 was also something I self-published a long time ago.

In closing I'll say that I hope we all stay dangerous and I'll leave you with the words of theMIND-

> When I was young/ I thought I'd grow up, be a cartoon/
> Used to be Rugrat/ Now I'm black Tommy Pickles/
> Trapped up in the costume/Trying to get out of that
> pardon my reach/But I need to change the channel/
> No eyes should see my battle/ These scenes ain't made
> for children/Lord help me, I've been feeling' grown.

Ben Passmore

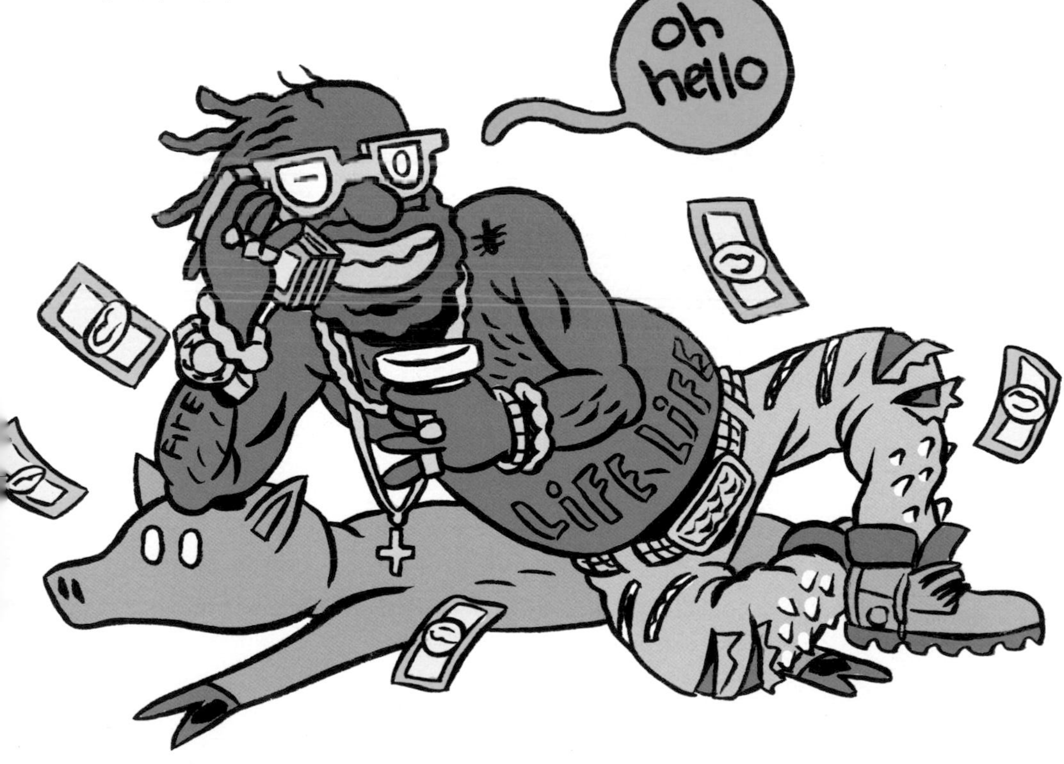
oh hello
FIRE
LIFE LIFE

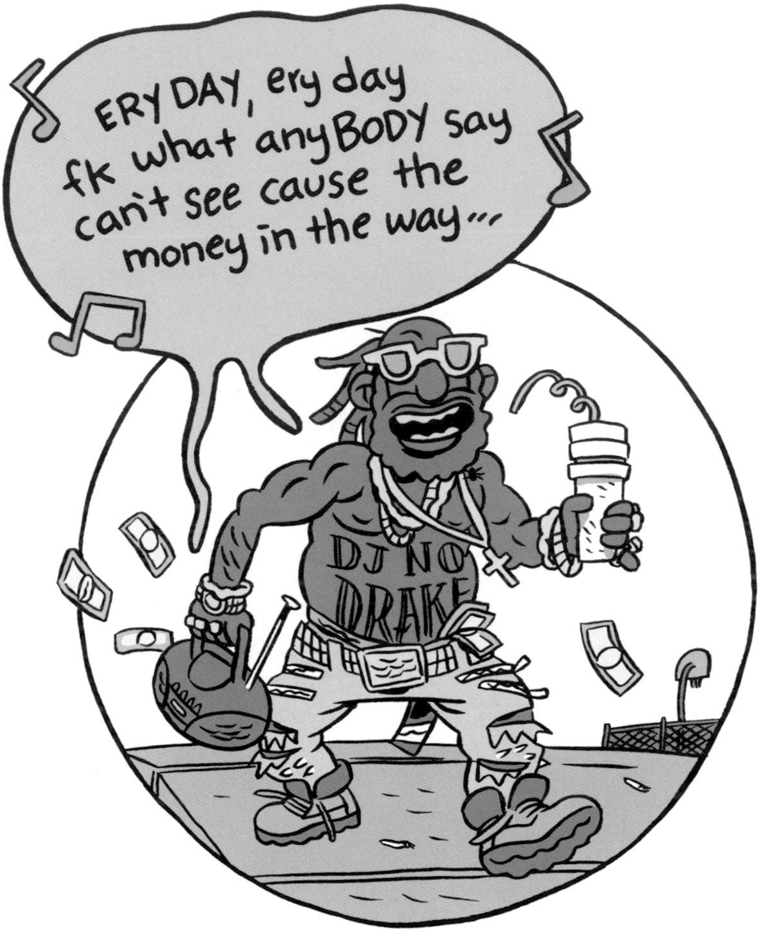
ERY DAY, ery day
fk what anyBODY say
can't see cause the
money in the way...
DJ NO DRAKE

TABLE OF CONTENTS

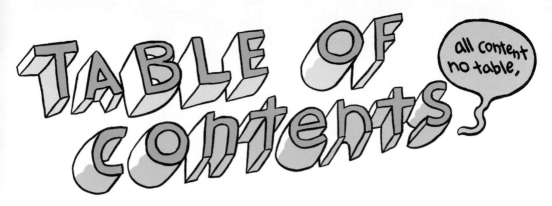

all content no table,

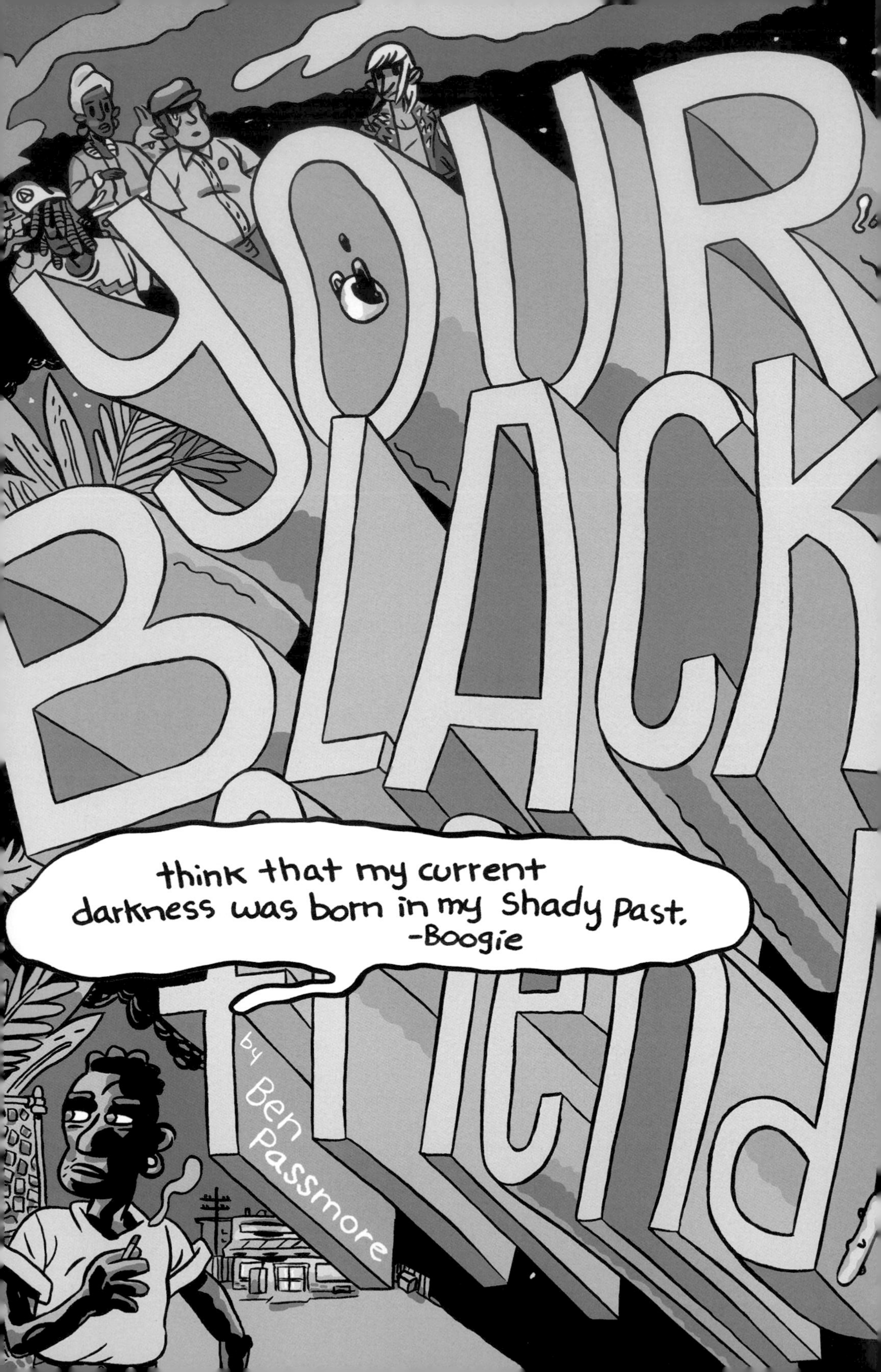
YOUR BLACK
think that my current darkness was born in my Shady past.
-Boogie
by Ben Passmore

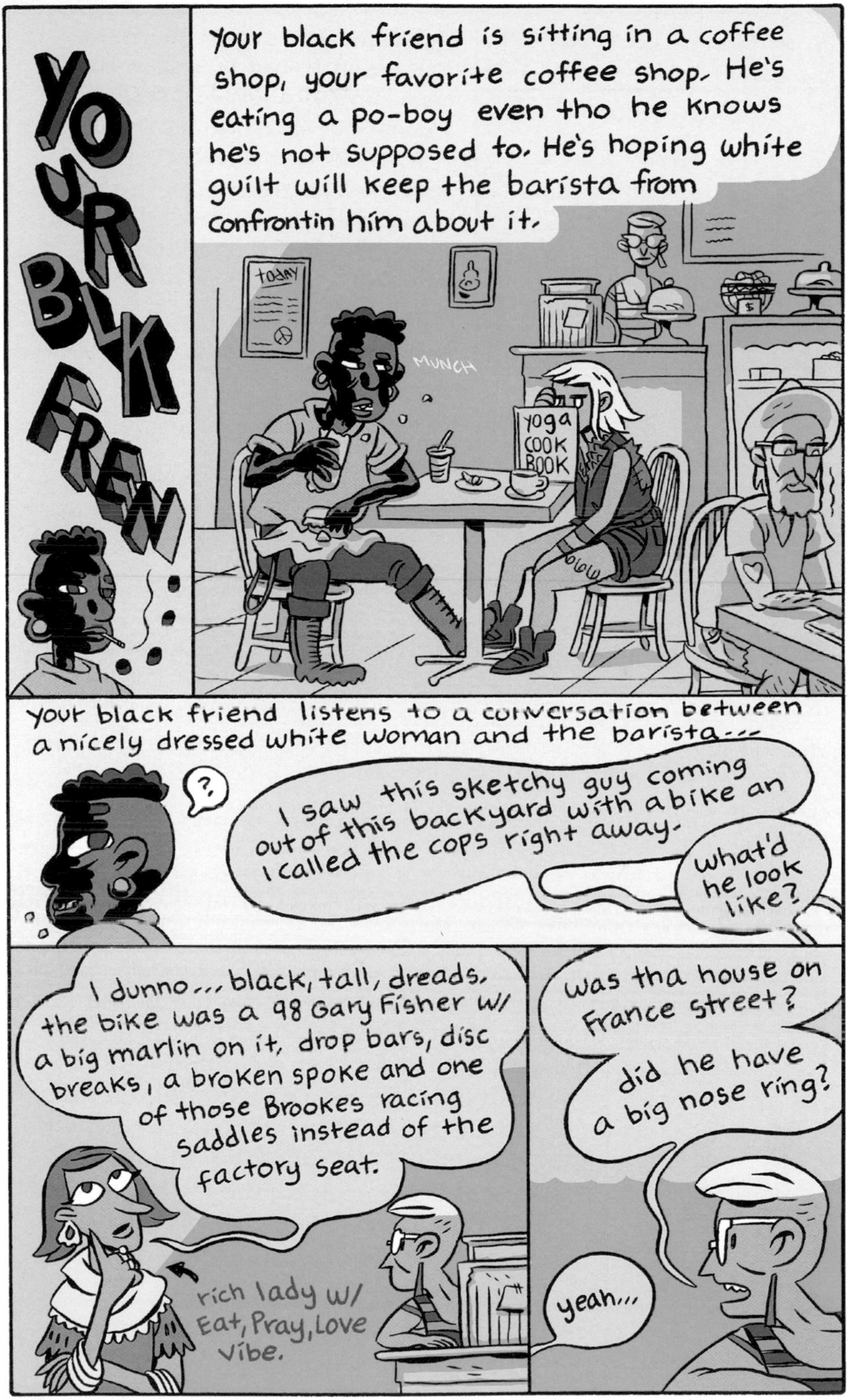
YOUR BLK FREN
Your black friend is sitting in a coffee shop, your favorite coffee shop. He's eating a po-boy even tho he knows he's not supposed to. He's hoping white guilt will keep the barista from confrontin him about it.
today
MUNCH
yoga COOK BOOK
$
your black friend listens to a conversation between a nicely dressed white woman and the barista...
?
I saw this sketchy guy coming out of this backyard with a bike an I called the cops right away.
what'd he look like?
I dunno... black, tall, dreads. the bike was a 98 Gary Fisher w/ a big marlin on it, drop bars, disc breaks, a broken spoke and one of those Brookes racing saddles instead of the factory seat.
rich lady w/ Eat, Pray, Love vibe.
was tha house on France street?
did he have a big nose ring?
yeah...

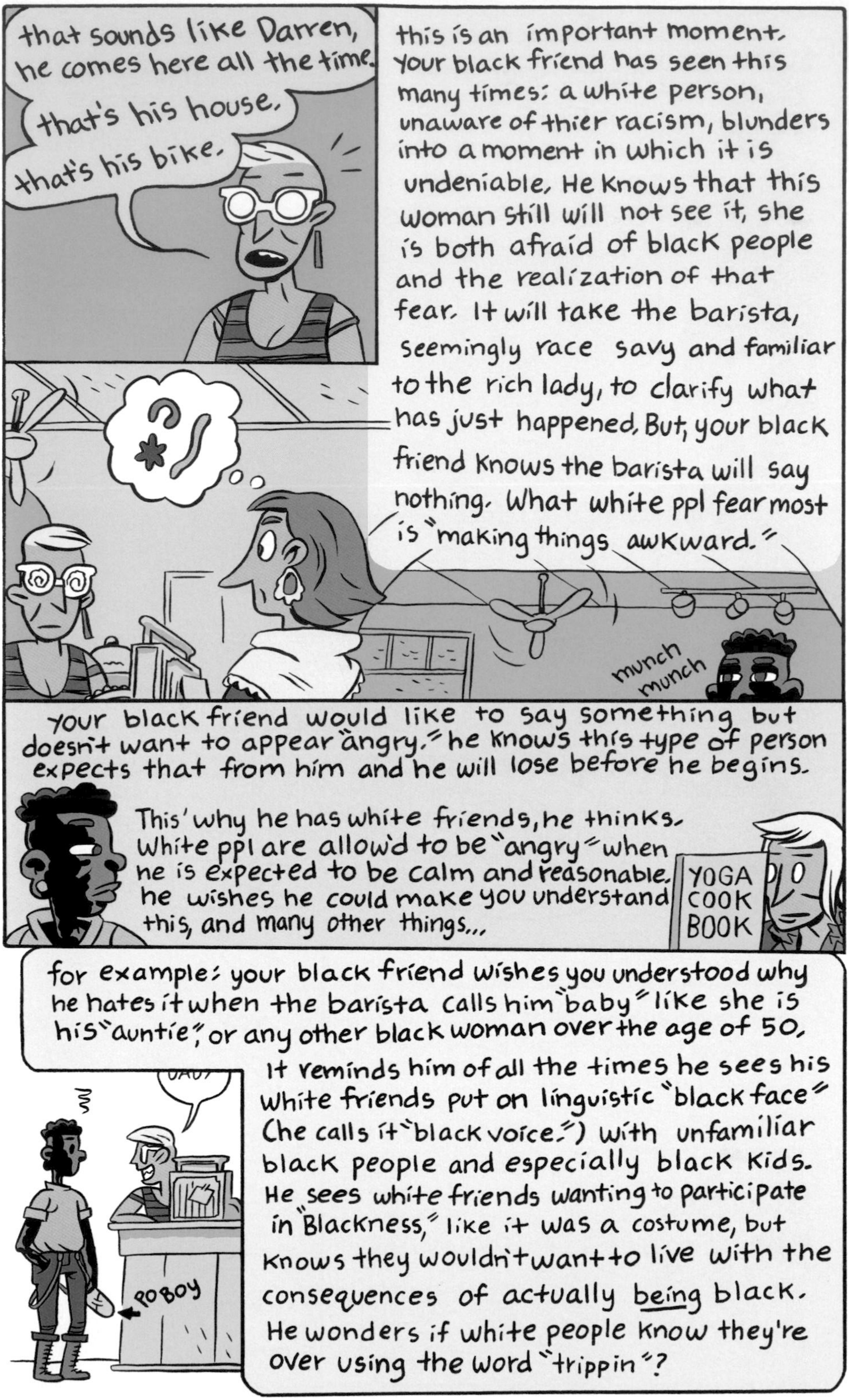
that sounds like Darren, he comes here all the time.
that's his house. that's his bike.
this is an important moment. Your black friend has seen this many times: a white person, unaware of thier racism, blunders into a moment in which it is undeniable. He knows that this woman still will not see it, she is both afraid of black people and the realization of that fear. It will take the barista, seemingly race savy and familiar to the rich lady, to clarify what has just happened. But, your black friend knows the barista will say nothing. What white ppl fear most is "making things awkward."
munch munch
your black friend would like to say something but doesn't want to appear "angry." he knows this type of person expects that from him and he will lose before he begins.
This' why he has white friends, he thinks. White ppl are allow'd to be "angry" when he is expected to be calm and reasonable. he wishes he could make you understand this, and many other things...
YOGA COOK BOOK
for example: your black friend wishes you understood why he hates it when the barista calls him "baby" like she is his "auntie", or any other black woman over the age of 50.
It reminds him of all the times he sees his White friends put on linguistic "black face" (he calls it "black voice.") with unfamiliar black people and especially black kids. He sees white friends wanting to participate in "Blackness," like it was a costume, but knows they wouldn't want to live with the consequences of actually being black. He wonders if white people know they're over using the word "trippin"?
POBOY

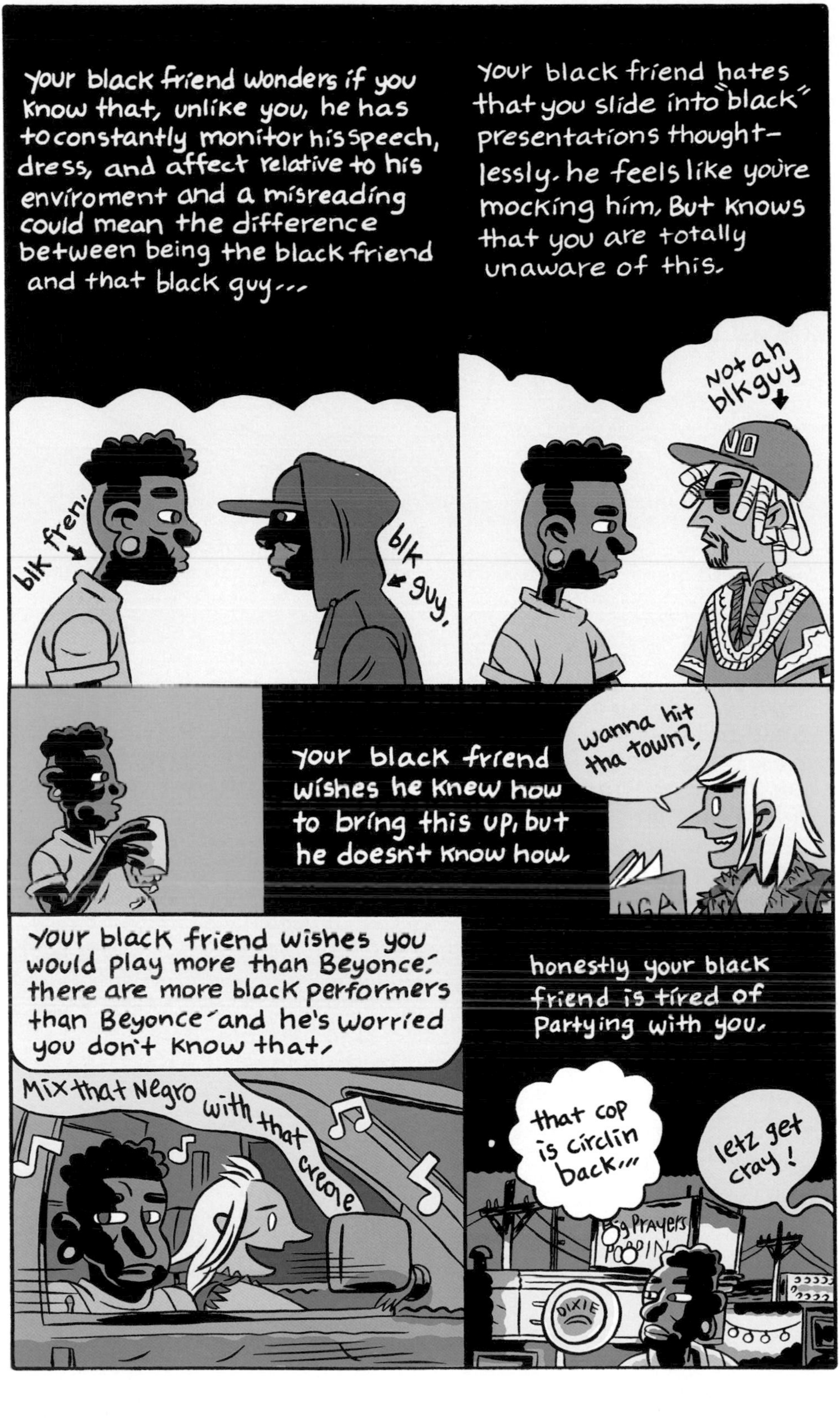
your black friend wonders if you know that, unlike you, he has to constantly monitor his speech, dress, and affect relative to his enviroment and a misreading could mean the difference between being the black friend and that black guy...
your black friend hates that you slide into "black" presentations thoughtlessly. he feels like you're mocking him. But knows that you are totally unaware of this.
blk fren.
blk guy.
Not ah blkguy
your black friend wishes he knew how to bring this up, but he doesn't know how.
wanna hit tha town?
your black friend wishes you would play more than Beyoncé. there are more black performers than Beyoncé and he's worried you don't know that.
Mix that Negro with that creole
honestly your black friend is tired of partying with you.
that cop is circlin back...
letz get cray!
Big Prayers
DIXIE

Your black friend doesn't really like your white friends, they wear dashikis and express their undying enthusiasm for the "Black Lives Matter Movement." Your black friend thinks wannabe Politicans hijacked the BLM, but your white friends ignore him. Your white friends are really bummed-out by negativity.

Irish ar black.

I do a lot of civil rights work?

hat goth

you seem really tense, wuts your sign?

ec nai

man, you're real street smart!

ugg

Your white friends compliment your black friends lips, skin and hair. He gets shit from his own black friends about his messy hair. He knows that your white friends would love that anecdote, it would seem like secret information to them.

fluffy!

oooh sexy.

Your white friends recommend a lot of black authors to your black friend and he's starting to feel like they're trying to "out black" him.

you know Amari Baraka?

I...

how bout Mummia Abu Jamal?

Bell HOOKS?

5

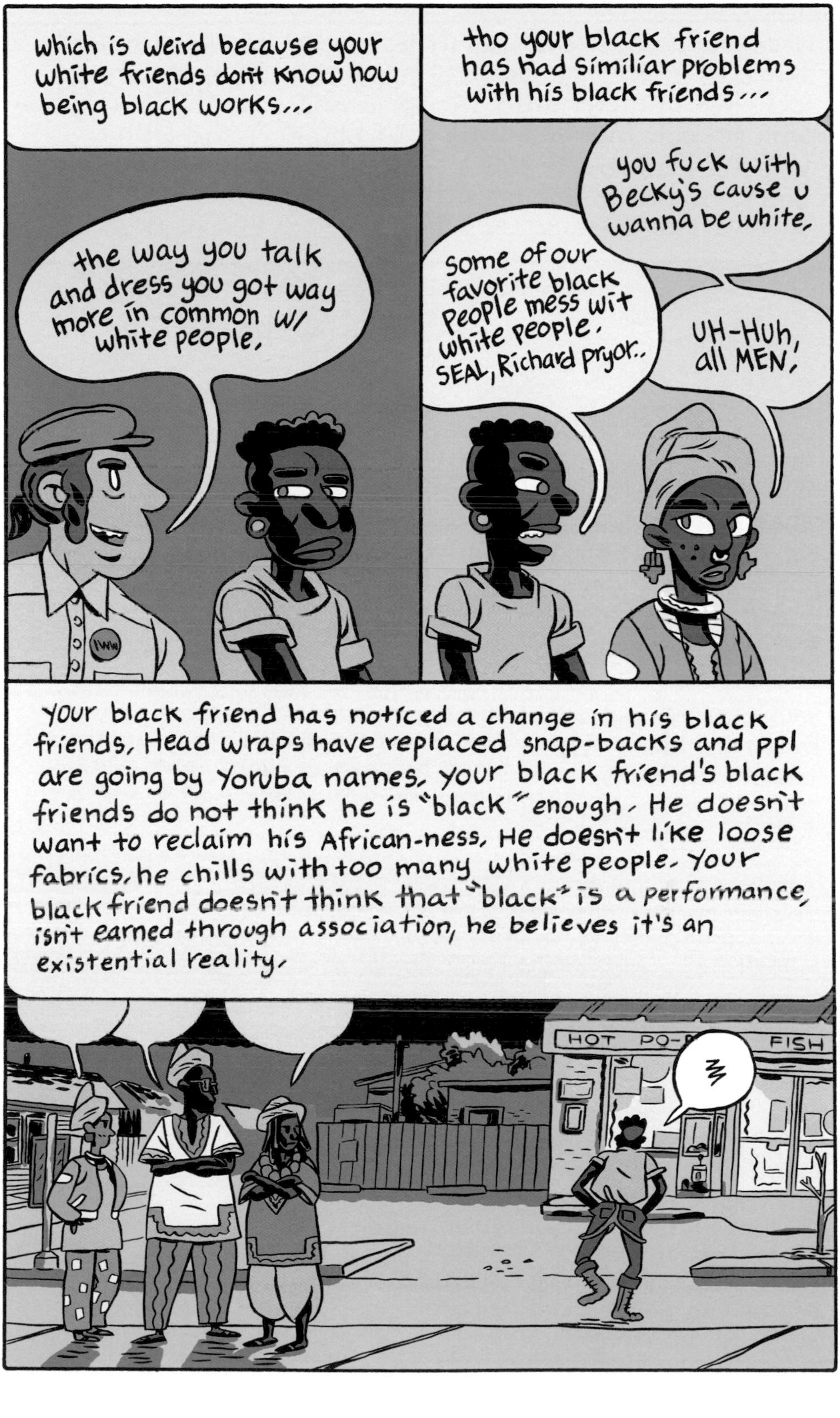
which is weird because your white friends don't know how being black works...
tho your black friend has had similiar problems with his black friends...
the way you talk and dress you got way more in common w/ white people,
you fuck with Becky's cause u wanna be white,
some of our favorite black people mess wit white people. SEAL, Richard pryor..
UH-HUh, all MEN,
IWW
Your black friend has noticed a change in his black friends, Head wraps have replaced snap-backs and ppl are going by Yoruba names, your black friend's black friends do not think he is "black" enough. He doesn't want to reclaim his African-ness, He doesn't like loose fabrics, he chills with too many white people. Your black friend doesn't think that "black" is a performance, isn't earned through association, he believes it's an existential reality,
HOT PO-P FISH

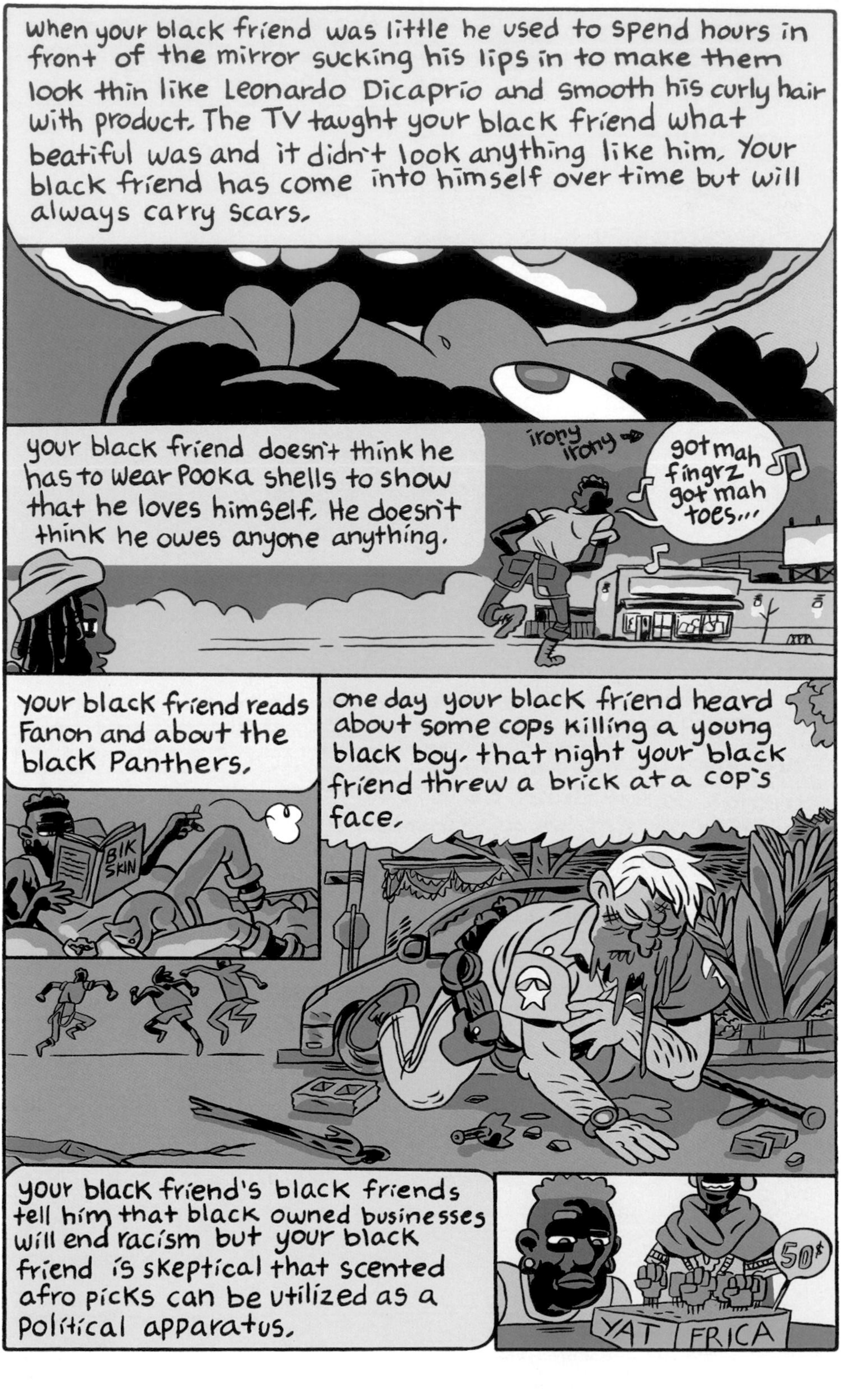
when your black friend was little he used to spend hours in front of the mirror sucking his lips in to make them look thin like Leonardo Dicaprio and smooth his curly hair with product. The TV taught your black friend what beatiful was and it didn't look anything like him. Your black friend has come into himself over time but will always carry scars.
your black friend doesn't think he has to wear Pooka shells to show that he loves himself. He doesn't think he owes anyone anything.
irony irony
got mah fingrz got mah toes...
your black friend reads Fanon and about the black Panthers.
BLK SKIN
one day your black friend heard about some cops killing a young black boy. that night your black friend threw a brick at a cop's face.
your black friend's black friends tell him that black owned businesses will end racism but your black friend is skeptical that scented afro picks can be utilized as a political apparatus.
50¢
YAT FRICA

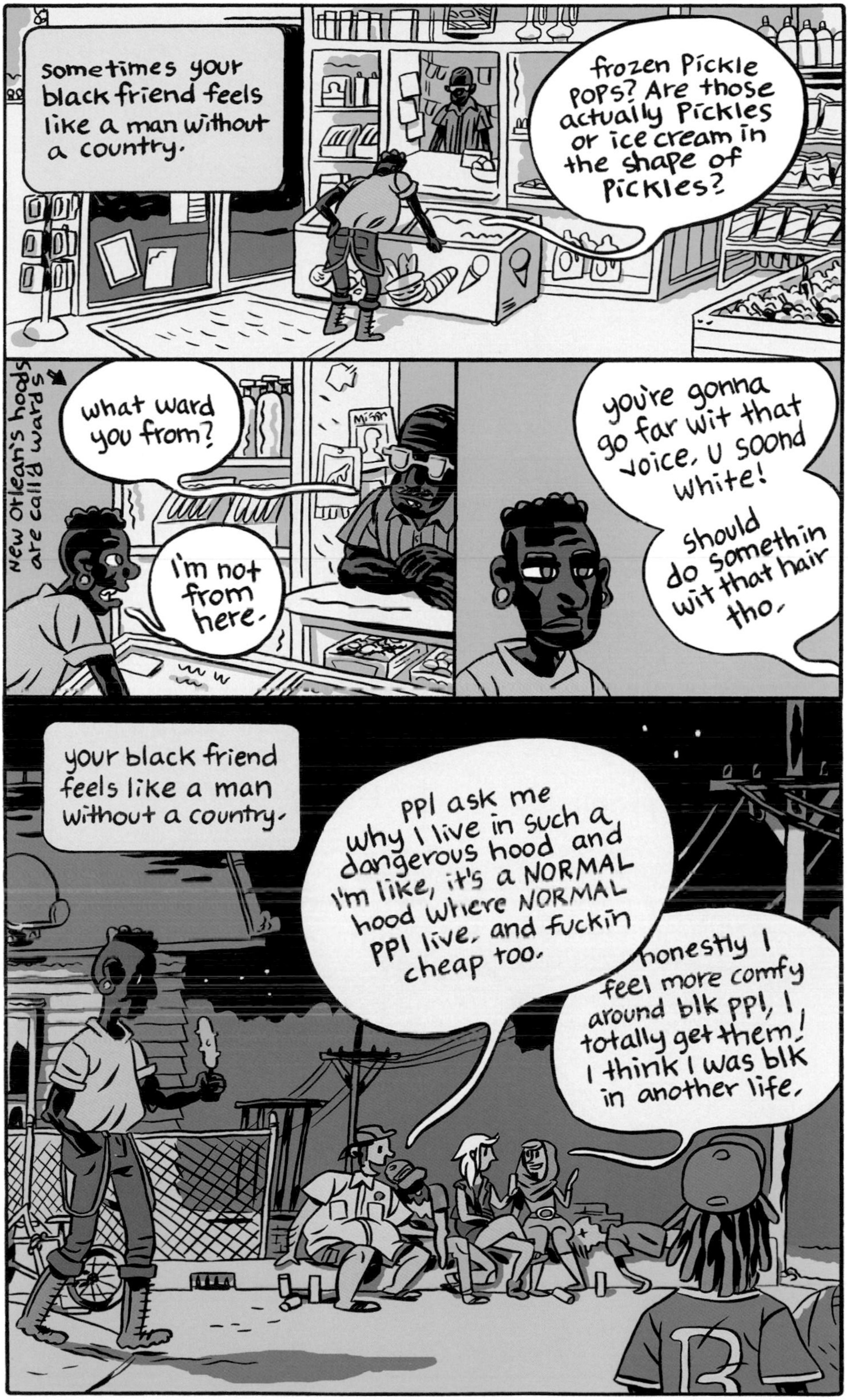
sometimes your black friend feels like a man without a country.
frozen Pickle POPS? Are those actually Pickles or ice cream in the shape of Pickles?
New Orlean's hoods are call'd wards
what ward you from?
I'm not from here.
you're gonna go far wit that voice. U soond white!
should do somethin wit that hair tho.
your black friend feels like a man without a country.
PPl ask me why I live in such a dangerous hood and I'm like, it's a NORMAL hood where NORMAL PPl live, and fuckin cheap too.
honestly I feel more comfy around blk PPl, I totally get them! I think I was blk in another life.

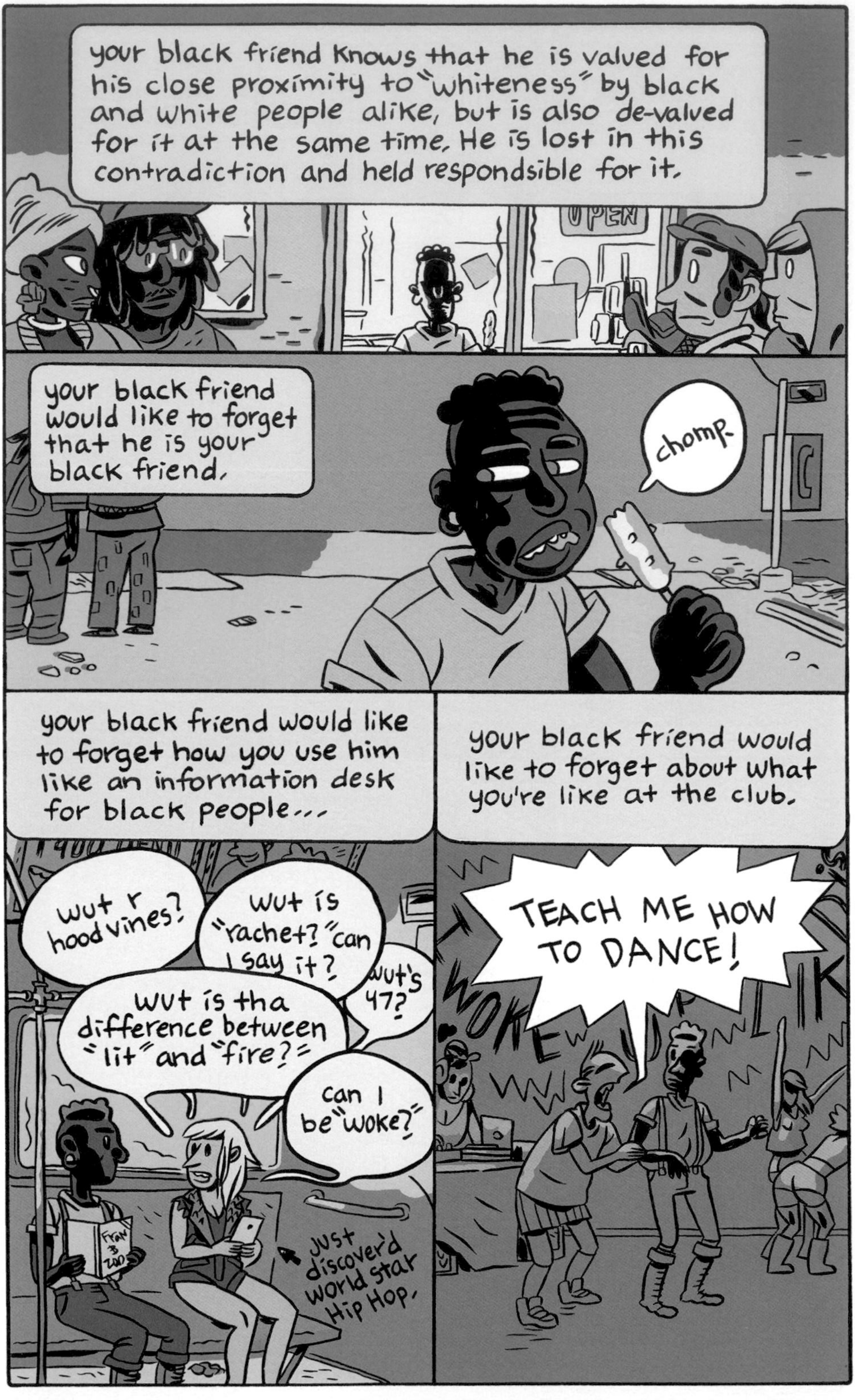
your black friend knows that he is valued for his close proximity to "whiteness" by black and white people alike, but is also de-valued for it at the same time. He is lost in this contradiction and held respondsible for it.
OPEN
your black friend would like to forget that he is your black friend.
chomp.
your black friend would like to forget how you use him like an information desk for black people...
wut r hood vines?
wut is "rachet?" can I say it?
wut's 47?
wut is tha difference between "lit" and "fire?"
can I be "woke?"
Fran & Zoo
just discover'd world star Hip Hop.
your black friend would like to forget about what you're like at the club.
TEACH ME HOW TO DANCE!

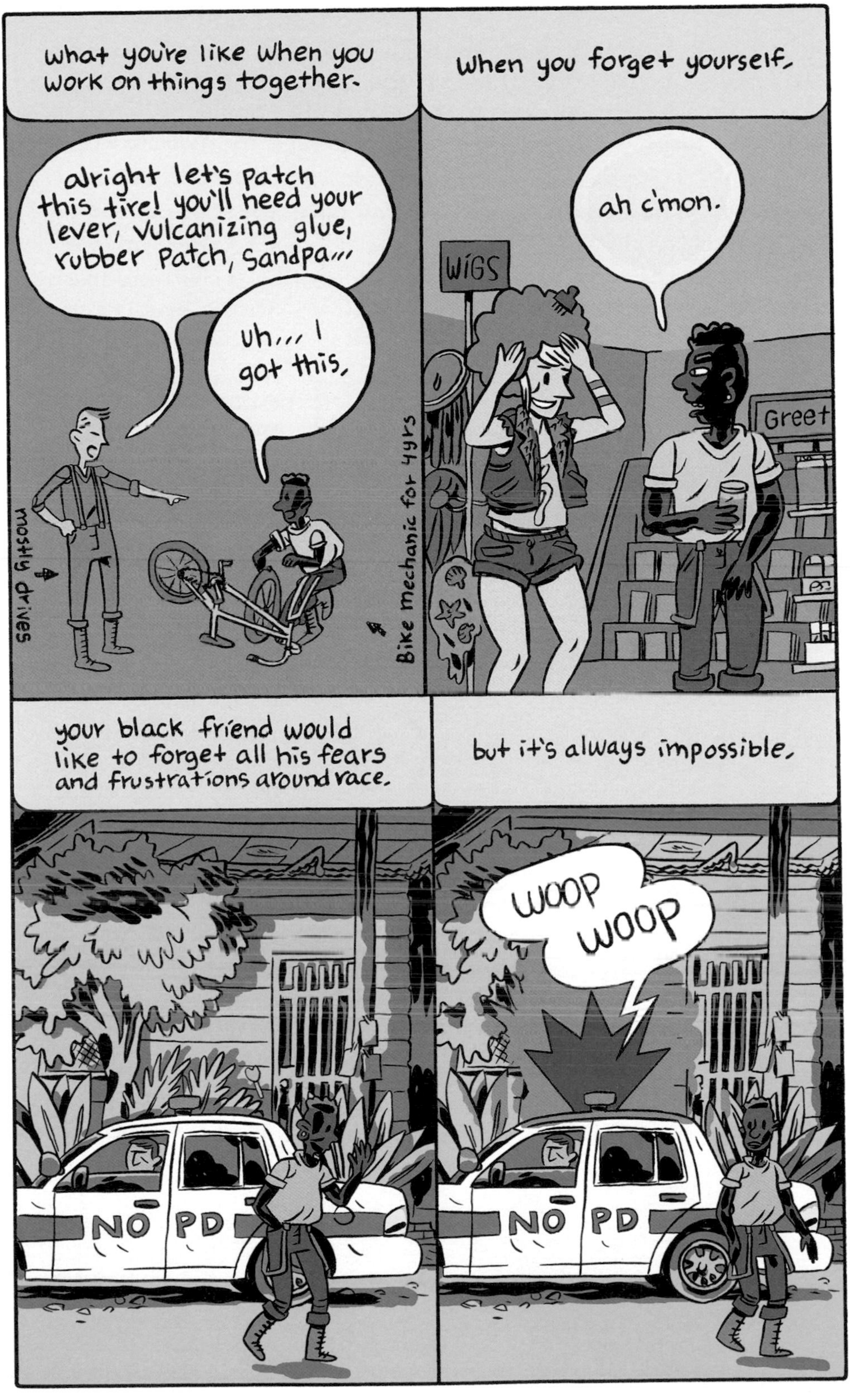
what you're like when you work on things together.
alright let's patch this tire! you'll need your lever, vulcanizing glue, rubber patch, sandpa...
uh... I got this.
mostly drives
Bike mechanic for 4yrs
when you forget yourself.
ah c'mon.
WIGS
Greet
your black friend would like to forget all his fears and frustrations around race.
NO PD
but it's always impossible.
WOOP WOOP
NO PD

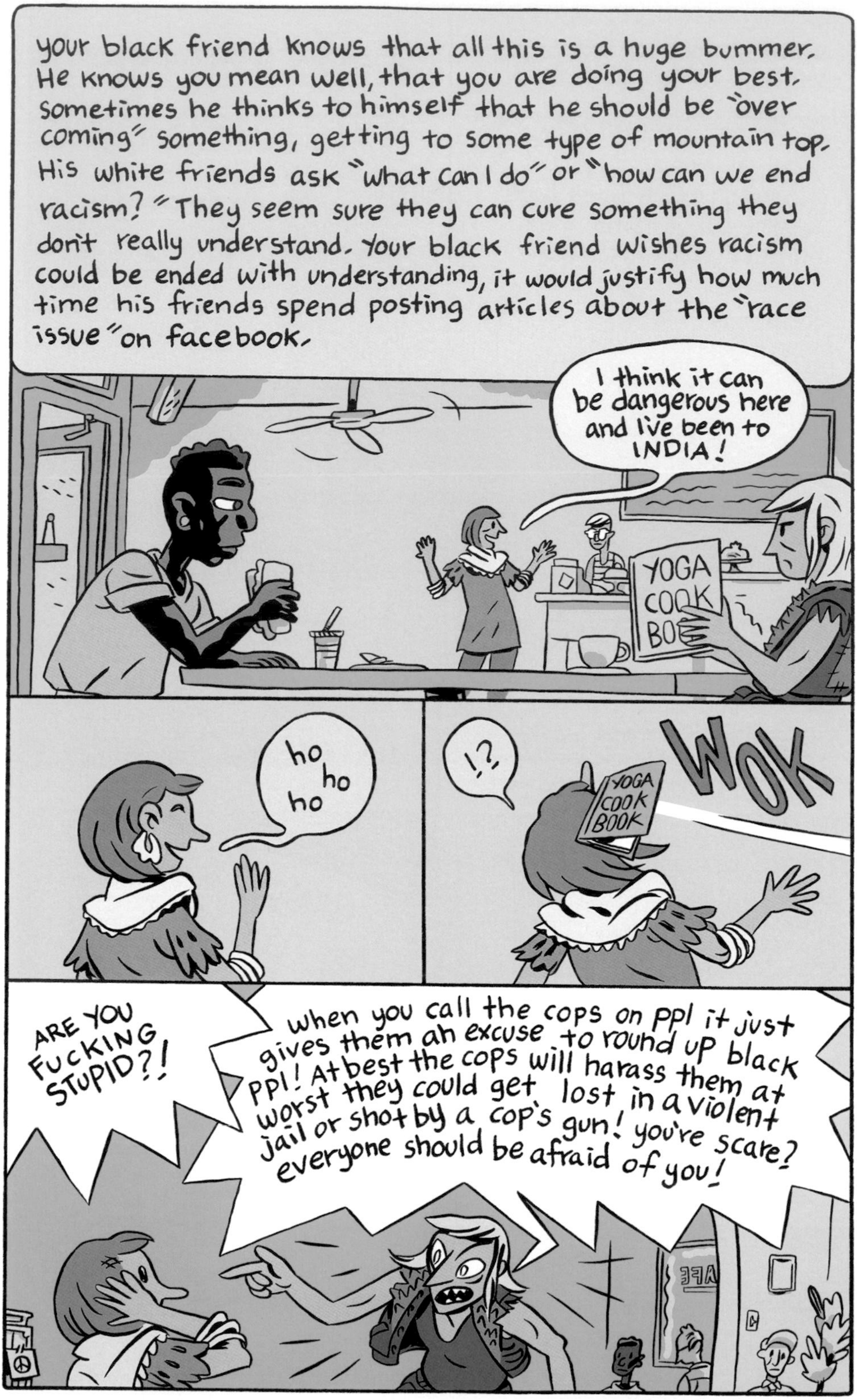
your black friend knows that all this is a huge bummer. He knows you mean well, that you are doing your best. Sometimes he thinks to himself that he should be "over coming" something, getting to some type of mountain top. His white friends ask "what can I do" or "how can we end racism?" They seem sure they can cure something they don't really understand. Your black friend wishes racism could be ended with understanding, it would justify how much time his friends spend posting articles about the "race issue" on facebook.
I think it can be dangerous here and I've been to INDIA!
YOGA COOK BOOK
ho ho ho
!?
YOGA COOK BOOK
WOK
ARE YOU FUCKING STUPID?!
when you call the cops on ppl it just gives them ah excuse to round up black ppl! At best the cops will harass them at worst they could get lost in a violent jail or shot by a cop's gun! you're scare? everyone should be afraid of you!

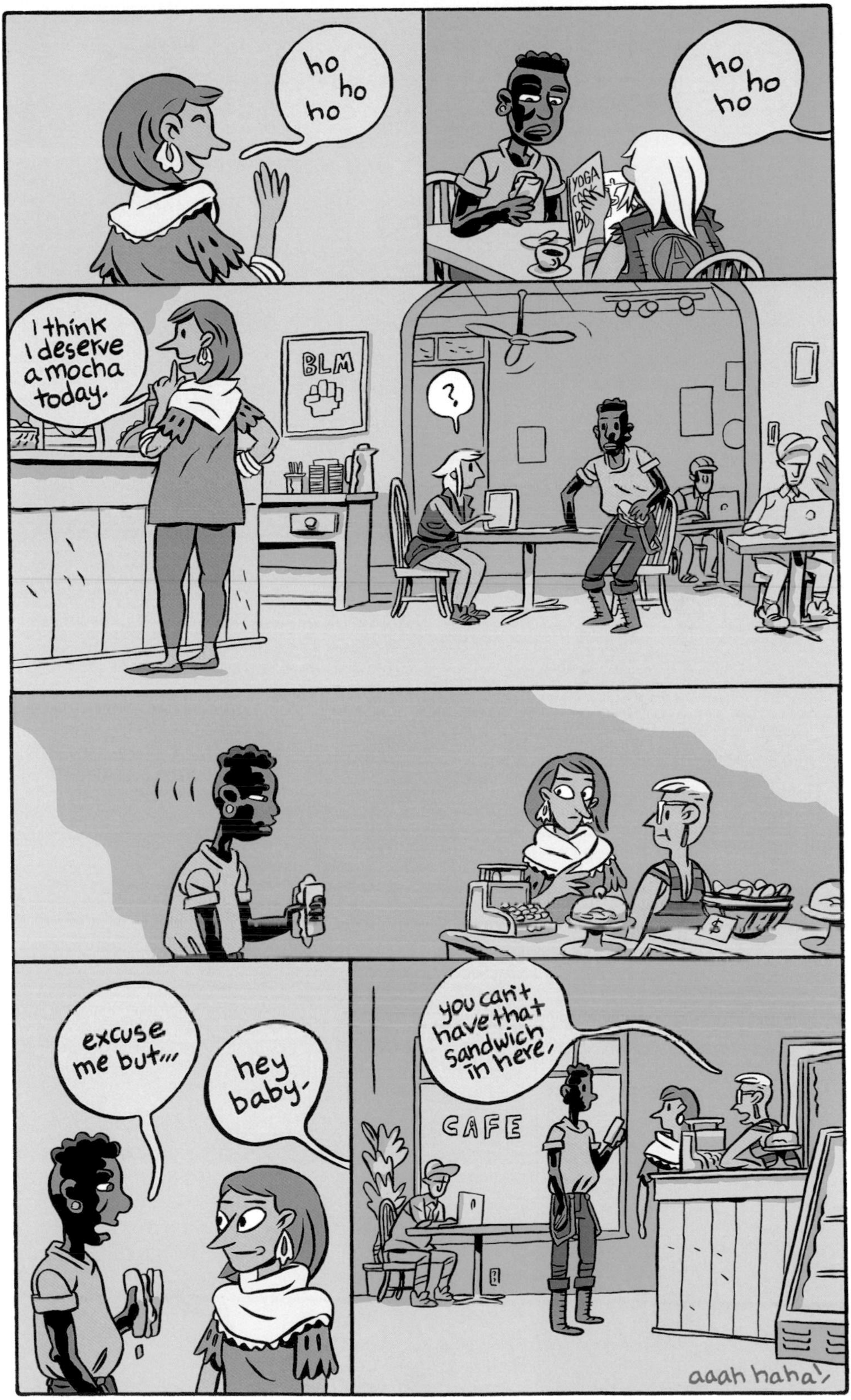

ho ho ho
ho ho ho
YOGA COOK BO
I think I deserve a mocha today.
BLM
?
excuse me but...
hey baby.
you can't have that sandwich in here.
CAFE
aaah haha!

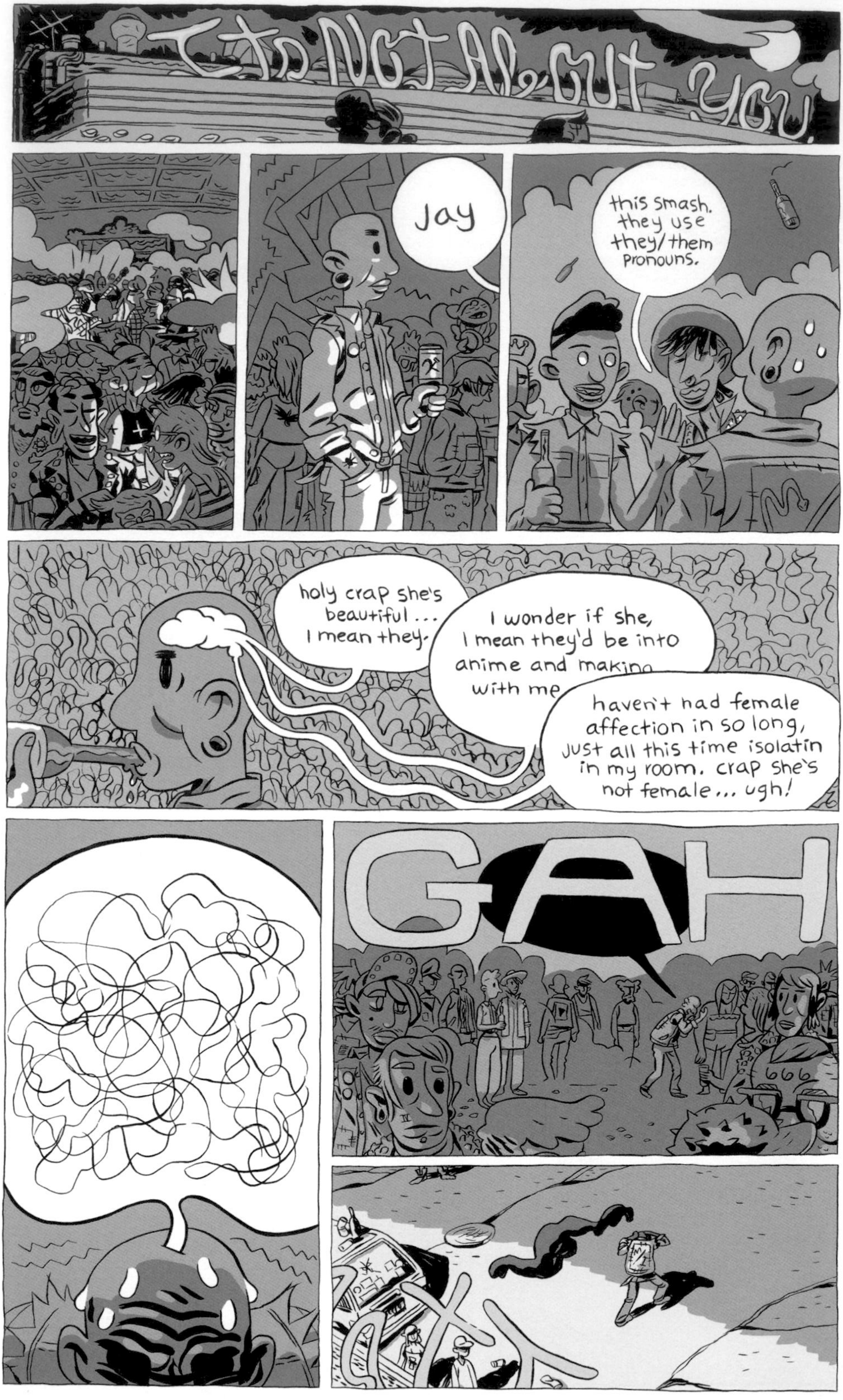
IT'S NOT ABOUT YOU.
JAY
this smash. they use they/them pronouns.
holy crap she's beautiful... I mean they.
I wonder if she, I mean they'd be into anime and making with me
haven't had female affection in so long, just all this time isolatin in my room. crap she's not female... ugh!
GAH

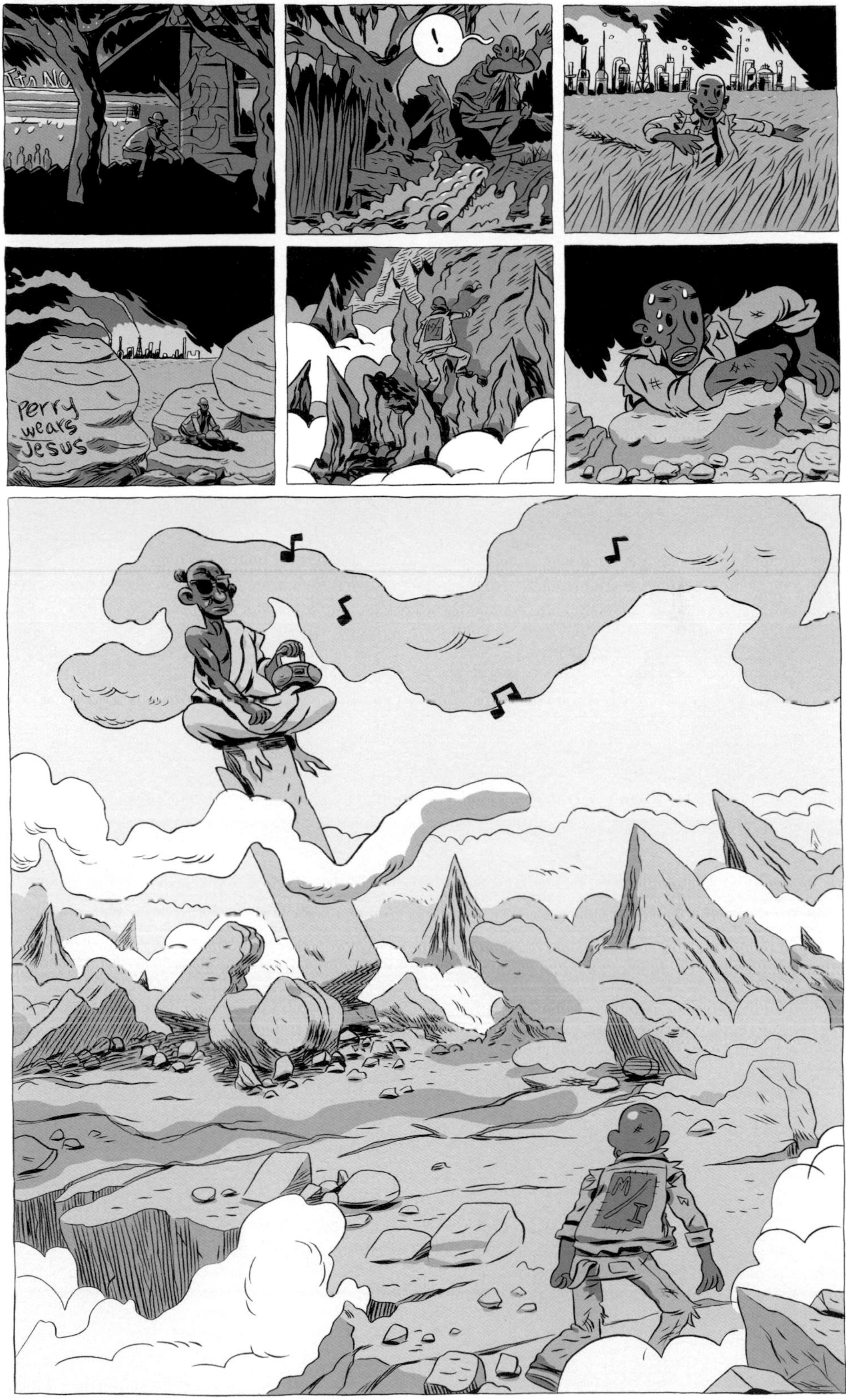
!
perry wears jesus

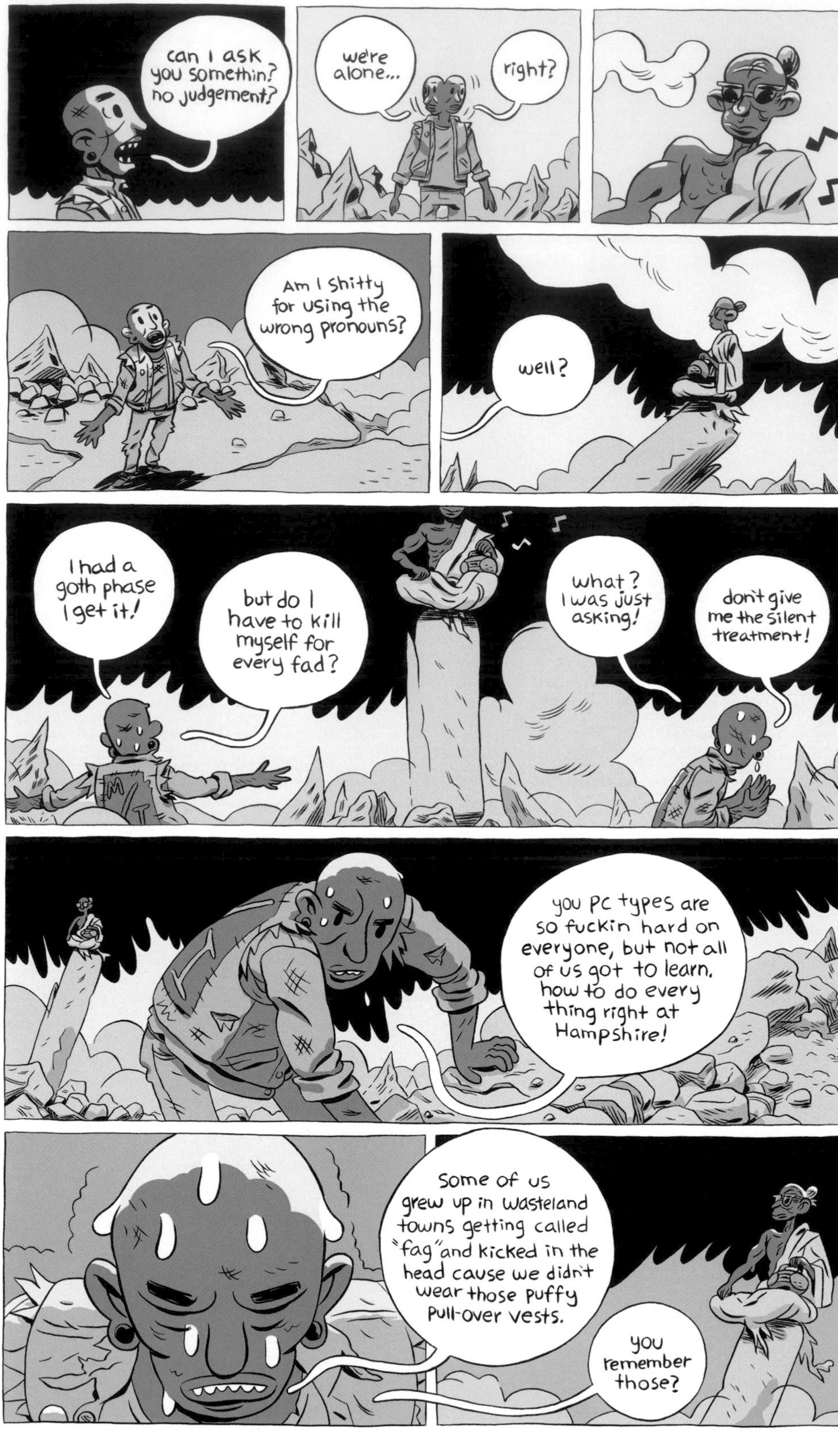
can I ask you somethin? no judgement?
we're alone...
right?
Am I shitty for using the wrong pronouns?
well?
I had a goth phase I get it!
but do I have to kill myself for every fad?
what? I was just asking!
don't give me the silent treatment!
you PC types are so fuckin hard on everyone, but not all of us got to learn how to do every thing right at Hampshire!
Some of us grew up in Wasteland towns getting called "fag" and kicked in the head cause we didn't wear those puffy pull-over vests.
you remember those?

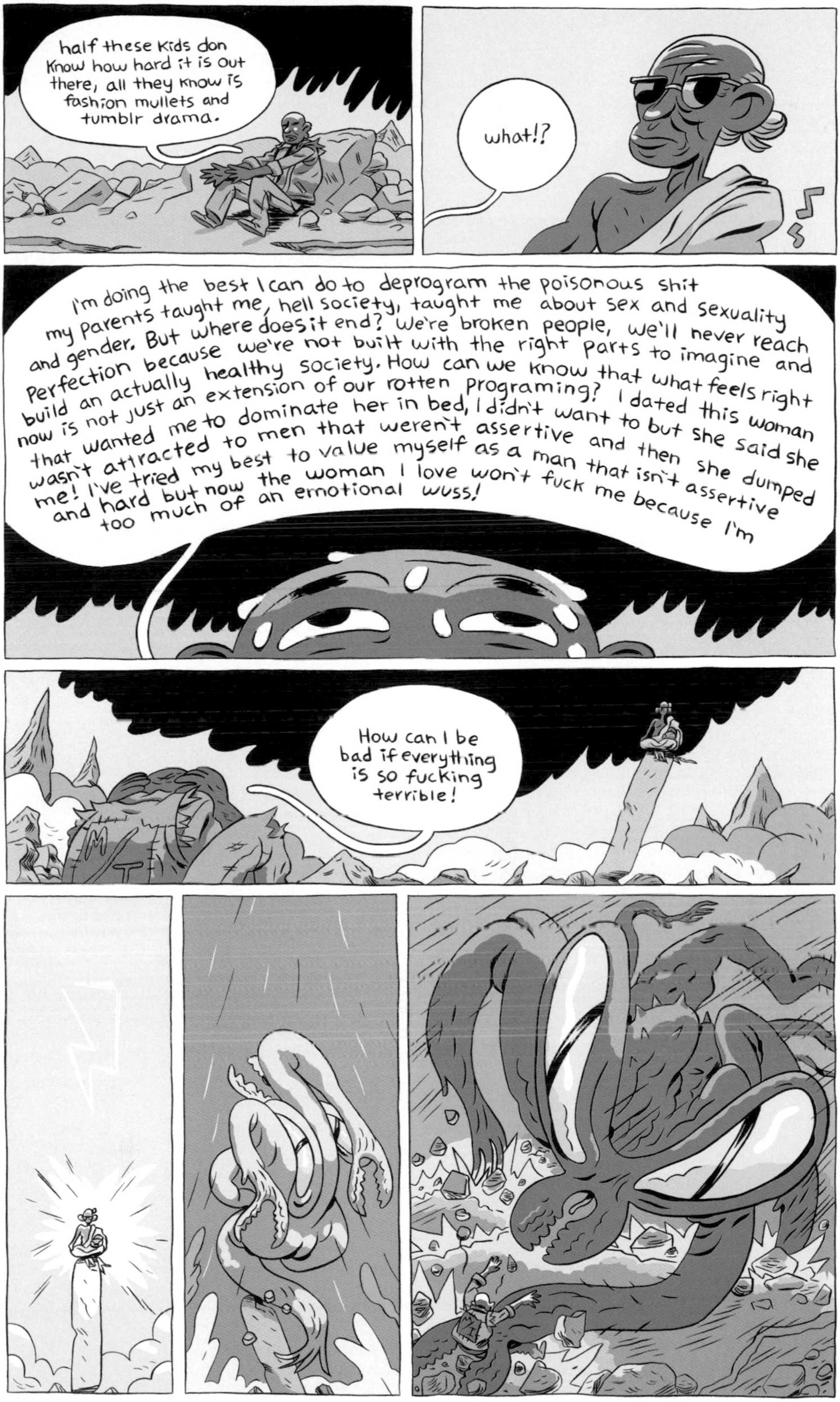
half these kids don know how hard it is out there, all they know is fashion mullets and tumblr drama.
what!?
I'm doing the best I can do to deprogram the poisonous shit my parents taught me, hell society, taught me about sex and sexuality and gender. But where does it end? We're broken people, we'll never reach perfection because we're not built with the right parts to imagine and build an actually healthy society. How can we know that what feels right now is not just an extension of our rotten programing? I dated this woman that wanted me to dominate her in bed, I didn't want to but she said she wasn't attracted to men that weren't assertive and then she dumped me! I've tried my best to value myself as a man that isn't assertive and hard but now the woman I love won't fuck me because I'm too much of an emotional wuss!
How can I be bad if everything is so fucking terrible!

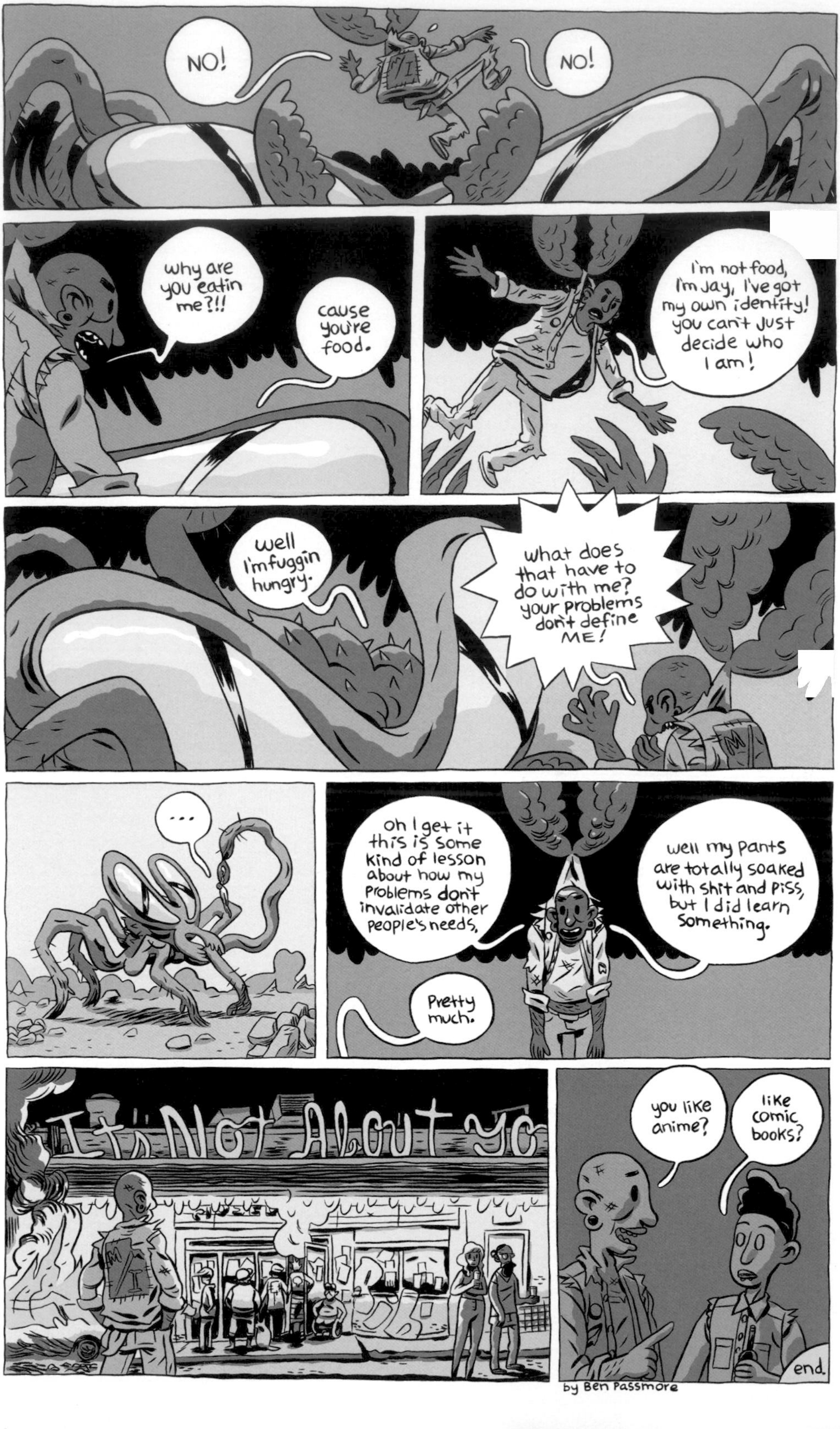
NO!
NO!
why are you eatin me?!!
cause you're food.
I'm not food, I'm Jay, I've got my own identity! you can't just decide who I am!
well I'm fuggin hungry.
what does that have to do with me? your problems don't define ME!
...
oh I get it this is some kind of lesson about how my problems don't invalidate other people's needs,
Pretty much.
well my pants are totally soaked with shit and piss, but I did learn something.
It's Not About Yo
you like anime?
like comic books?
end.

by Ben Passmore

ok stoopd!

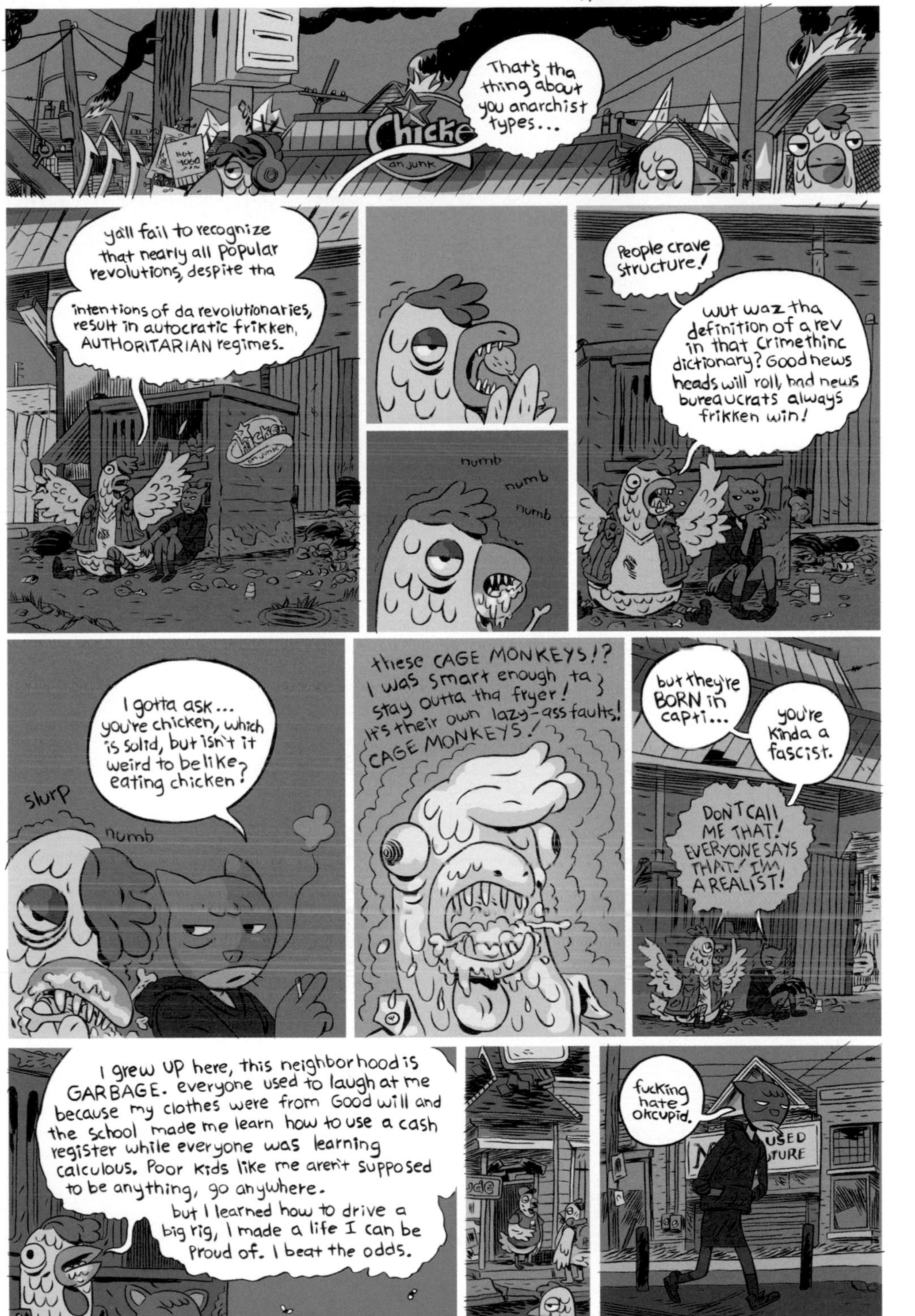
That's tha thing about you anarchist types...
Chicken an junk
y'all fail to recognize that nearly all popular revolutions, despite tha
intentions of da revolutionaries, result in autocratic frikken, AUTHORITARIAN regimes.
numb numb numb
People crave structure!
wut waz tha definition of a rev in that Crimethinc dictionary? Good news heads will roll, bad news bureaucrats always frikken win!
I gotta ask... you're chicken, which is solid, but isn't it weird to be like, eating chicken?
slurp
numb
these CAGE MONKEYS!? I was smart enough ta stay outta tha fryer! It's their own lazy-ass faults! CAGE MONKEYS!
but they're BORN in capti...
you're kinda a fascist.
DON'T CALL ME THAT! EVERYONE SAYS THAT! I'M A REALIST!
I grew up here, this neighborhood is GARBAGE. everyone used to laugh at me because my clothes were from Good will and the school made me learn how to use a cash register while everyone was learning calculous. Poor kids like me aren't supposed to be anything, go anywhere.
but I learned how to drive a big rig, I made a life I can be proud of. I beat the odds.
fucking hate okcupid.

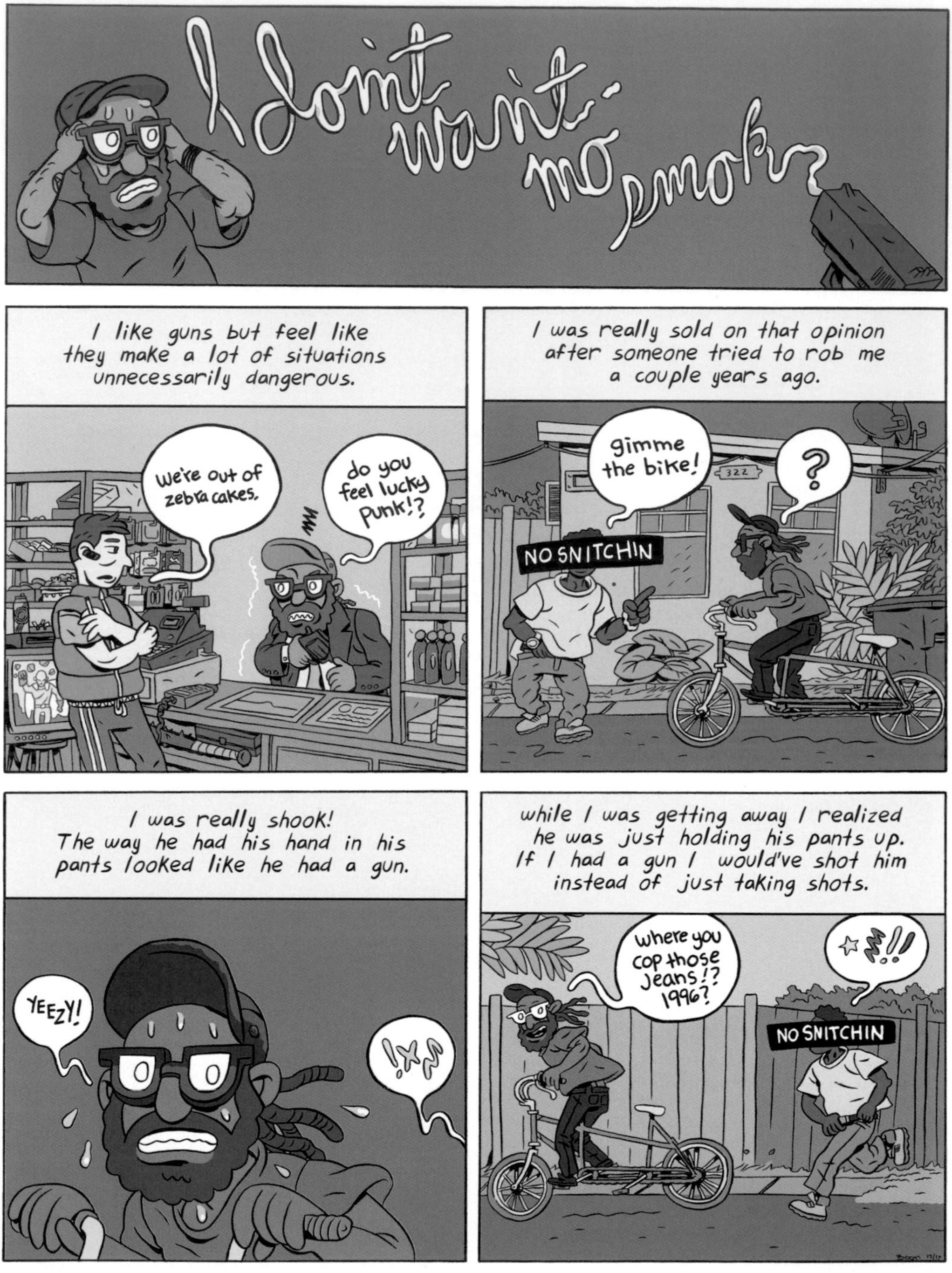
I don't want no smoke
I like guns but feel like they make a lot of situations unnecessarily dangerous.
We're out of zebra cakes.
do you feel lucky punk!?
I was really sold on that opinion after someone tried to rob me a couple years ago.
gimme the bike!
322
?
NO SNITCHIN
I was really shook! The way he had his hand in his pants looked like he had a gun.
YEEZY!
while I was getting away I realized he was just holding his pants up. If I had a gun I would've shot him instead of just taking shots.
where you cop those jeans!? 1996?
NO SNITCHIN

from tha bowelz of DAYGLOAYHOLE presents Art is Shit

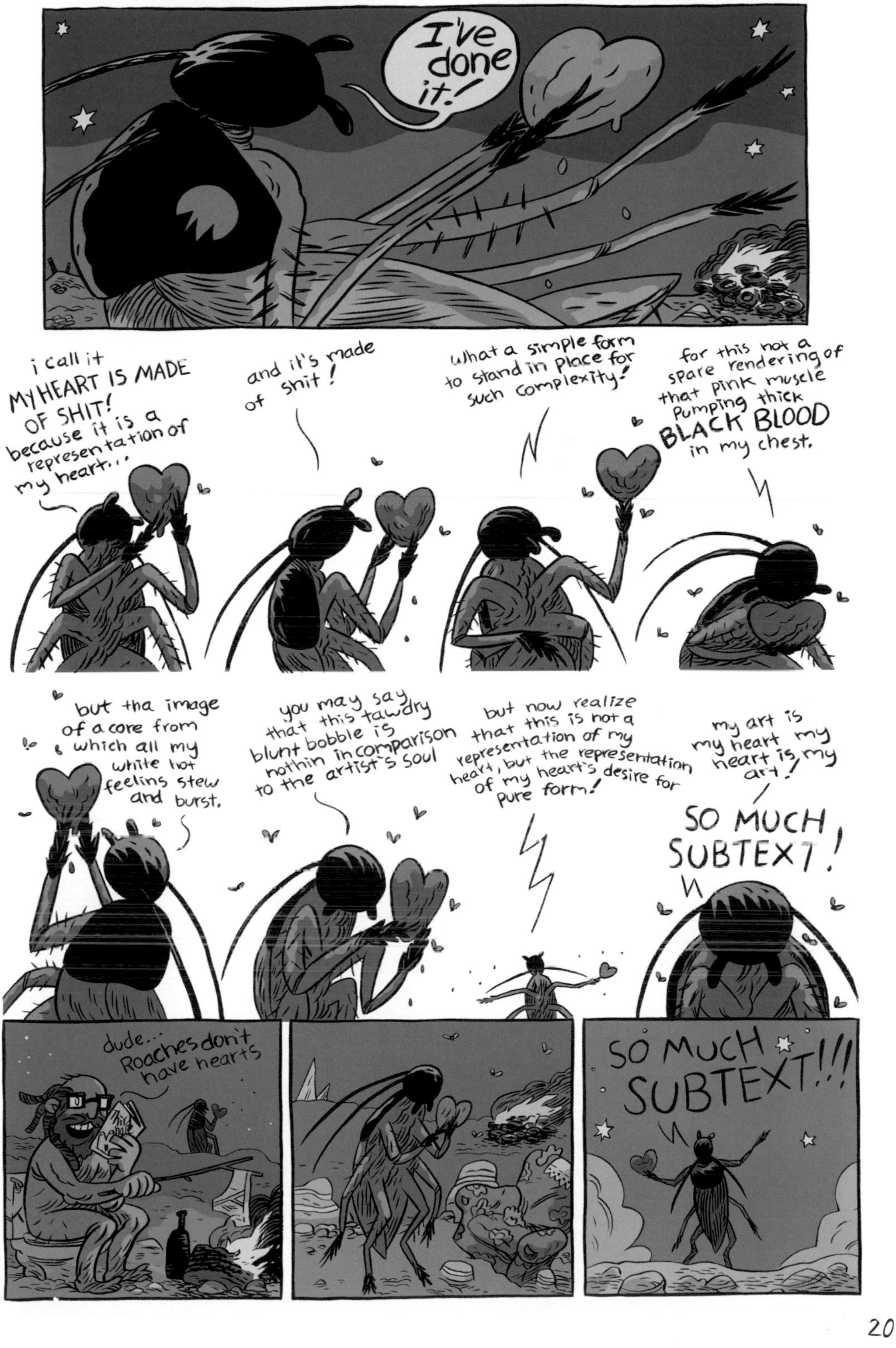

I've done it!
i call it MY HEART IS MADE OF SHIT! because it is a representation of my heart...
and it's made of shit!
what a simple form to stand in place for such complexity!
for this not a spare rendering of that pink muscle pumping thick BLACK BLOOD in my chest.
but tha image of a core from which all my white hot feelins stew and burst.
you may say that this tawdry blunt bobble is nothin in comparison to the artist's soul
but now realize that this is not a representation of my heart, but the representation of my heart's desire for pure form!
my art is my heart my heart is my art!
SO MUCH SUBTEXT!
dude... Roaches don't have hearts
SO MUCH SUBTEXT!!!

A LETTER FROM A STONE MOUNTAIN JAIL

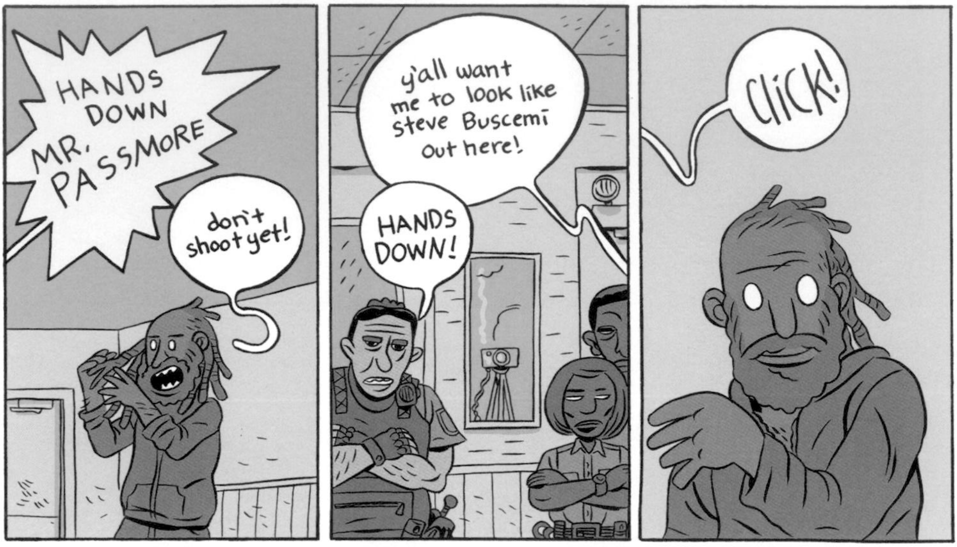
HANDS DOWN MR. PASSMORE
don't shoot yet!
y'all want me to look like Steve Buscemi out here!
HANDS DOWN!
CLICK!

On April 23, 2016 the Klu Klux Klan, sundry skinheads, and some ``history not hate`` pro-confederate monument people (cough. racists. cough.) decided to celebrate years of the Klan by convening on top of the Stone Mountain in Stone Mountain, GA, a giant piece of quartz monzonite with some sore losers carved into it.

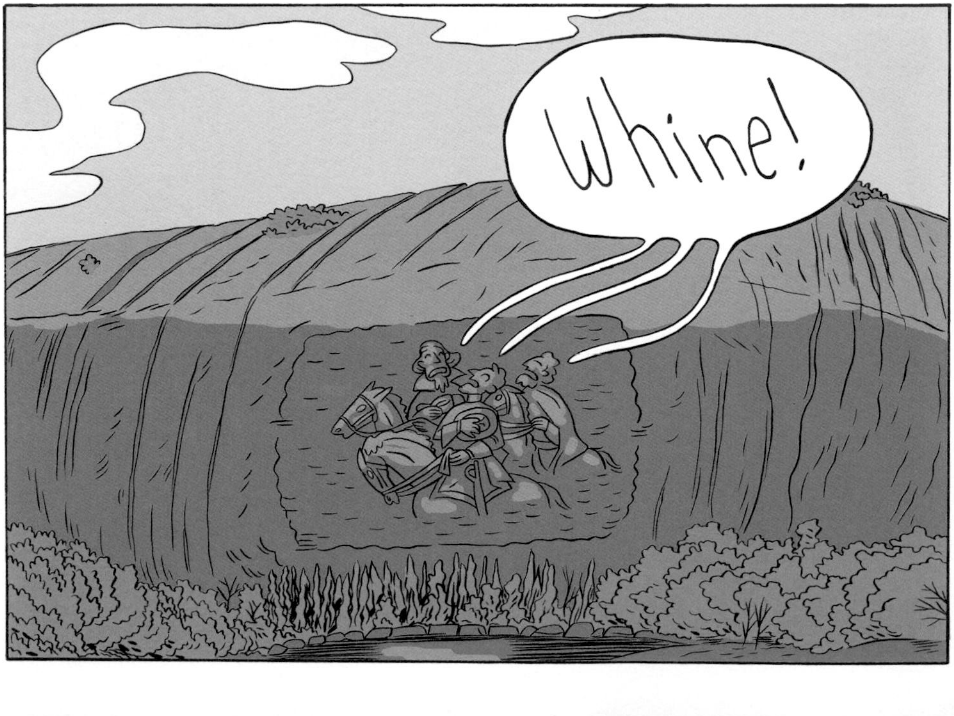
Whine!

I went to Stone Mountain because I'd been welling up with anger and frustration with every new news story, image, and video of black people being murdered in the streets.

I was angry at the second false imprisonment of my friend. After he spent a year and a half in prison for a crime he didn't commit.

Angry at the lighting fast destruction of countless black communities in New Orleans in favor of hip white businesses.

RUSTIC PICKEL

white ppl from Santa cruz

Jail

Angry at the juvenile prison facility that was built at the end of my block in the poor black neighborhood I live in.

I needed to push back against some part of the spectacle of white supremacy and I knew I'd find friends in Georgia to do that with me

soggy meat,

you'd better eat that you won't get nothin else for a while.

NBdy wuz HEre

the march was only 200 to 300 people, but an impressive array of black power folks, anarchists, and sign laiden liberals.

police

bury the KLAN

BLM!

bath facism

BEN

SMASH

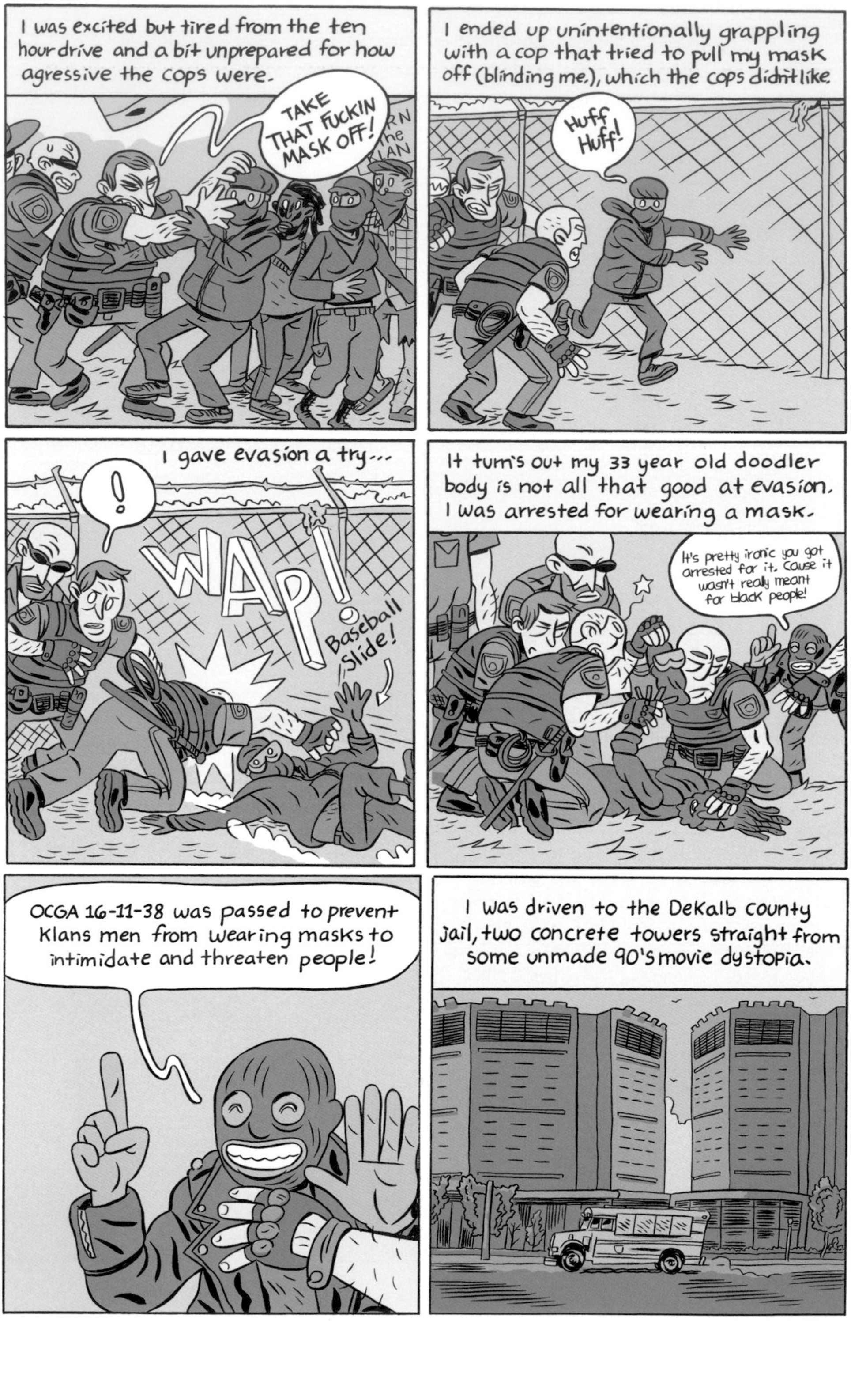

I was excited but tired from the ten hour drive and a bit unprepared for how agressive the cops were.
TAKE THAT FUCKIN MASK OFF!
I ended up unintentionally grappling with a cop that tried to pull my mask off (blinding me.), which the cops didn't like.
Huff Huff!
I gave evasion a try...
!
WAP!
Baseball Slide!
It turn's out my 33 year old doodler body is not all that good at evasion. I was arrested for wearing a mask.
It's pretty ironic you got arrested for it. Cause it wasn't really meant for black people!
OCGA 16-11-38 was passed to prevent Klans men from wearing masks to intimidate and threaten people!
I was driven to the DeKalb county jail, two concrete towers straight from some unmade 90's movie dystopia.

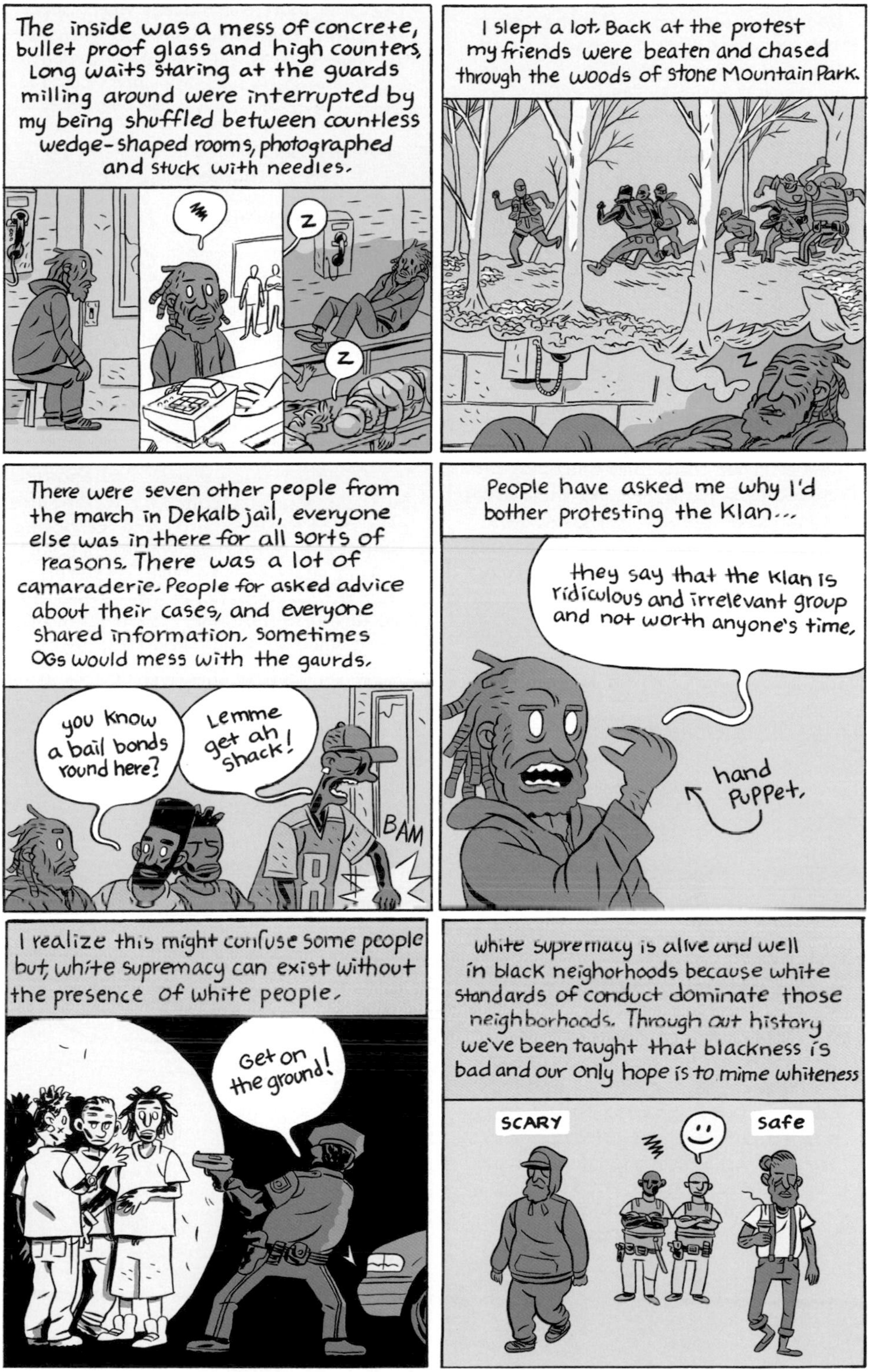
The inside was a mess of concrete, bullet proof glass and high counters, Long waits staring at the guards milling around were interrupted by my being shuffled between countless wedge-shaped rooms, photographed and stuck with needles.
Z
Z
I slept a lot. Back at the protest my friends were beaten and chased through the woods of Stone Mountain Park.
Z
There were seven other people from the march in Dekalb jail, everyone else was in there for all sorts of reasons. There was a lot of camaraderie. People for asked advice about their cases, and everyone shared information. Sometimes OGs would mess with the gaurds.
you know a bail bonds round here?
Lemme get ah shack!
BAM
People have asked me why I'd bother protesting the Klan...
they say that the klan is ridiculous and irrelevant group and not worth anyone's time.
hand puppet.
I realize this might confuse some people but, white supremacy can exist without the presence of white people.
Get on the ground!
white supremacy is alive and well in black neighorhoods because white standards of conduct dominate those neighborhoods. Through out history we've been taught that blackness is bad and our only hope is to mime whiteness
SCARY
Safe

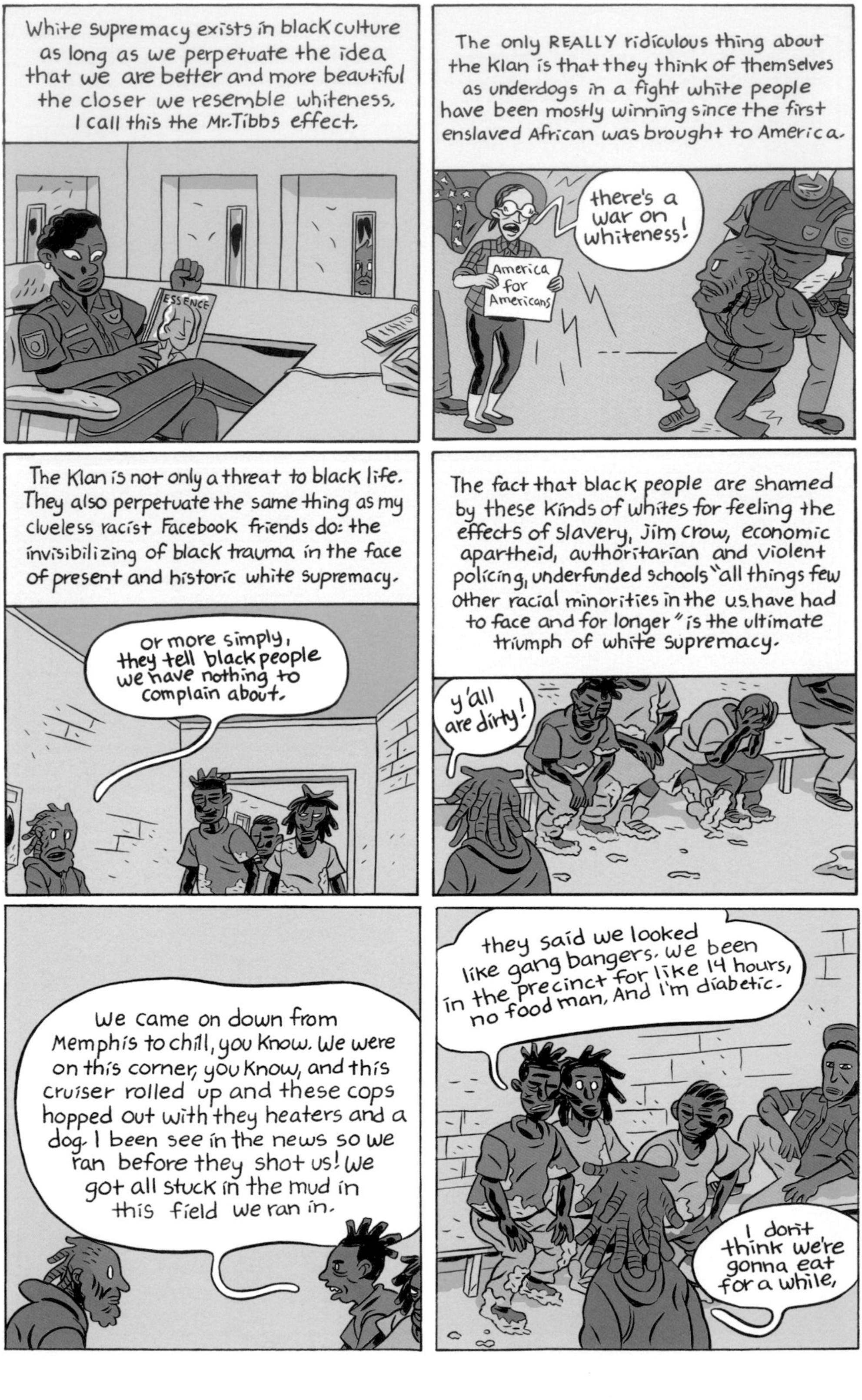
White supremacy exists in black culture as long as we perpetuate the idea that we are better and more beautiful the closer we resemble whiteness. I call this the Mr. Tibbs effect.
ESSENCE
The only REALLY ridiculous thing about the Klan is that they think of themselves as underdogs in a fight white people have been mostly winning since the first enslaved African was brought to America.
there's a war on whiteness!
America for Americans
The Klan is not only a threat to black life. They also perpetuate the same thing as my clueless racist Facebook friends do: the invisibilizing of black trauma in the face of present and historic white supremacy.
or more simply, they tell black people we have nothing to complain about.
The fact that black people are shamed by these kinds of whites for feeling the effects of slavery, Jim Crow, economic apartheid, authoritarian and violent policing, underfunded schools "all things few other racial minorities in the U.S. have had to face and for longer" is the ultimate triumph of white supremacy.
y'all are dirty!
We came on down from Memphis to chill, you know. We were on this corner, you know, and this cruiser rolled up and these cops hopped out with they heaters and a dog. I been see in the news so we ran before they shot us! We got all stuck in the mud in this field we ran in.
they said we looked like gang bangers. we been in the precinct for like 14 hours, no food man. And I'm diabetic.
I don't think we're gonna eat for a while.

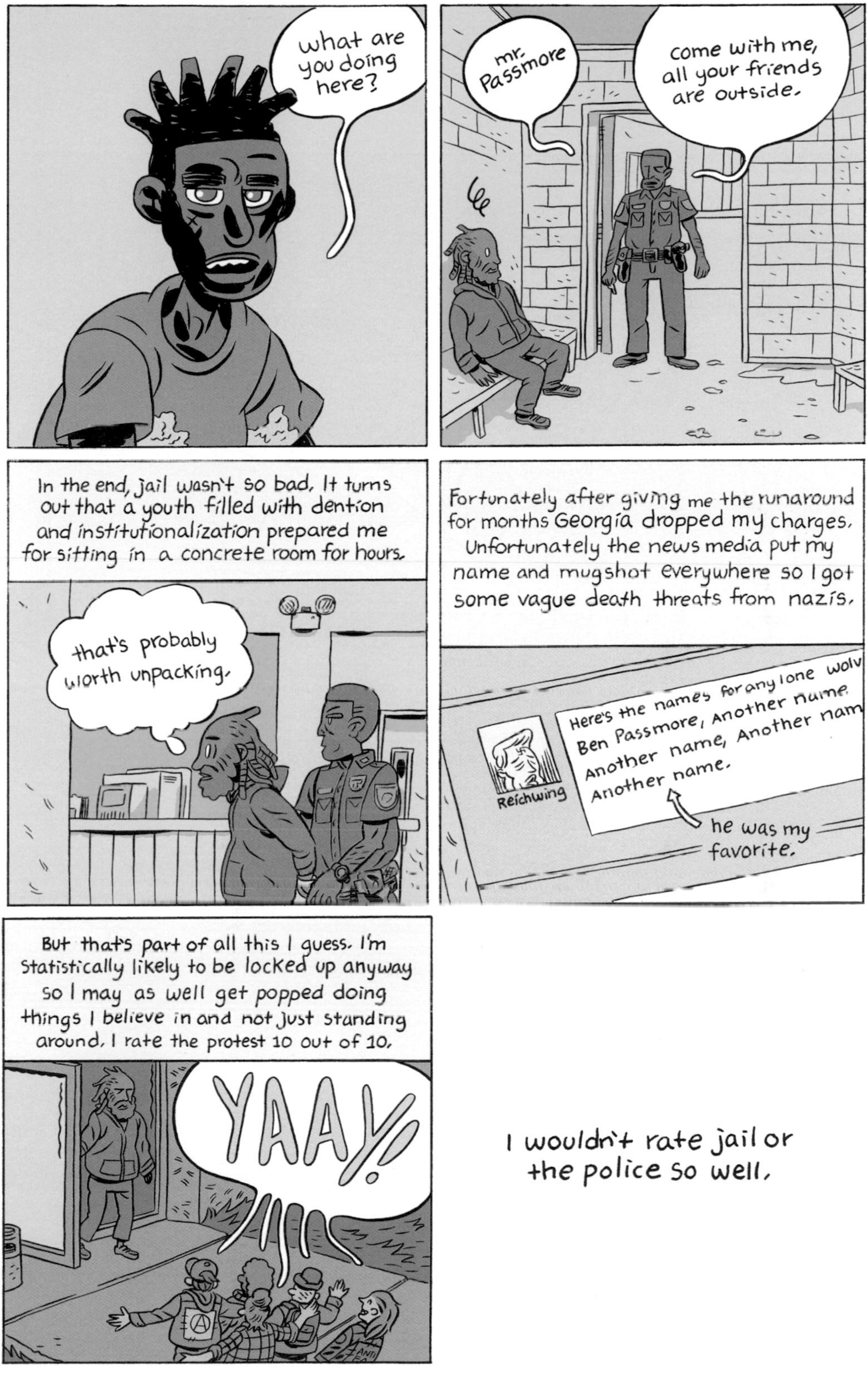
what are you doing here?
mr. Passmore
come with me, all your friends are outside.
In the end, jail wasn't so bad. It turns out that a youth filled with dention and institutionalization prepared me for sitting in a concrete room for hours.
that's probably worth unpacking.
Fortunately after giving me the runaround for months Georgia dropped my charges. Unfortunately the news media put my name and mugshot everywhere so I got some vague death threats from nazis.
Reichwing
Here's the names for any lone wolv
Ben Passmore, Another name.
Another name, Another nam
Another name.
he was my favorite.
But that's part of all this I guess. I'm statistically likely to be locked up anyway so I may as well get popped doing things I believe in and not just standing around. I rate the protest 10 out of 10.
YAAY!

I wouldn't rate jail or the police so well.

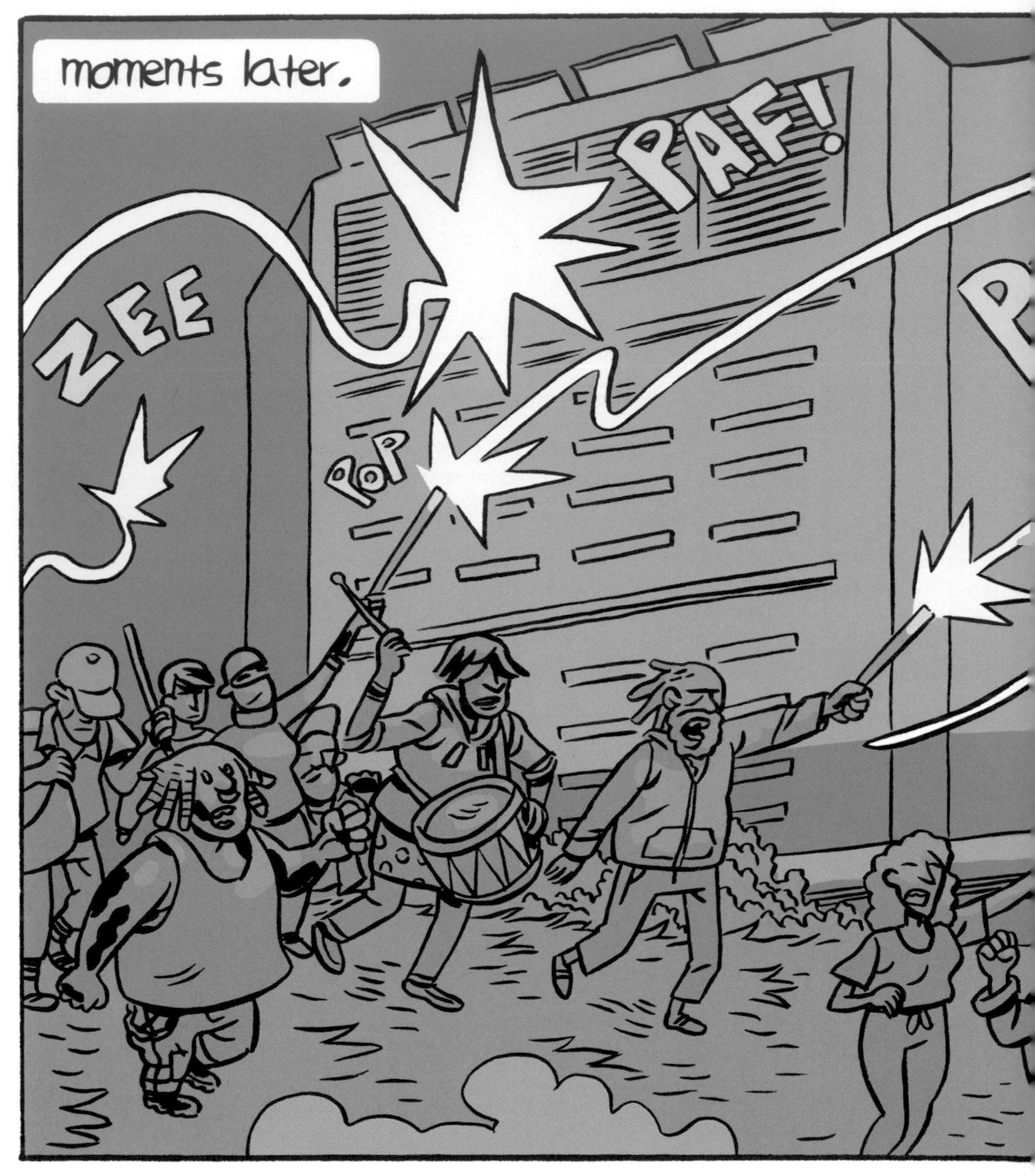
moments later.
PAF!
ZEE
POP

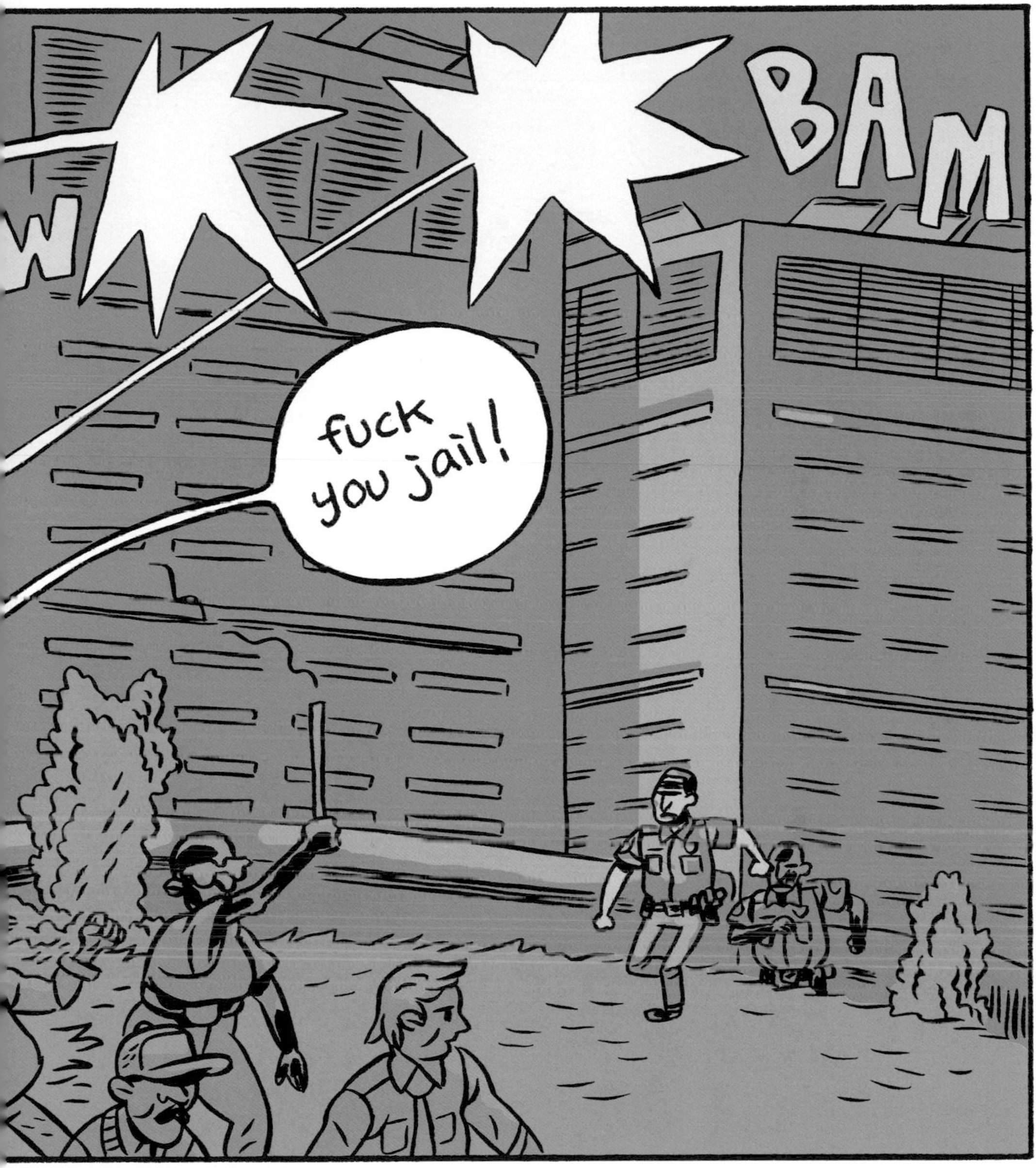
W
BAM
fuck you jail!

Since Trump's election I've been to several protests around his election, his executive orders, or pro-Trump rallies. While I feel pretty lukewarm about protests generally, I've been to a bunch over the years. So I'm well acquainted with the protest culture of the left.

your brave author,

My Poetry will solve this whole thing.

I didn't give us permission to march in the street!

this is a PEACEFUL protest!!!

NOT WITH HATE

NOT my Pres

♡TRUMP'S HATE!

Punch your LOCAL FASCIST

Do I still have to do this?

Protests can be one of those rare situations when previously disempowered people find self-determination, but I've been seeing a lot of preference for performance over substance lately.

It's very important that we all play dead!

What happened? Maybe a lot of revisionist thinking around the Civil Rights movement has people thinking that nice speeches will shake the dust off the brokers of power and make them fix everything? The reality is that the history of change in the US is a story of communities acting autonomously and the state playing catch-up.

Put respect on my feels!

direct Angela Davis quote...

Hopefully in time we'll see more actions that focus on making things happen. Not all of the marches I've been to have been lame. The airport protests against Trump's Muslim ban were inspiring, and in Philadelphia I saw almost a hundred black clad Anti-fascists circle and then shut-down a teensy pro-Trump rally.

MAGA

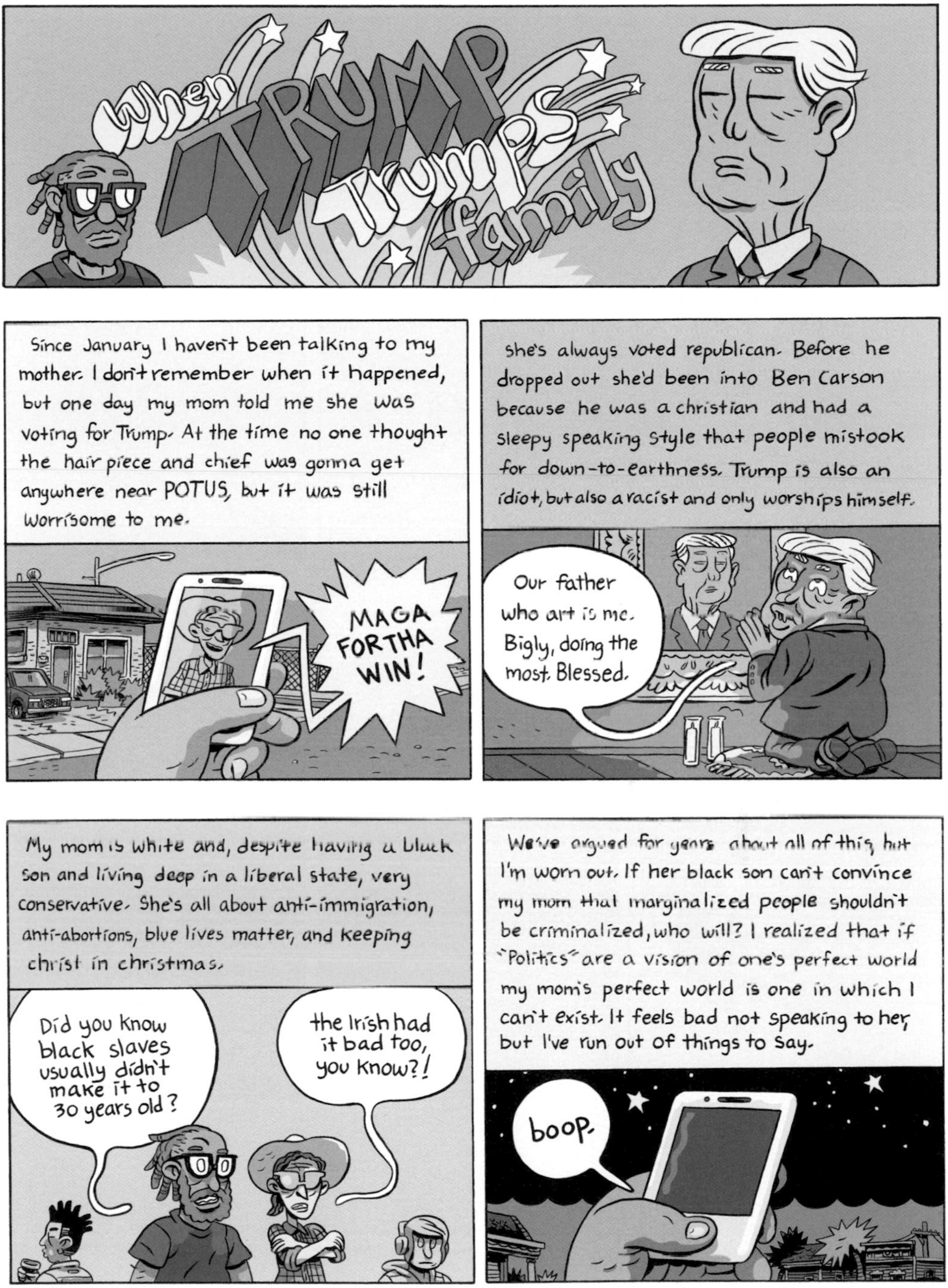
When TRUMP Trumps family
Since January I haven't been talking to my mother. I don't remember when it happened, but one day my mom told me she was voting for Trump. At the time no one thought the hair piece and chief was gonna get anywhere near POTUS, but it was still worrisome to me.
MAGA FOR THA WIN!
She's always voted republican. Before he dropped out she'd been into Ben Carson because he was a christian and had a sleepy speaking style that people mistook for down-to-earthness. Trump is also an idiot, but also a racist and only worships himself.
Our father who art is me. Bigly, doing the most. Blessed.
My mom is white and, despite having a black son and living deep in a liberal state, very conservative. She's all about anti-immigration, anti-abortions, blue lives matter, and keeping christ in christmas.
Did you know black slaves usually didn't make it to 30 years old?
the Irish had it bad too, you know?!
We've argued for years about all of this but I'm worn out. If her black son can't convince my mom that marginalized people shouldn't be criminalized, who will? I realized that if "Politics" are a vision of one's perfect world my mom's perfect world is one in which I can't exist. It feels bad not speaking to her, but I've run out of things to say.
boop.

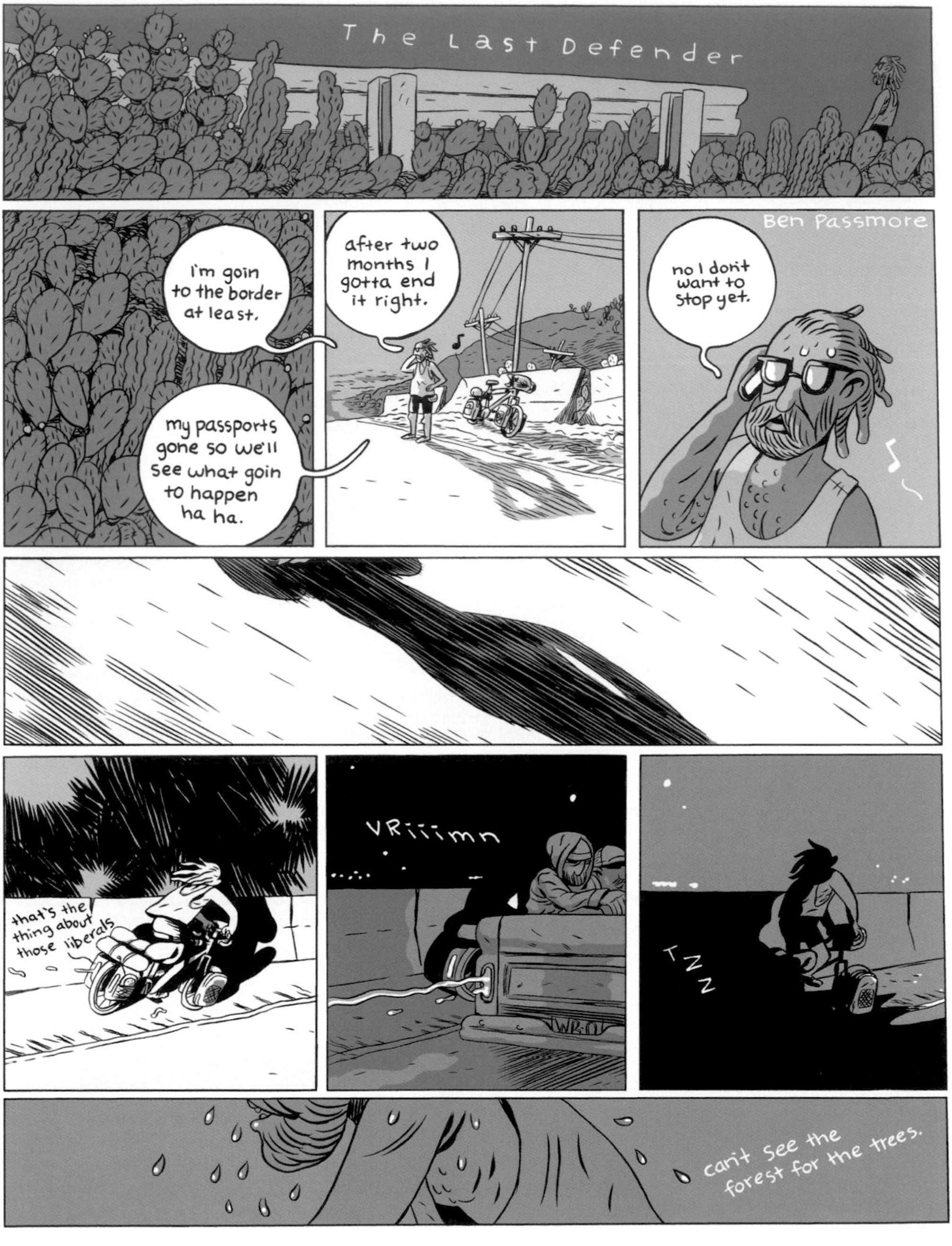
The Last Defender
I'm goin to the border at least.
my passports gone so we'll see what goin to happen ha ha.
after two months I gotta end it right.
Ben Passmore
no I don't want to stop yet.
that's the thing about those liberals
VRiiimn
TZZ
can't see the forest for the trees.

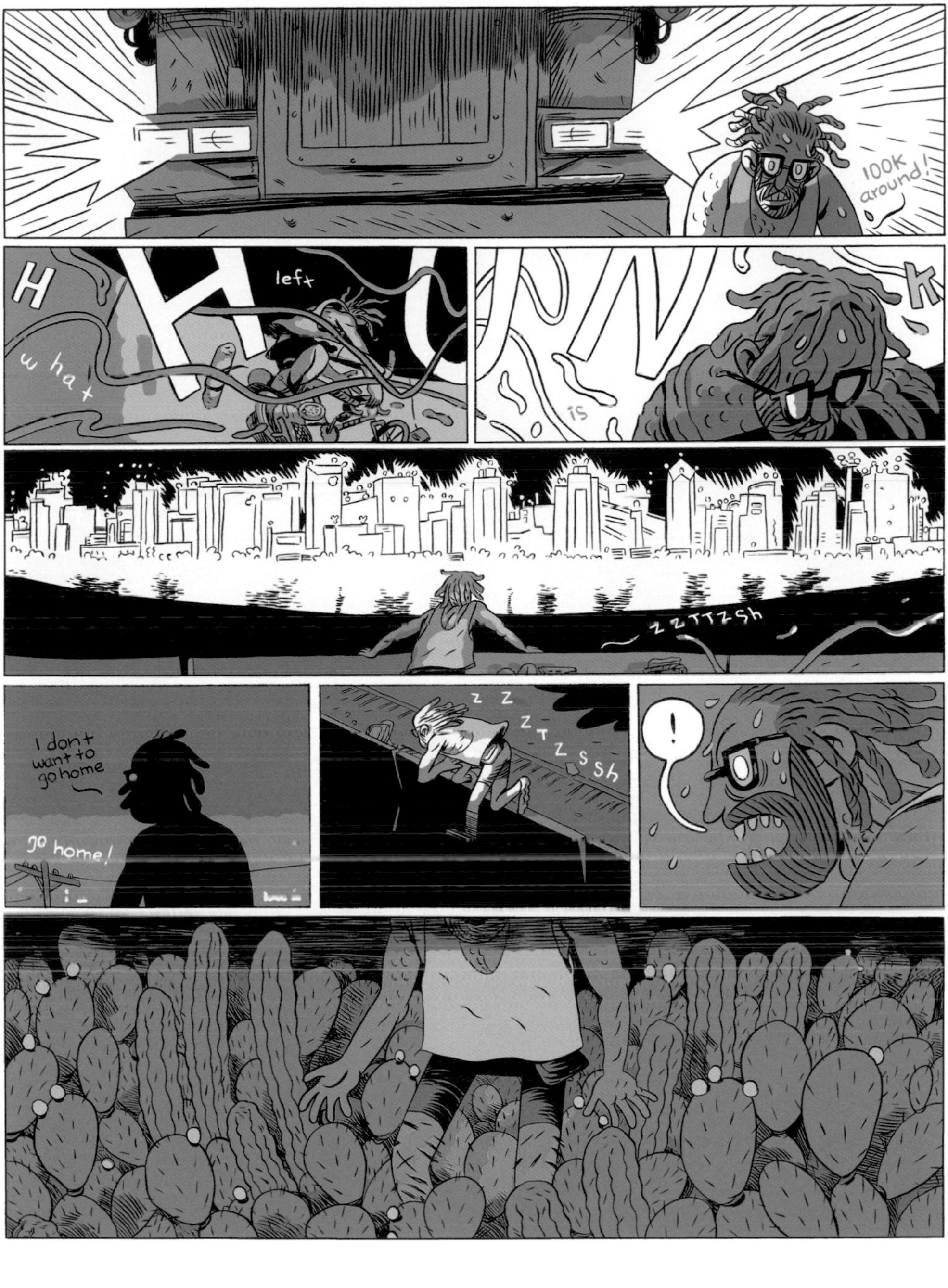

lOOK around!
H
left
what
is
k
zzTTTzSh
I don't want to go home
go home!
z z zTzssh
!

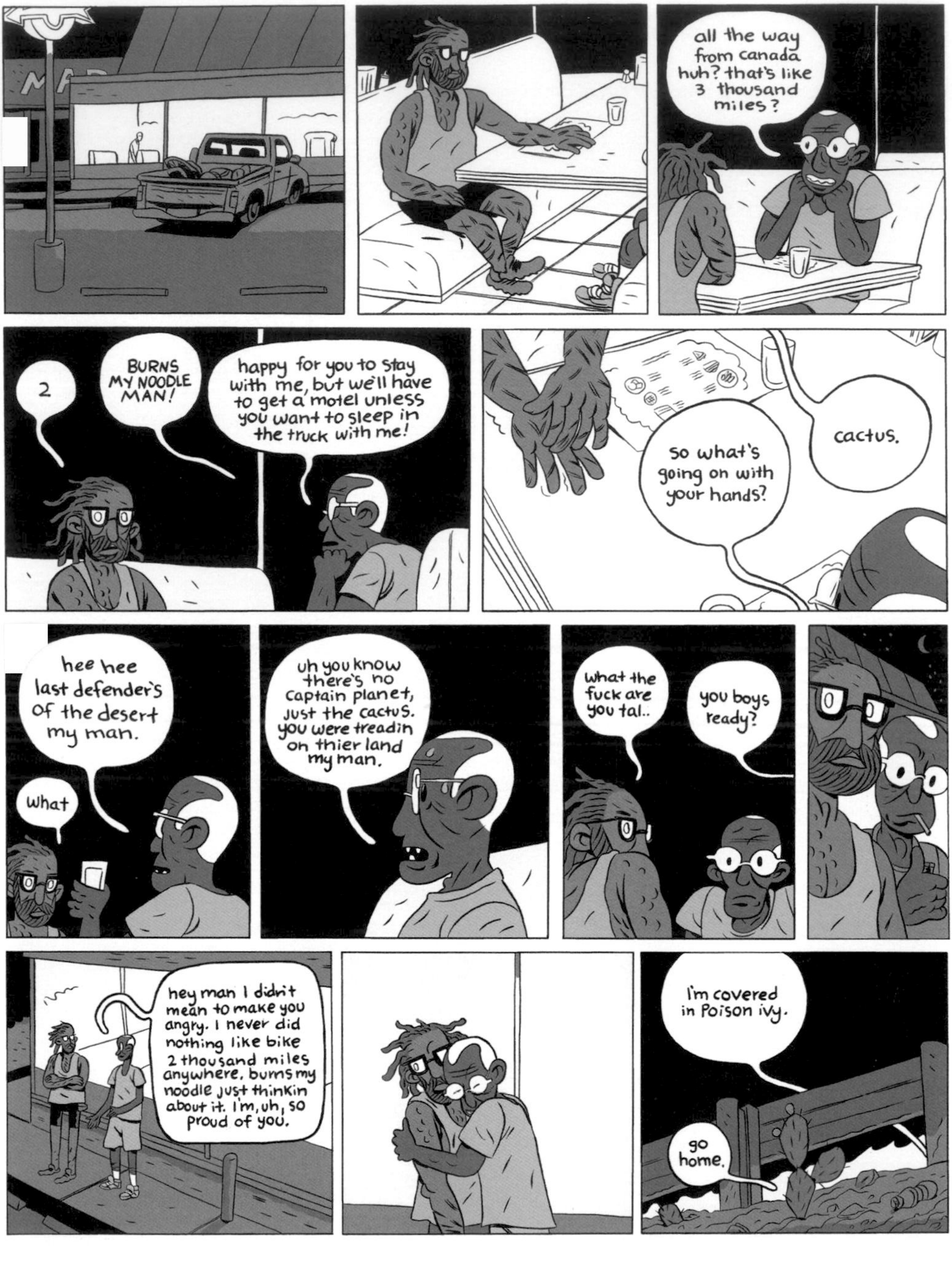
all the way from canada huh? that's like 3 thousand miles?
2
BURNS MY NOODLE MAN!
happy for you to stay with me, but we'll have to get a motel unless you want to sleep in the truck with me!
so what's going on with your hands?
cactus.
hee hee last defender's of the desert my man.
what
uh you know there's no captain planet, just the cactus. you were treadin on thier land my man.
what the fuck are you tal..
you boys ready?
hey man I didn't mean to make you angry. I never did nothing like bike 2 thousand miles anywhere. burns my noodle just thinkin about it. I'm, uh, so proud of you.
I'm covered in Poison ivy.
go home.

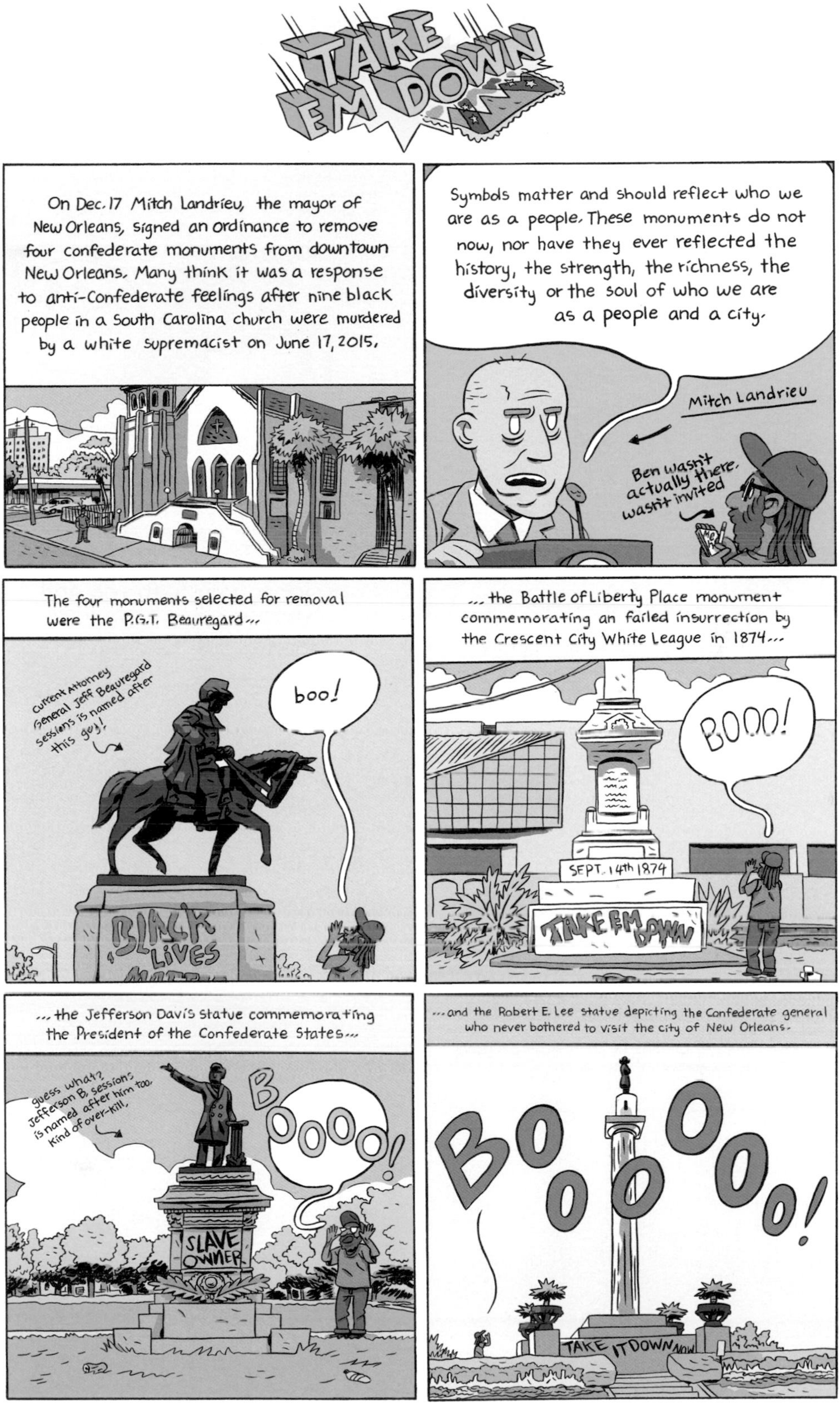
TAKE EM DOWN
On Dec. 17 Mitch Landrieu, the mayor of New Orleans, signed an ordinance to remove four confederate monuments from downtown New Orleans. Many think it was a response to anti-Confederate feelings after nine black people in a South Carolina church were murdered by a white supremacist on June 17, 2015.
Symbols matter and should reflect who we are as a people. These monuments do not now, nor have they ever reflected the history, the strength, the richness, the diversity or the soul of who we are as a people and a city.
Mitch Landrieu
Ben wasn't actually there. wasn't invited
The four monuments selected for removal were the P.G.T. Beauregard...
current Attorney General Jeff Beauregard Sessions is named after this guy!
boo!
BLACK LIVES
...the Battle of Liberty Place monument commemorating an failed insurrection by the Crescent City White League in 1874...
BOOO!
SEPT. 14th 1874
TAKE EM DOWN
...the Jefferson Davis statue commemorating the President of the Confederate States...
guess what? Jefferson B. Sessions is named after him too. Kind of over-kill.
BOOOO!
SLAVE OWNER
...and the Robert E. Lee statue depicting the Confederate general who never bothered to visit the city of New Orleans.
BOOOOOOO!
TAKE IT DOWN NOW

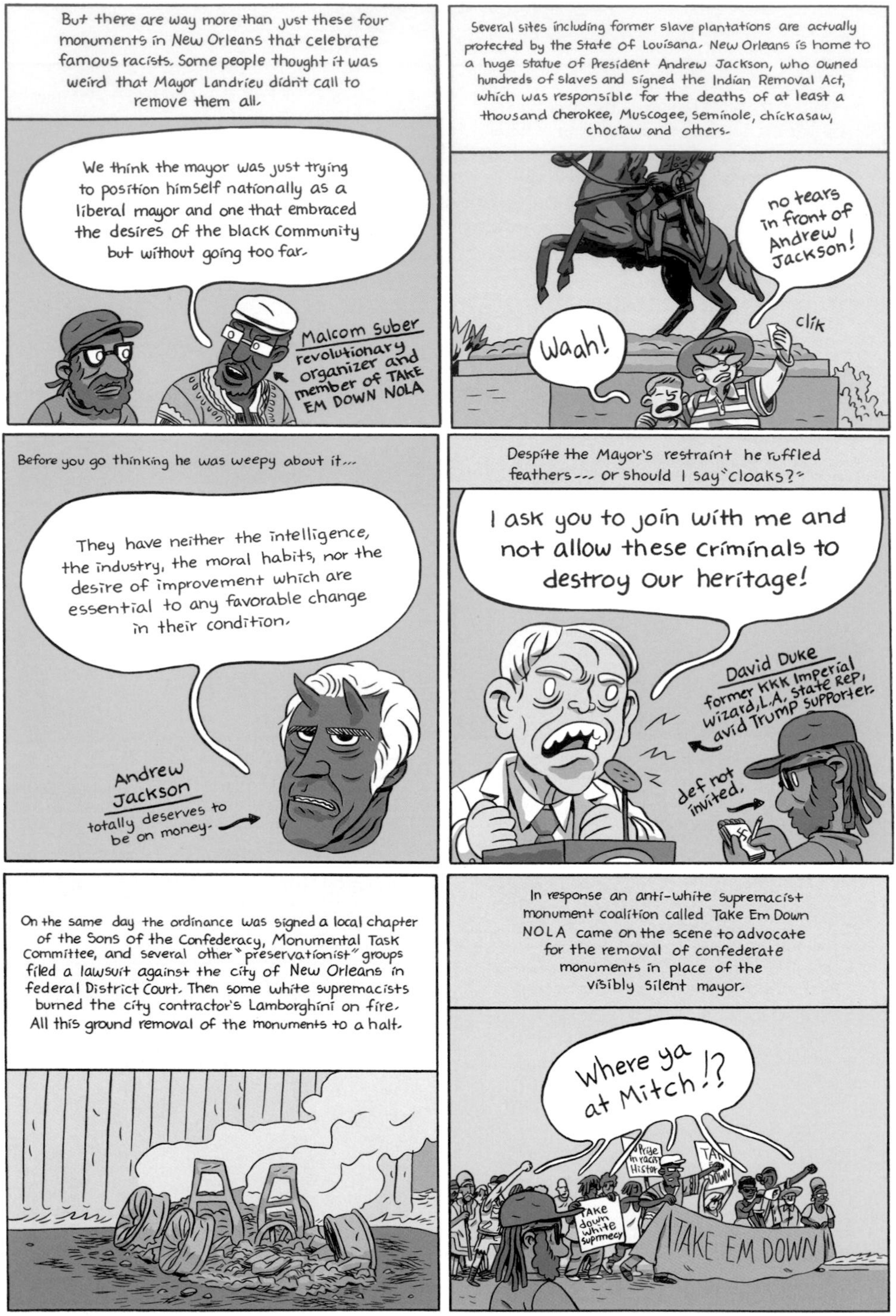
But there are way more than just these four monuments in New Orleans that celebrate famous racists. Some people thought it was weird that Mayor Landrieu didn't call to remove them all.
We think the mayor was just trying to position himself nationally as a liberal mayor and one that embraced the desires of the black community but without going too far.
Malcom Suber revolutionary organizer and member of TAKE EM DOWN NOLA
Several sites including former slave plantations are actually protected by the State of Louisana. New Orleans is home to a huge statue of President Andrew Jackson, who owned hundreds of slaves and signed the Indian Removal Act, which was responsible for the deaths of at least a thousand Cherokee, Muscogee, Seminole, Chickasaw, Choctaw and others.
no tears in front of Andrew Jackson!
clik
Waah!
Before you go thinking he was weepy about it...
They have neither the intelligence, the industry, the moral habits, nor the desire of improvement which are essential to any favorable change in their condition.
Andrew Jackson
totally deserves to be on money.
Despite the Mayor's restraint he ruffled feathers... or should I say "cloaks?"
I ask you to join with me and not allow these criminals to destroy our heritage!
David Duke
former KKK Imperial Wizard, L.A. State Rep, avid Trump supporter.
def not invited.
On the same day the ordinance was signed a local chapter of the Sons of the Confederacy, Monumental Task Committee, and several other "preservationist" groups filed a lawsuit against the city of New Orleans in federal District Court. Then some white supremacists burned the city contractor's Lamborghini on fire. All this ground removal of the monuments to a halt.
In response an anti-white supremacist monument coalition called Take Em Down NOLA came on the scene to advocate for the removal of confederate monuments in place of the visibly silent mayor.
Where ya at Mitch!?
Pride in racist History
TAKE DOWN
Take down white suprmecy
TAKE EM DOWN

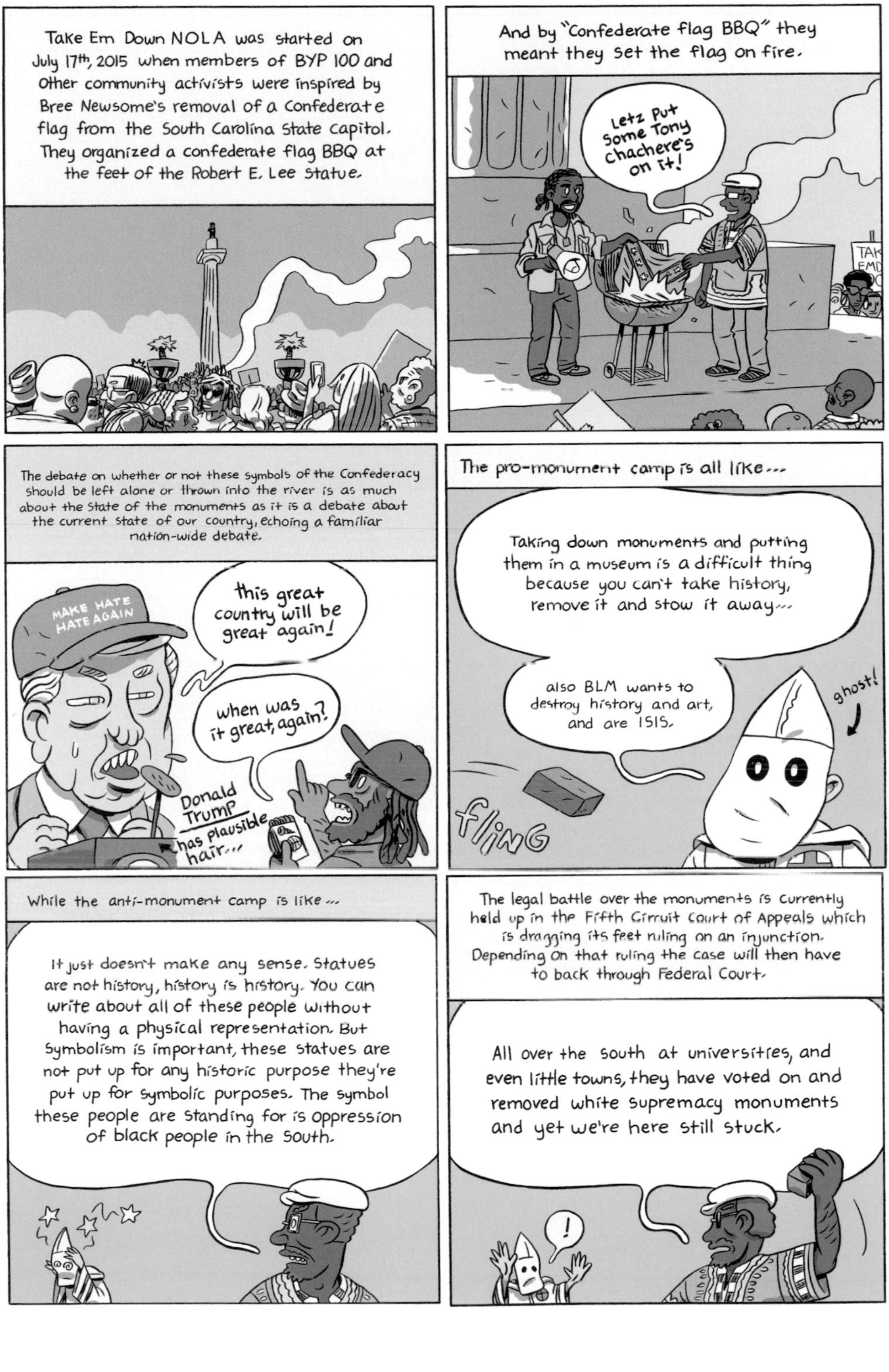

Take Em Down NOLA was started on July 17th, 2015 when members of BYP 100 and other community activists were inspired by Bree Newsome's removal of a Confederate flag from the South Carolina State Capitol. They organized a confederate flag BBQ at the feet of the Robert E. Lee statue.
And by "Confederate flag BBQ" they meant they set the flag on fire.
Letz Put Some Tony Chachere's on it!
The debate on whether or not these symbols of the Confederacy should be left alone or thrown into the river is as much about the state of the monuments as it is a debate about the current state of our country, echoing a familiar nation-wide debate.
MAKE HATE HATE AGAIN
this great country will be great again!
when was it great, again?
Donald Trump has plausible hair...
The pro-monument camp is all like...
Taking down monuments and putting them in a museum is a difficult thing because you can't take history, remove it and stow it away...
also BLM wants to destroy history and art, and are ISIS.
ghost!
fling
While the anti-monument camp is like...
It just doesn't make any sense. Statues are not history, history is history. You can write about all of these people without having a physical representation. But Symbolism is important, these statues are not put up for any historic purpose they're put up for symbolic purposes. The symbol these people are standing for is oppression of black people in the South.
The legal battle over the monuments is currently held up in the Fifth Circuit Court of Appeals which is dragging its feet ruling on an injunction. Depending on that ruling the case will then have to back through Federal Court.
All over the south at universities, and even little towns, they have voted on and removed white supremacy monuments and yet we're here still stuck.
!

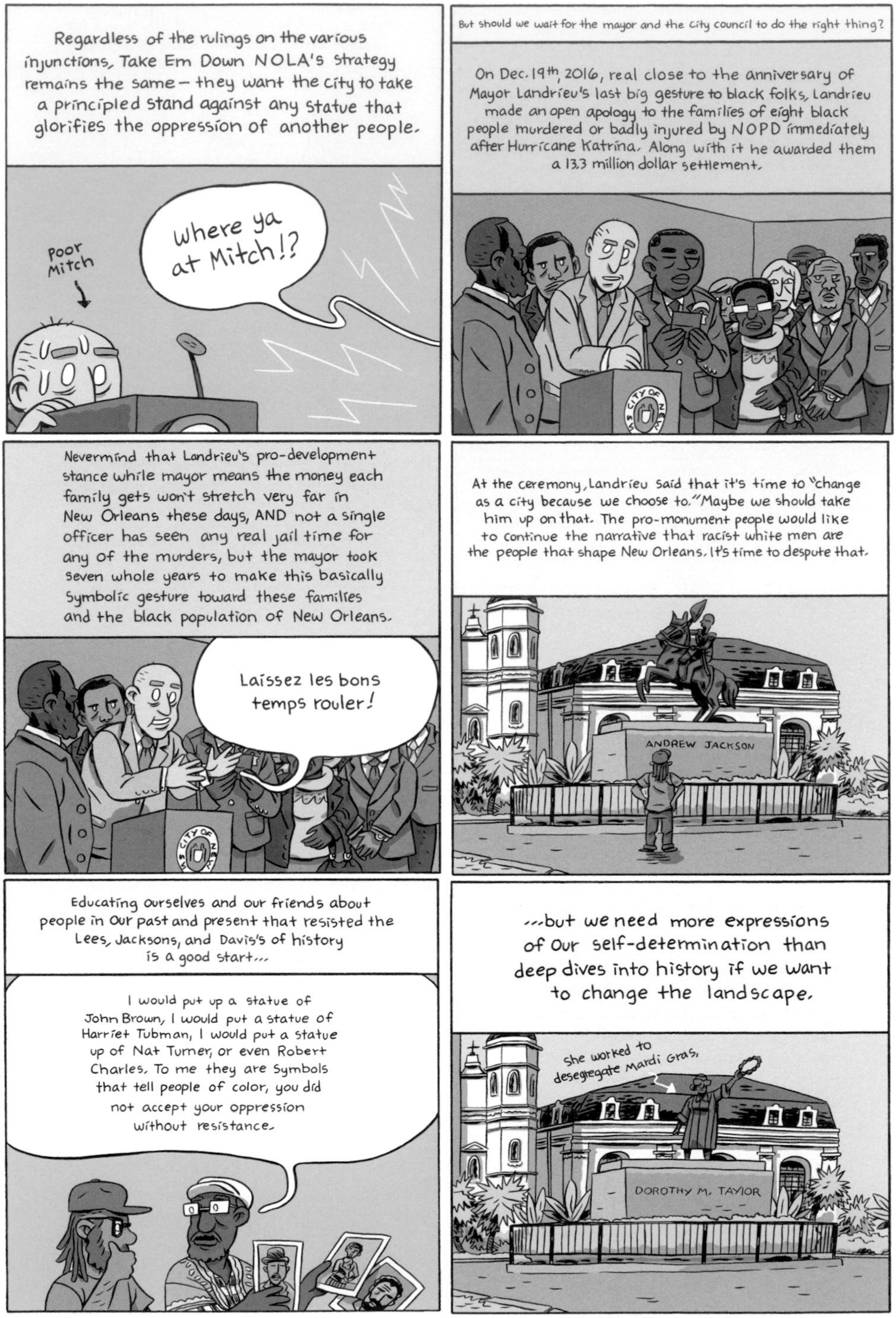
Regardless of the rulings on the various injunctions, Take Em Down NOLA's strategy remains the same — they want the city to take a principled stand against any statue that glorifies the oppression of another people.
Poor Mitch
Where ya at Mitch!?
But should we wait for the mayor and the city council to do the right thing?
On Dec. 19th, 2016, real close to the anniversary of Mayor Landrieu's last big gesture to black folks, Landrieu made an open apology to the families of eight black people murdered or badly injured by NOPD immediately after Hurricane Katrina. Along with it he awarded them a 13.3 million dollar settlement.
Nevermind that Landrieu's pro-development stance while mayor means the money each family gets won't stretch very far in New Orleans these days, AND not a single officer has seen any real jail time for any of the murders, but the mayor took seven whole years to make this basically symbolic gesture toward these families and the black population of New Orleans.
Laissez les bons temps rouler!
At the ceremony, Landrieu said that it's time to "change as a city because we choose to." Maybe we should take him up on that. The pro-monument people would like to continue the narrative that racist white men are the people that shape New Orleans. It's time to despute that.
ANDREW JACKSON
Educating ourselves and our friends about people in our past and present that resisted the Lees, Jacksons, and Davis's of history is a good start...
I would put up a statue of John Brown, I would put a statue of Harriet Tubman, I would put a statue up of Nat Turner, or even Robert Charles. To me they are symbols that tell people of color, you did not accept your oppression without resistance.
...but we need more expressions of our self-determination than deep dives into history if we want to change the landscape.
She worked to desegregate Mardi Gras.
DOROTHY M. TAYLOR

Black people have been gaslighted in America. We're simultaneously told that we'll find equality and success now that slavery is gone (by the way it's not), while simultaneously living amongst countless shrines to the people that enslaved us.

Also you gotta ask yourself, who are these shrines for?

def not us.

Or as one of my favorites said...

What what people have to do, is to try and find out in their own hearts why it was necessary to have the "Nigger" in the first place.

James Baldwin
Poet, novelist, not your negro.

If these monuments are symbols of white supremacy then how they are removed will be just as symbolic. If these monuments are celebrations of white supremacy then maybe their destruction should also be a celebration

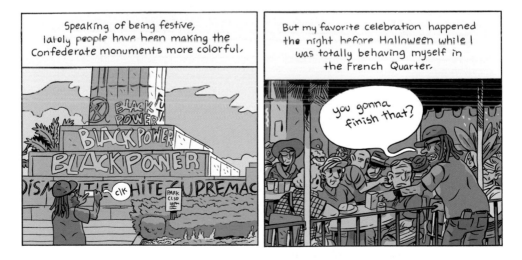

Speaking of being festive, lately people have been making the Confederate monuments more colorful.

BLACK POWER
BLACK POWER
BLACK POWER
DISMANTLE WHITE SUPREMAC

clk

PARK CLSD

But my favorite celebration happened the night before Halloween while I was totally behaving myself in the French Quarter.

you gonna finish that?

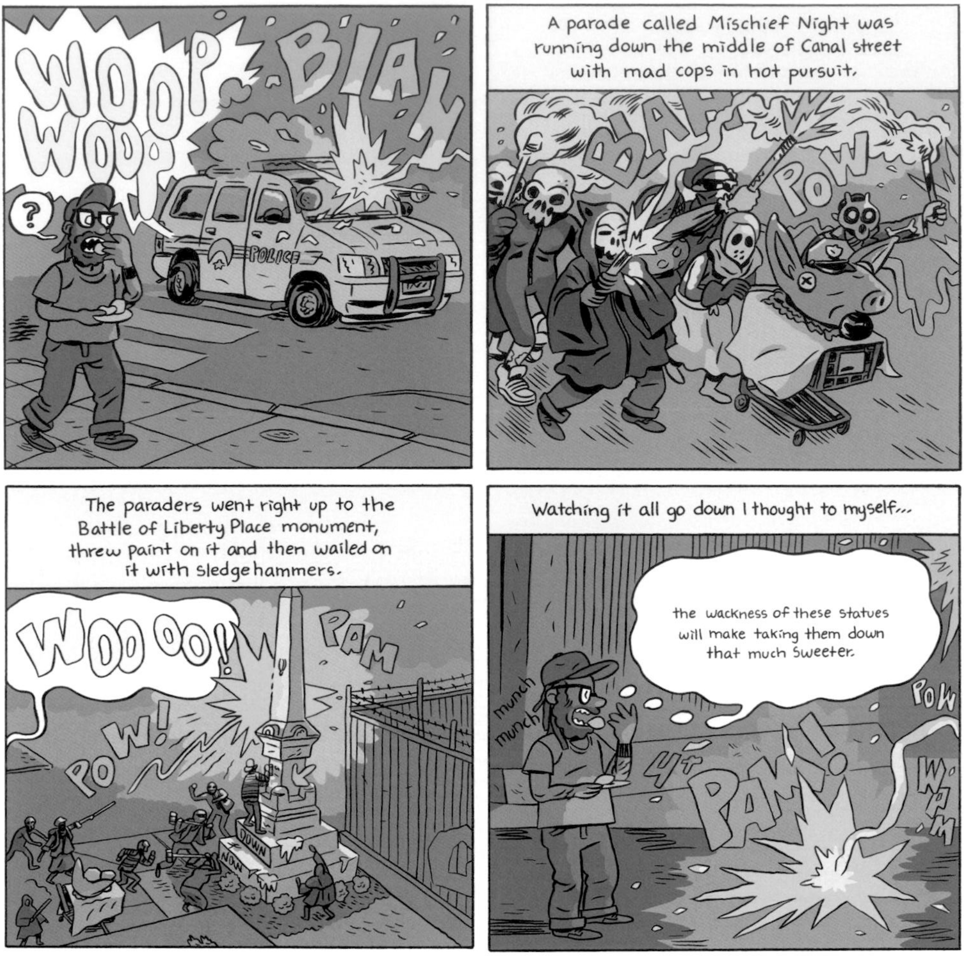
WOOP WOOP
BLAM
?
A parade called Mischief Night was running down the middle of Canal street with mad cops in hot pursuit.
BLAM
POW
The paraders went right up to the Battle of Liberty Place monument, threw paint on it and then wailed on it with sledgehammers.
WOOOO!
PAM
POW!
Watching it all go down I thought to myself...
the wackness of these statues will make taking them down that much sweeter.
munch munch
POW
PAM!
WAM

In the future, it would be nice to see Our country celebrate the people who were really responsible for our freedoms. In the meantime, it's up to us to be our own symbols of liberation.

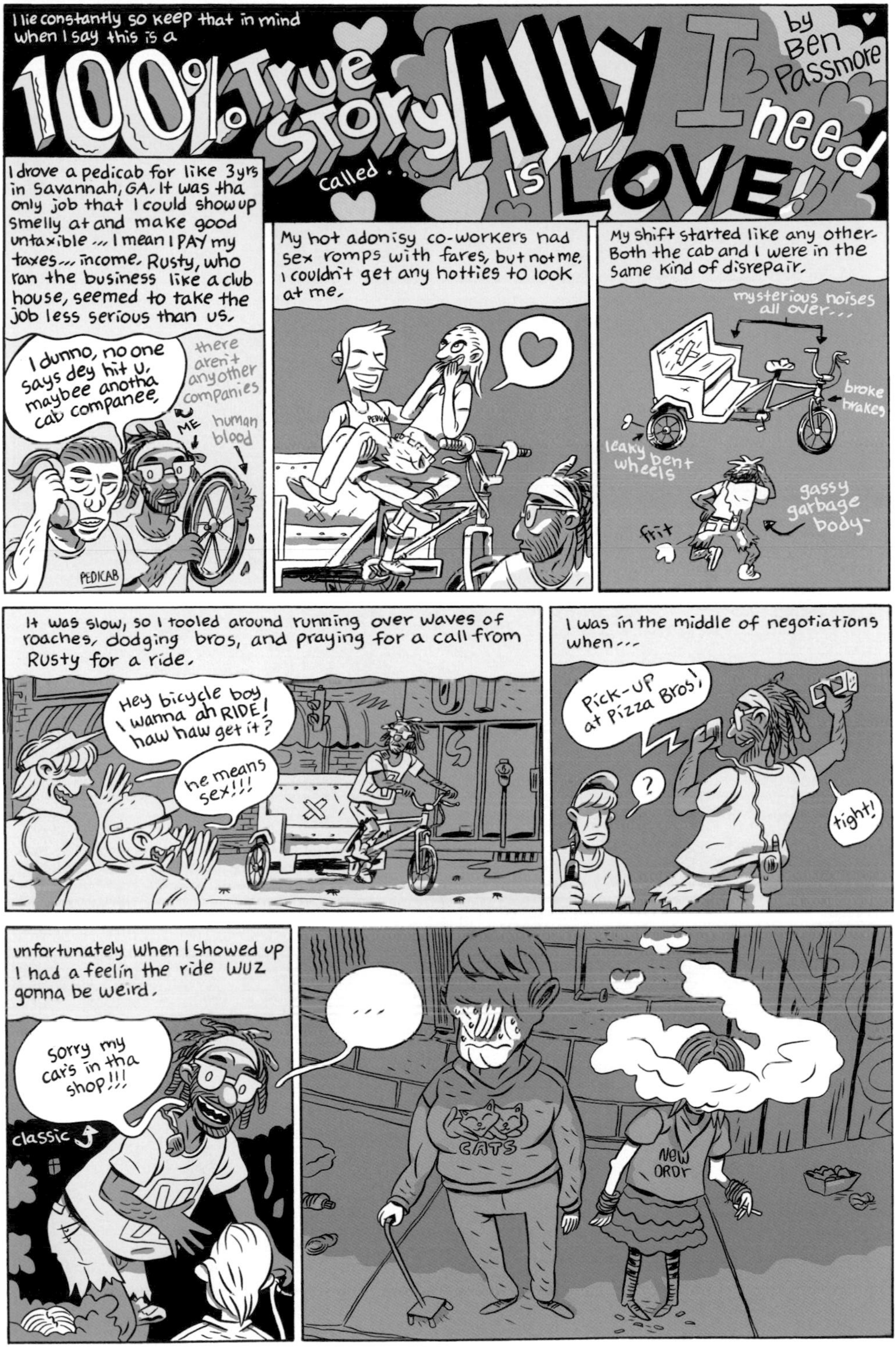
I lie constantly so keep that in mind when I say this is a
100% True Story called . . . ALL I need IS LOVE!
by Ben Passmore
I drove a pedicab for like 3yrs in Savannah, GA. It was tha only job that I could show up smelly at and make good untaxible ... I mean I PAY my taxes ... income. Rusty, who ran the business like a club house, seemed to take the job less serious than us.
I dunno, no one says dey hit u, maybee anotha cab companee.
there aren't any other companies
ME
human blood
PEDICAB
My hot adonisy co-workers had sex romps with fares, but not me. I couldn't get any hotties to look at me.
My shift started like any other. Both the cab and I were in the same kind of disrepair.
mysterious noises all over...
broke brakes
leaky bent wheels
gassy garbage body
frit
It was slow, so I tooled around running over waves of roaches, dodging bros, and praying for a call from Rusty for a ride.
Hey bicycle boy I wanna ah RIDE! haw haw get it?
he means sex!!!
I was in the middle of negotiations when...
Pick-up at Pizza Bros!
?
tight!
unfortunately when I showed up I had a feelin the ride WUZ gonna be weird.
Sorry my cars in tha shop!!!
classic
...
CATS
NEW ORDR

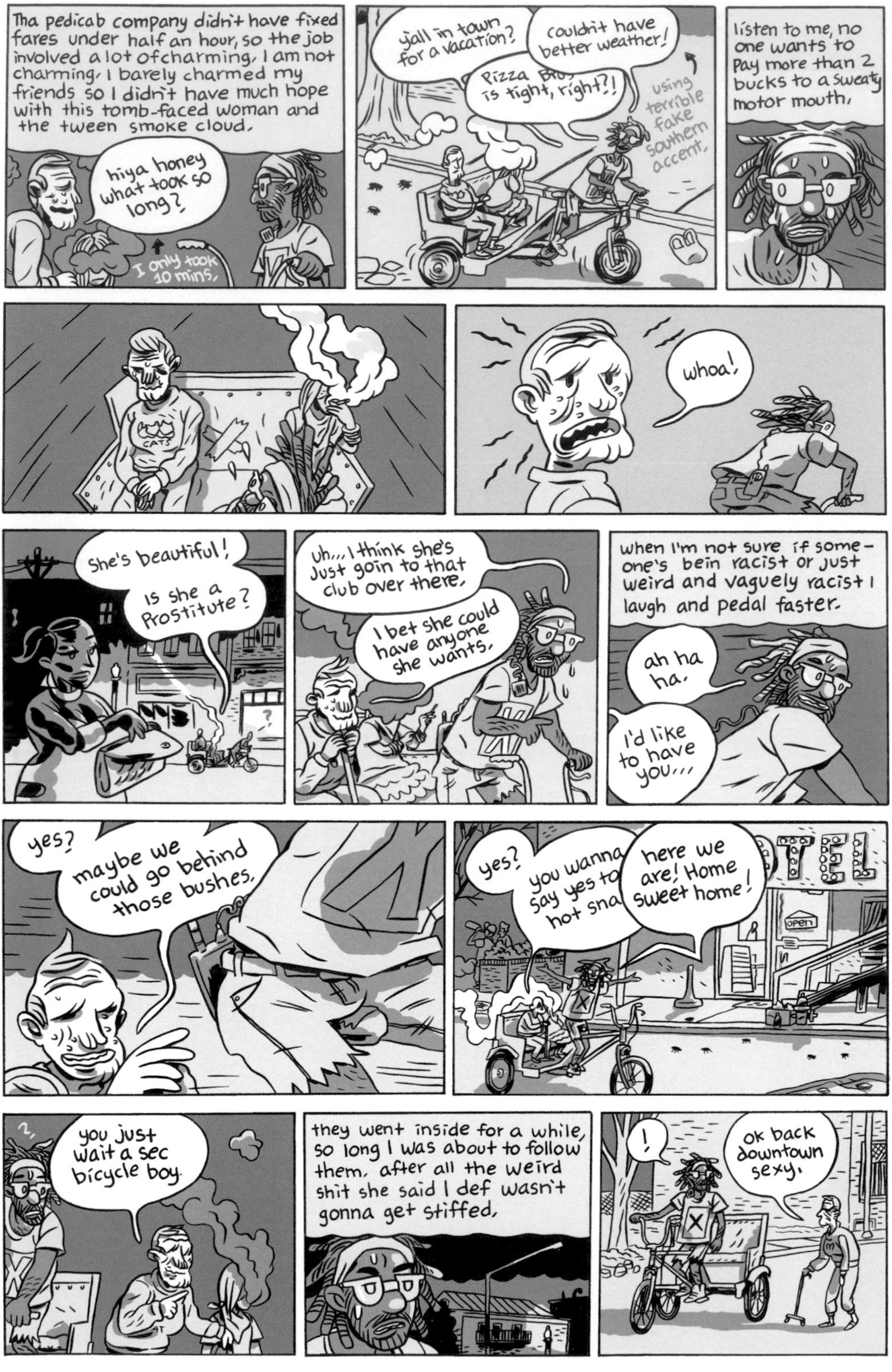
Tha pedicab company didn't have fixed fares under half an hour, so the job involved a lot of charming, I am not charming, I barely charmed my friends so I didn't have much hope with this tomb-faced woman and the tween smoke cloud,
hiya honey what took so long?
I only took 10 mins,
y'all in town for a vacation?
couldn't have better weather!
Pizza Bro, is tight, right?!
using terrible fake southern accent,
listen to me, no one wants to pay more than 2 bucks to a sweaty motor mouth,
whoa!
She's beautiful!
Is she a prostitute?
uh,,, I think she's just goin to that club over there,
I bet she could have anyone she wants,
when I'm not sure if some-one's bein racist or just weird and vaguely racist I laugh and pedal faster.
ah ha ha,
I'd like to have you,,,
yes?
maybe we could go behind those bushes,
yes?
you wanna say yes to hot sna
here we are! Home sweet home!
you just wait a sec bicycle boy.
they went inside for a while, so long I was about to follow them, after all the weird shit she said I def wasn't gonna get stiffed,
!
ok back downtown sexy,

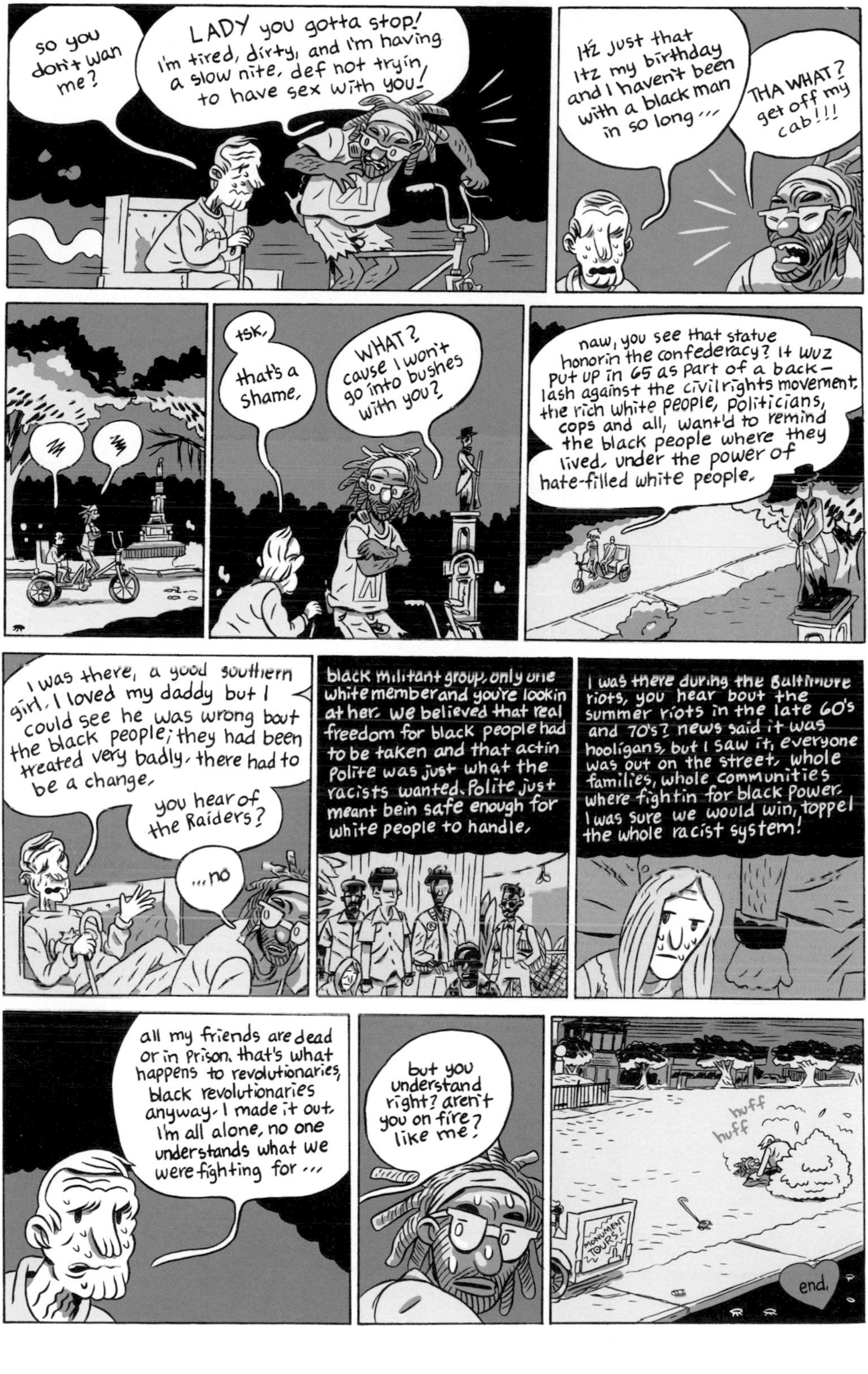
so you don't wan me?
LADY you gotta stop! I'm tired, dirty, and I'm having a slow nite, def not tryin to have sex with you!
Itz just that Itz my birthday and I haven't been with a black man in so long ...
THA WHAT? get off my cab!!!
tsk,
that's a shame,
WHAT? cause I won't go into bushes with you?
naw, you see that statue honorin the confederacy? It wuz put up in 65 as part of a back-lash against the civilrights movement, the rich white people, politicians, cops and all, want'd to remind the black people where they lived, under the power of hate-filled white people.
I was there, a good southern girl, I loved my daddy but I could see he was wrong bout the black people; they had been treated very badly, there had to be a change,
you hear of the Raiders?
...no
black militant group, only one white member and you're lookin at her. We believed that real freedom for black people had to be taken and that actin Polite was just what the racists wanted. Polite just meant bein safe enough for white people to handle,
I was there during the Baltimore riots, you hear bout the summer riots in the late 60's and 70's? news said it was hooligans, but I saw it, everyone was out on the street, whole families, whole communities where fightin for black Power. I was sure we would win, toppel the whole racist system!
all my friends are dead or in Prison. that's what happens to revolutionaries, black revolutionaries anyway. I made it out. I'm all alone, no one understands what we were fighting for ...
but you understand right? aren't you on fire like me?
huff
huff
MONUMENT TOURS!
end.

Whose free speech?

As you probably know, on August 12th and 13th a horde of Nazis, white-supremacists, mansplainers, and others that comprise the "Alt-Right" descended on Charlottesville, VA, in response to the city's decision to remove the confederate monuments.

"What brings us together is that we are white, we are people, we will not be replaced!"

Richard Spencer
coined the term "Alt-Right," famously face-punched.

100% MAYO

Even though they were outnumbered by baton, mace, shield and gun wielding goons, ...

...anti-racists and anti-fascists came out to rebuff the Alt-Right.

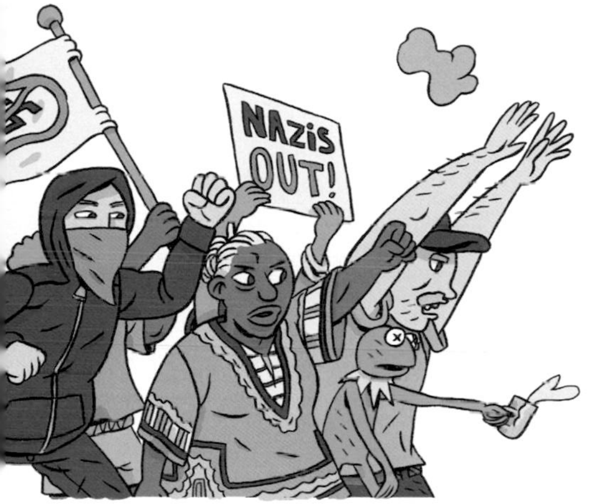
NAZIS
OUT!

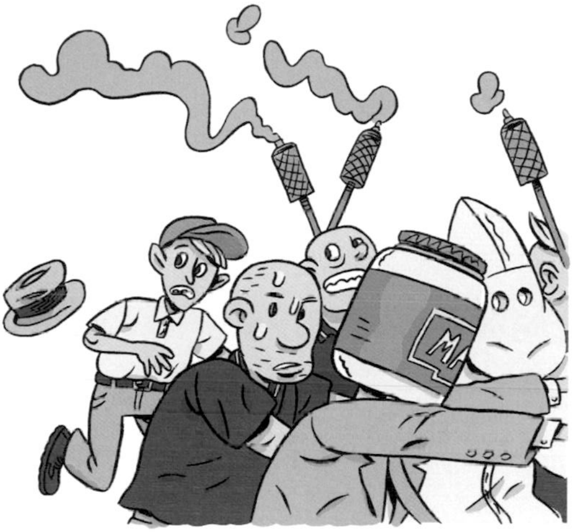

But they couldn't stop a man who'd marched with neo-nazis and white-supremacists, driving his car into a large group of counter-protestors, Killing 32 year-old Heather Heyer and injuring over nineteen other people.

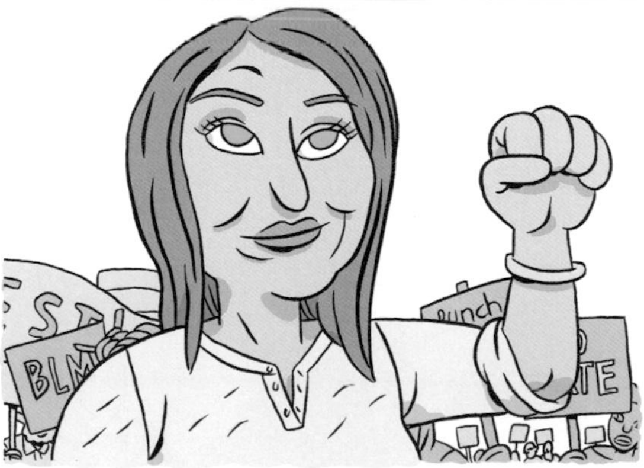
punch

Heather's death is a tragedy and charlottesville is a wake-up call for the whole country.

The city had anticipated some sort of mess and had attempted to move the Alt-Right rally before it started, but the American civil liberties Union stepped in.

"...the city of Charlottesville asked for that to be moved to a park about a mile and a half away...We were unfortunately sued by the ACLU. And the judge ruled against us." (cnn.com)

Terry McAuliffe
Virginia Governor

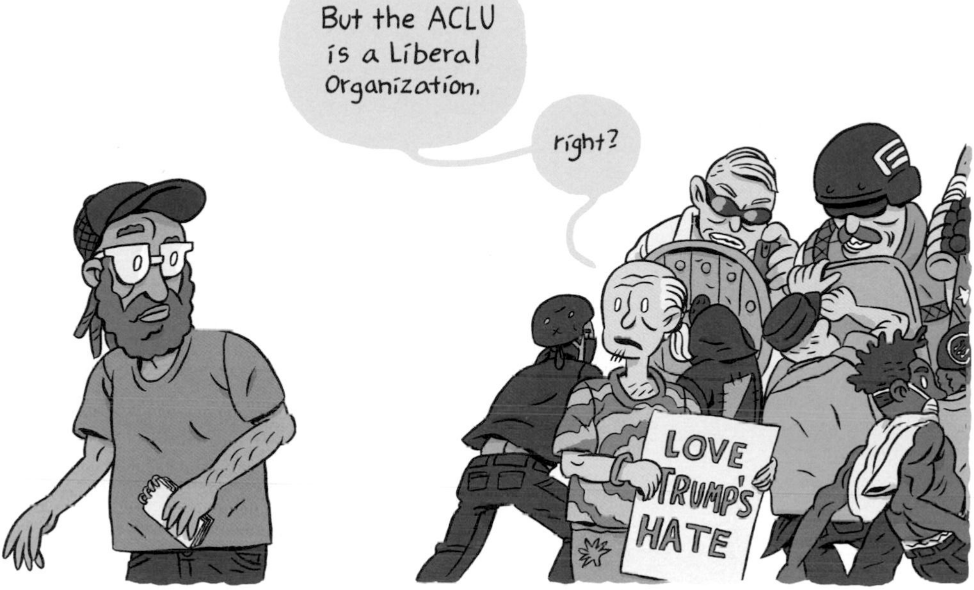
But the ACLU is a Liberal Organization.
right?
LOVE TRUMP'S HATE

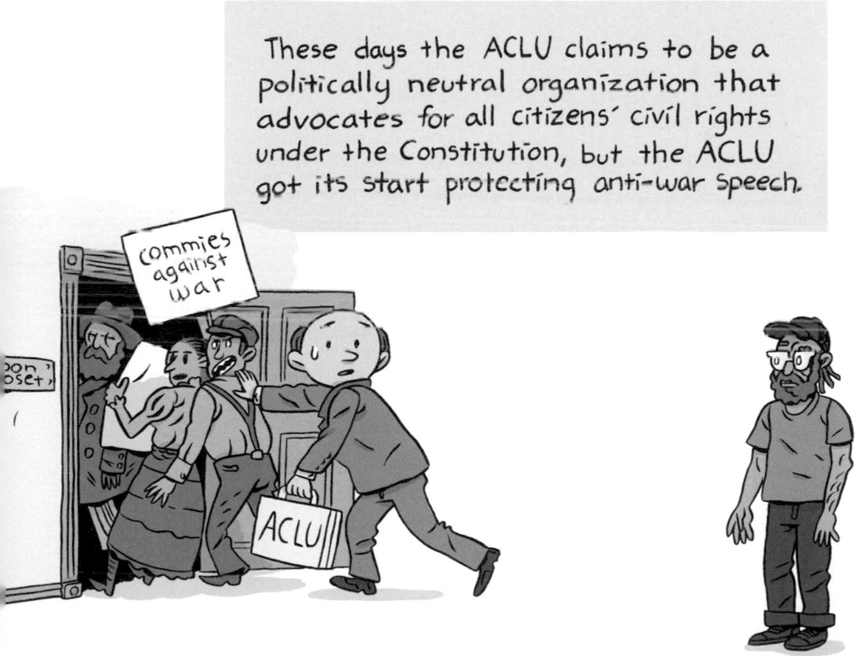
These days the ACLU claims to be a politically neutral organization that advocates for all citizens' civil rights under the Constitution, but the ACLU got its start protecting anti-war speech.
commies against war
ACLU

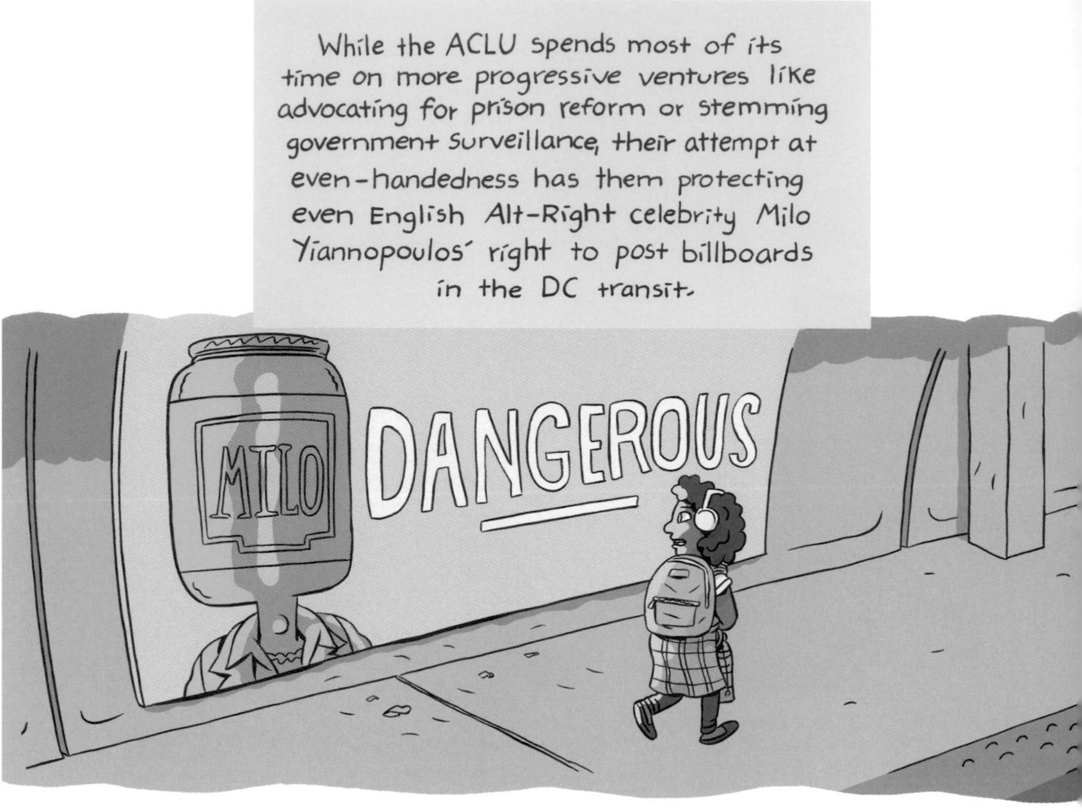
While the ACLU spends most of its time on more progressive ventures like advocating for prison reform or stemming government surveillance, their attempt at even-handedness has them protecting even English Alt-Right celebrity Milo Yiannopoulos' right to post billboards in the DC transit.
MILO
DANGEROUS

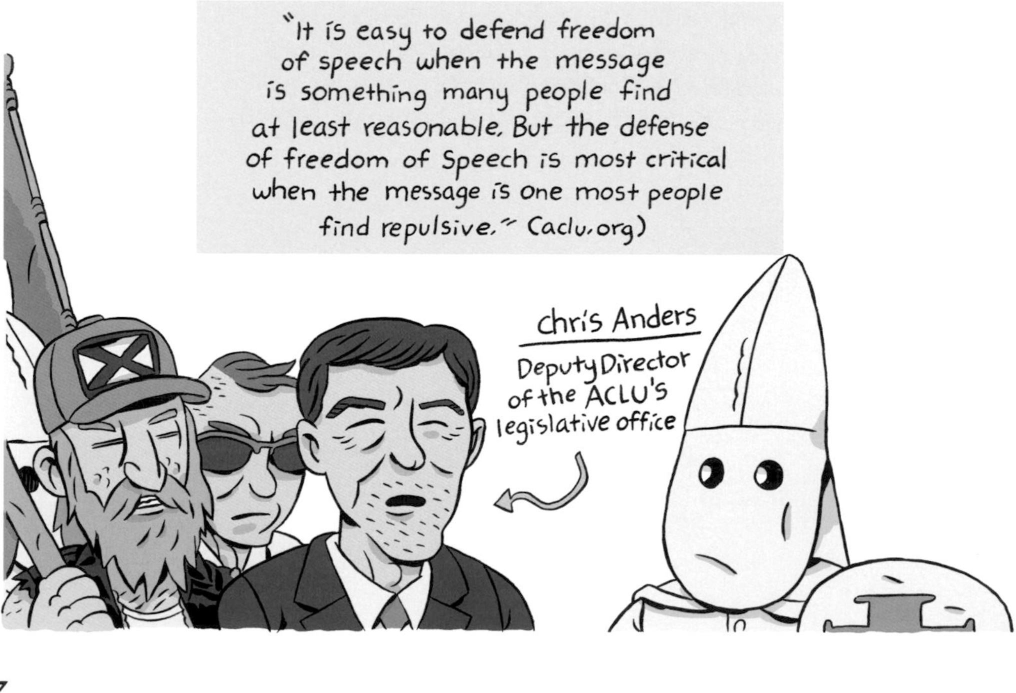
"It is easy to defend freedom of speech when the message is something many people find at least reasonable. But the defense of freedom of Speech is most critical when the message is one most people find repulsive." (aclu.org)
Chris Anders
Deputy Director of the ACLU's legislative office

Ander's response plays into a narrative I've seen the Right creating for itself during the rise of Trump that they are the advocates of "speech" and the Left just want to end debate. That debate itself is the most important thing for society.

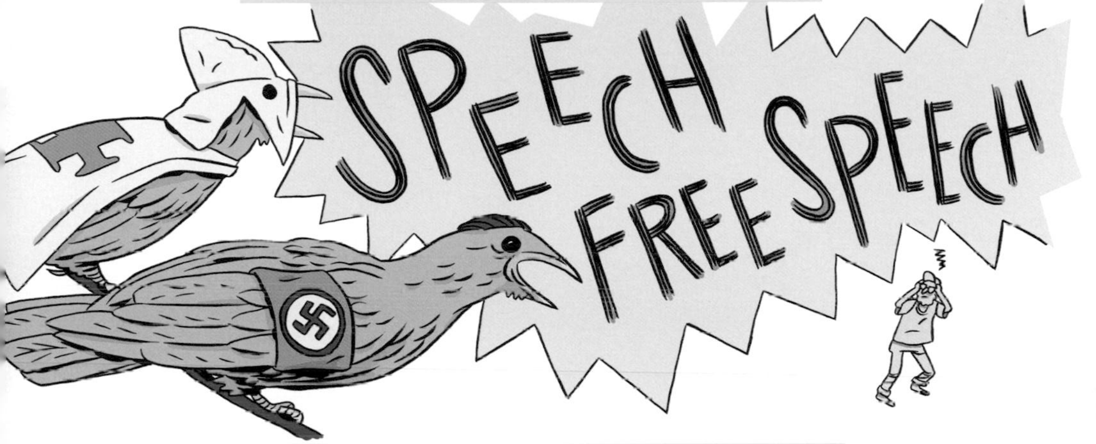
SPEECH
FREE SPEECH

It's a little ironic that the Right sees themselves as the champions of "free-speech." Starting in the early 1900's everyone from the International Workers of the World, the American Communist Party and conscientious objectors fought with the US government in long legal battles to protect antiwar during World War One.

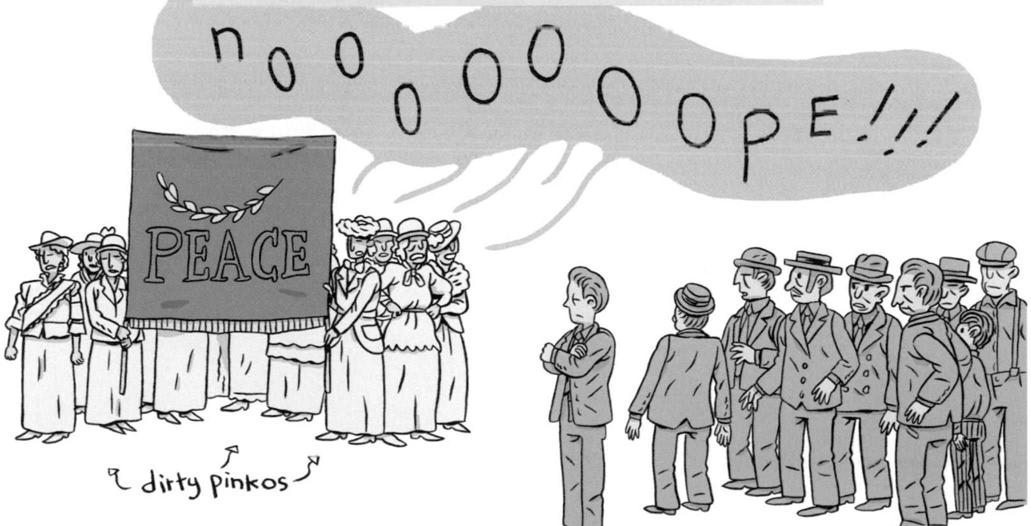
nooooooope!!!
PEACE
dirty pinkos

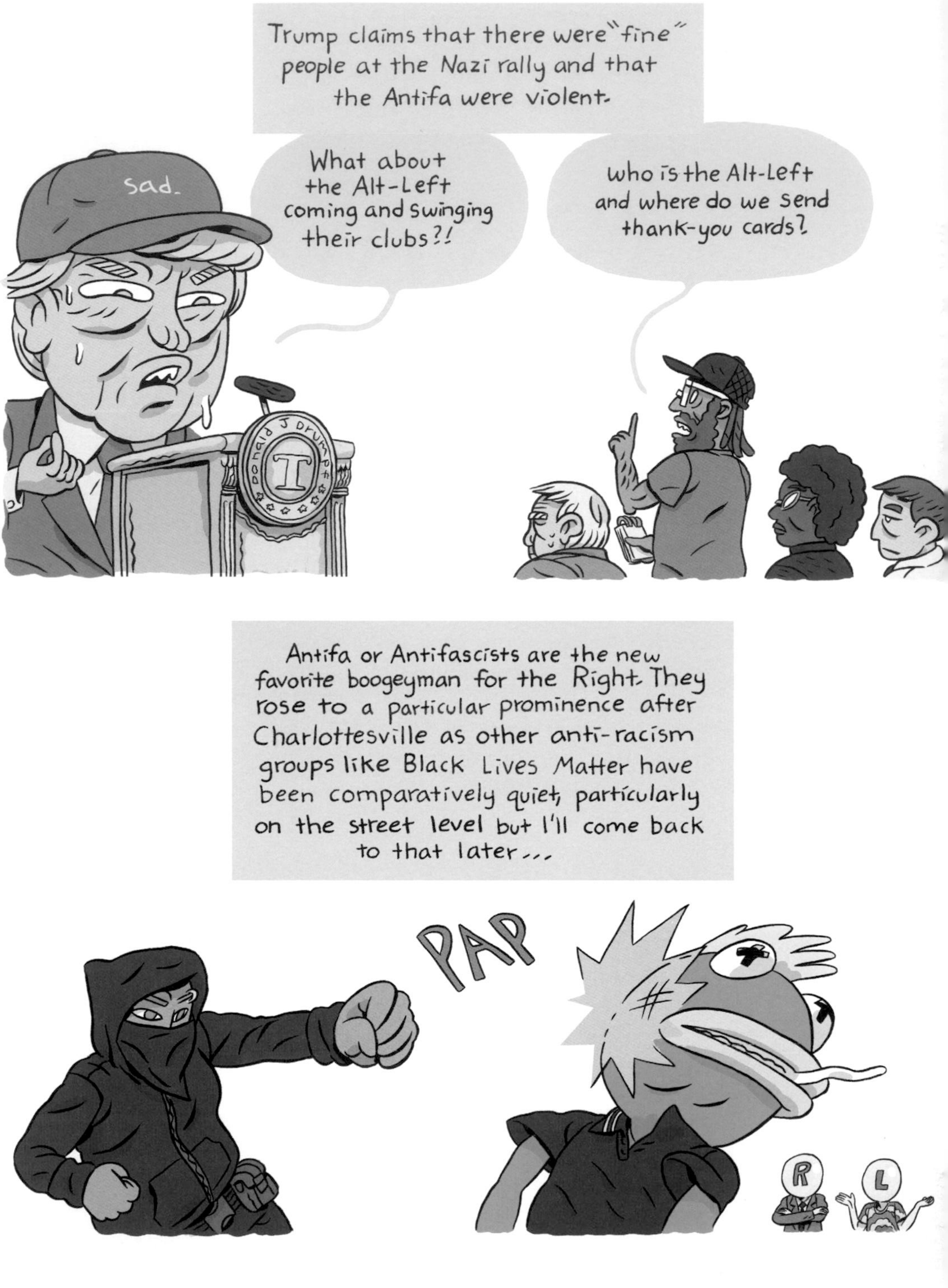

Trump claims that there were "fine" people at the Nazi rally and that the Antifa were violent.
sad.
What about the Alt-Left coming and swinging their clubs?!
Who is the Alt-Left and where do we send thank-you cards?
Antifa or Antifascists are the new favorite boogeyman for the Right. They rose to a particular prominence after Charlottesville as other anti-racism groups like Black Lives Matter have been comparatively quiet, particularly on the street level but I'll come back to that later...
PAP
R
L

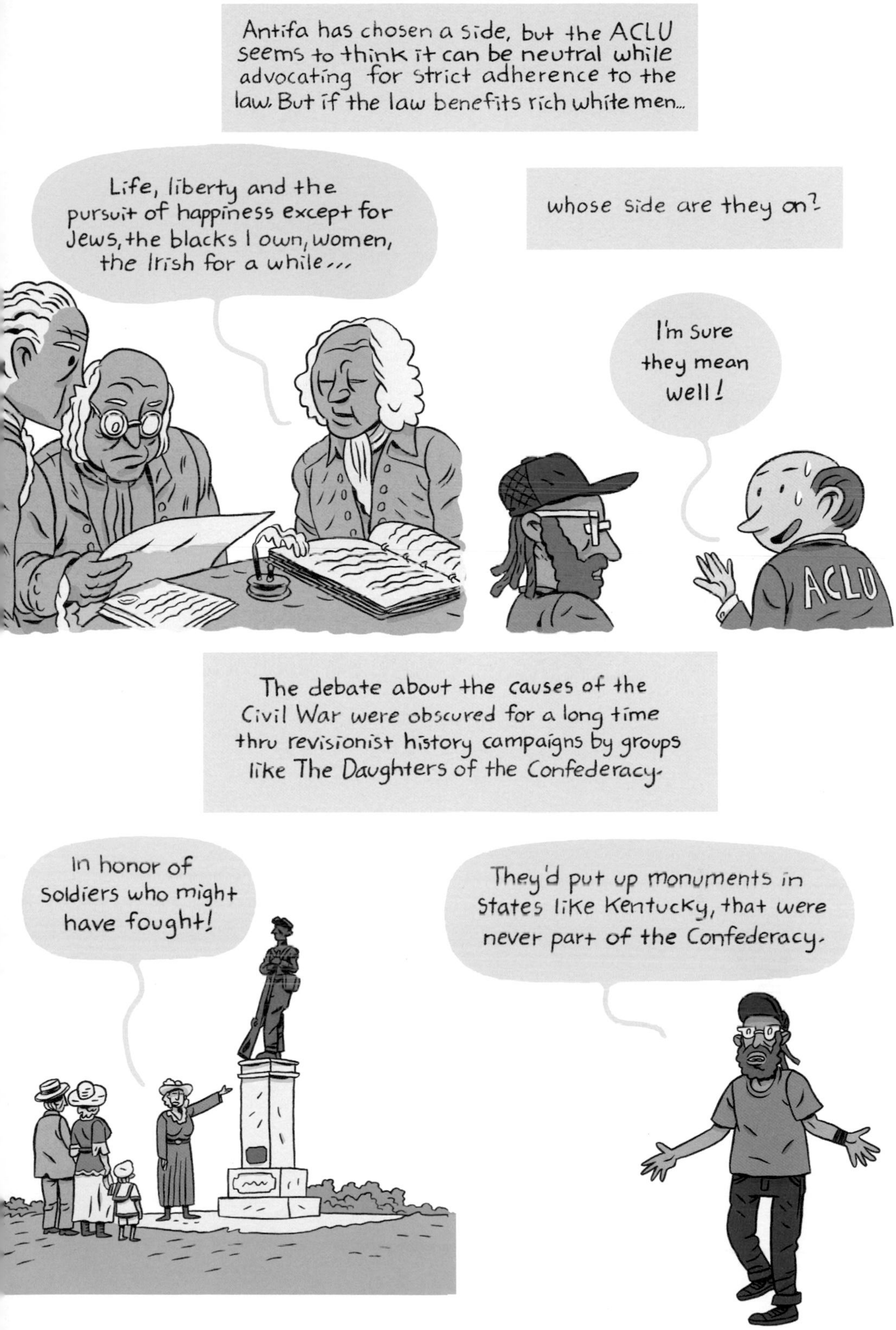
Antifa has chosen a side, but the ACLU seems to think it can be neutral while advocating for strict adherence to the law. But if the law benefits rich white men...
Life, liberty and the pursuit of happiness except for Jews, the blacks I own, women, the Irish for a while...
whose side are they on?
I'm sure they mean well!
ACLU
The debate about the causes of the Civil War were obscured for a long time thru revisionist history campaigns by groups like The Daughters of the Confederacy.
In honor of soldiers who might have fought!
They'd put up monuments in states like Kentucky, that were never part of the Confederacy.

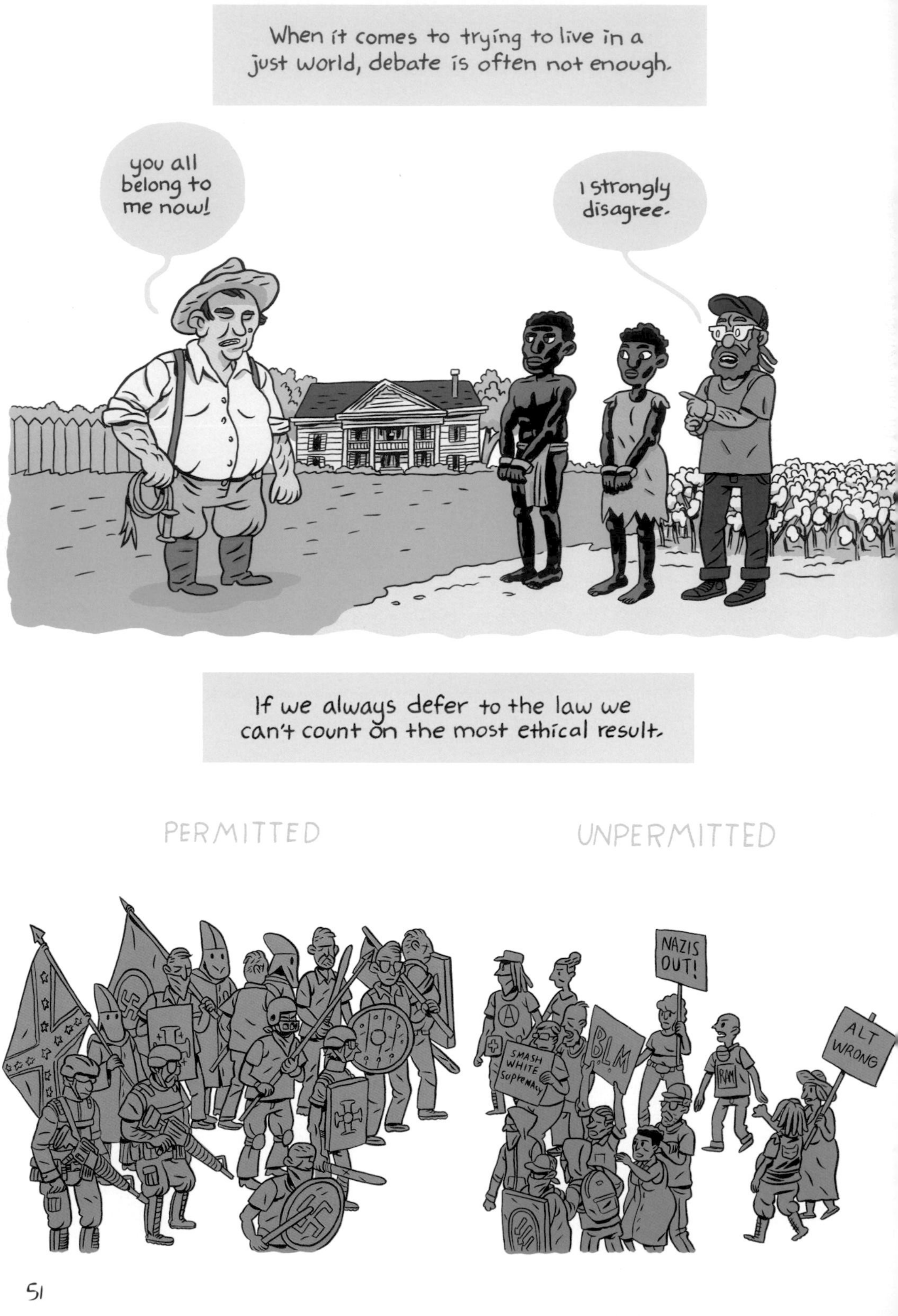
When it comes to trying to live in a just world, debate is often not enough.
you all belong to me now!
I strongly disagree.
If we always defer to the law we can't count on the most ethical result.
PERMITTED
UNPERMITTED
NAZIS OUT!
SMASH WHITE supremacy
BLM
ALT WRONG

Most media portray non-violent protesters as sturdy and wise speech jockeys and everyone else as weak-willed and reactionary. The reality is the history of left-wing struggle is as full of peaceful marches and sit-ins as it is more spirited rebellion.

WE DON'T NEED NO WA-TER...

Who's to say we would have collective bargaining if it wasn't for union strikes that battled factory owners, or Black Lives Matter without the gun-toting Black Panther Party? The Left needs decide if it wants to be respectable or revolutionary, because we can't always be both.

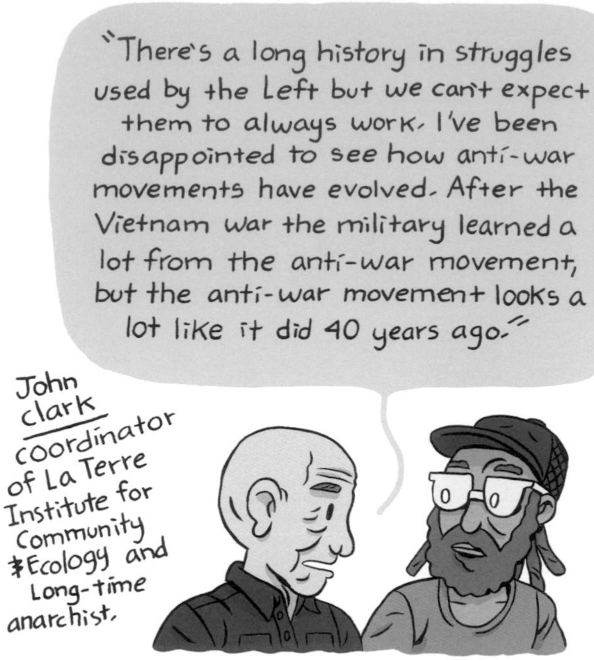
"There's a long history in struggles used by the Left but we can't expect them to always work. I've been disappointed to see how anti-war movements have evolved. After the Vietnam war the military learned a lot from the anti-war movement, but the anti-war movement looks a lot like it did 40 years ago."
John clark
coordinator of La Terre Institute for Community & Ecology and Long-time anarchist.

After Freddie Gray was killed in police custody in 2015, I went to a march organized by B.L.M folks where people planned to stage a die-in after someone read poetry. It seemed like the organizers wanted to invoke the drama of a Civil Rights era sit-in...

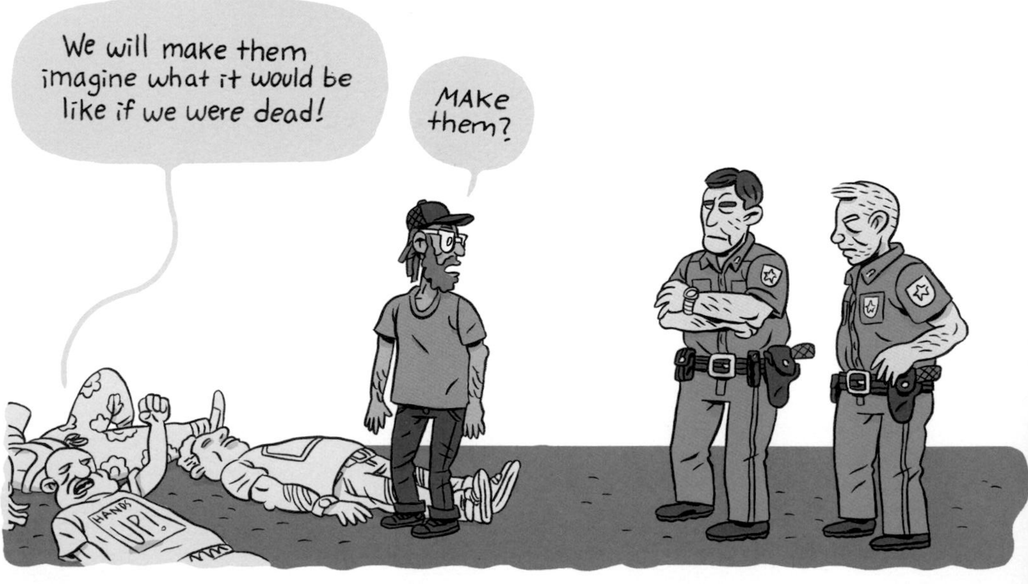
We will make them imagine what it would be like if we were dead!
MAKe them?
HANDS UP!

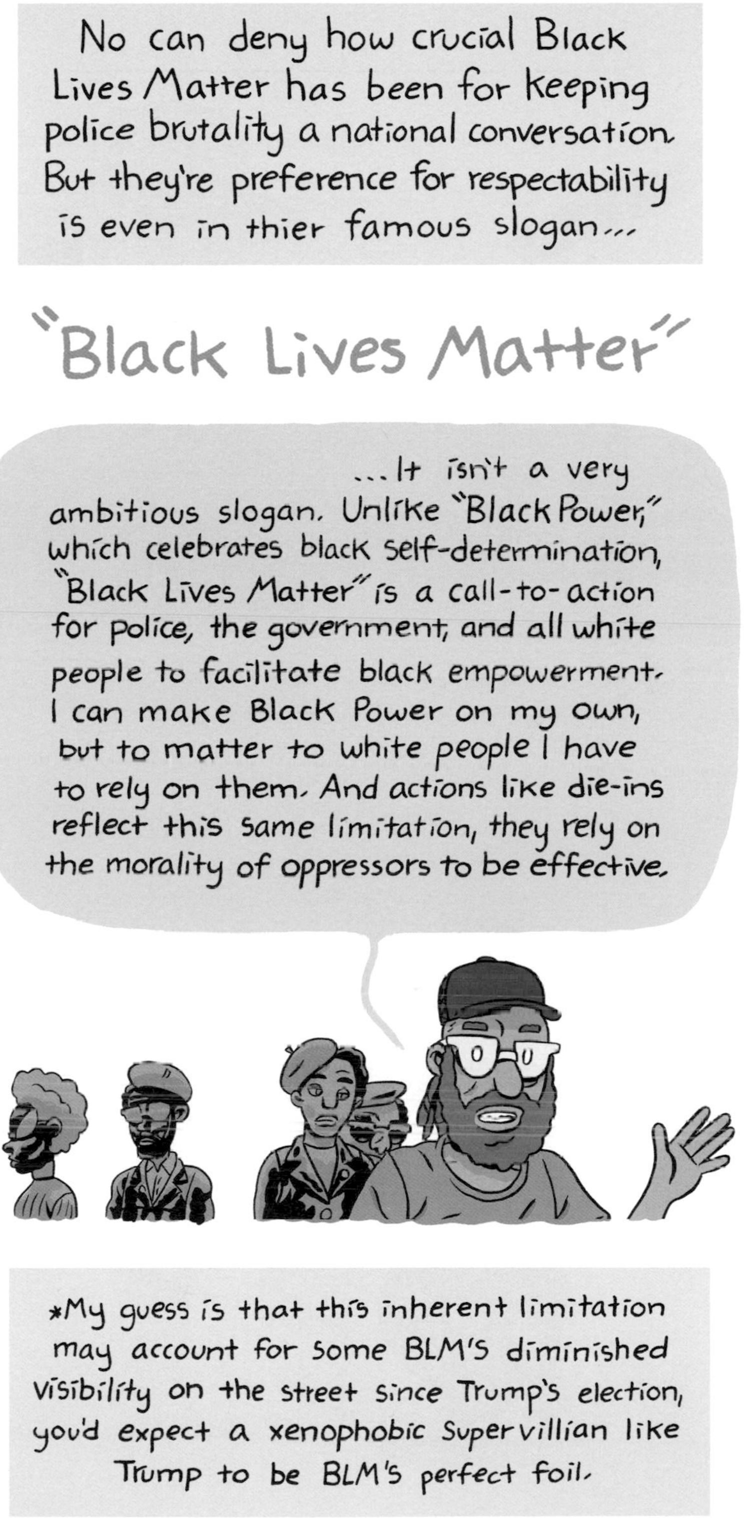
No can deny how crucial Black Lives Matter has been for keeping police brutality a national conversation. But they're preference for respectability is even in thier famous slogan...
"Black Lives Matter"
...It isn't a very ambitious slogan. Unlike "Black Power," which celebrates black self-determination, "Black Lives Matter" is a call-to-action for police, the government, and all white people to facilitate black empowerment. I can make Black Power on my own, but to matter to white people I have to rely on them. And actions like die-ins reflect this same limitation, they rely on the morality of oppressors to be effective.
*My guess is that this inherent limitation may account for some BLM'S diminished visibility on the street since Trump's election, you'd expect a xenophobic Supervillian like Trump to be BLM'S perfect foil.

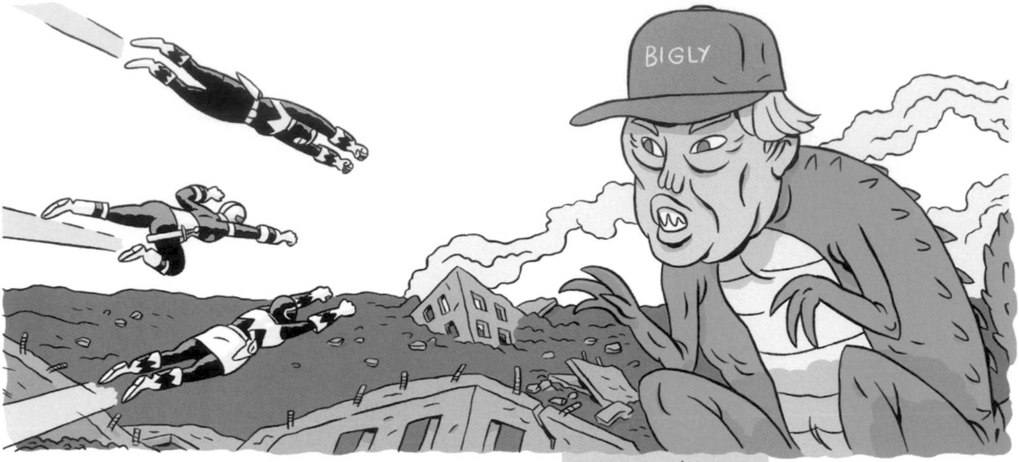
BIGLY

* I contacted several BLM chapters but they declined to comment.

For black people's part, I think our community spends a lot of time shaming itself for behavior that play into white racists' vision of us.

"There's a lot of 'respectability' politics in general in the black community, a lot of poverty shaming, a lot of slut shaming, It just naturally happens because the black community has for so long been in a struggle for survival, and for so long had to choose the 'best' representative in order to shine for us."
(Antigravity Magazine March 2015)

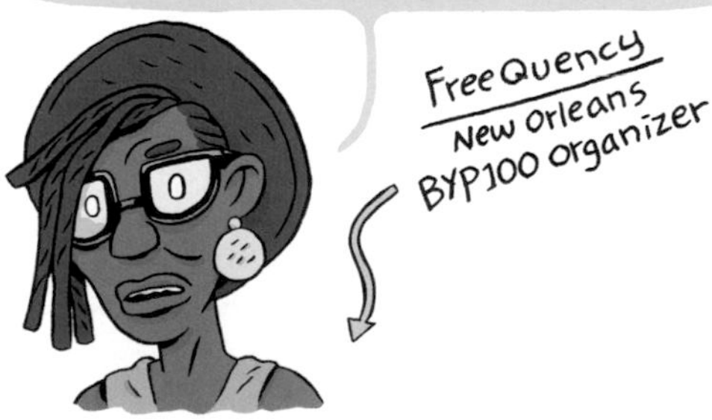
FreeQuency
New Orleans
BYP100 organizer

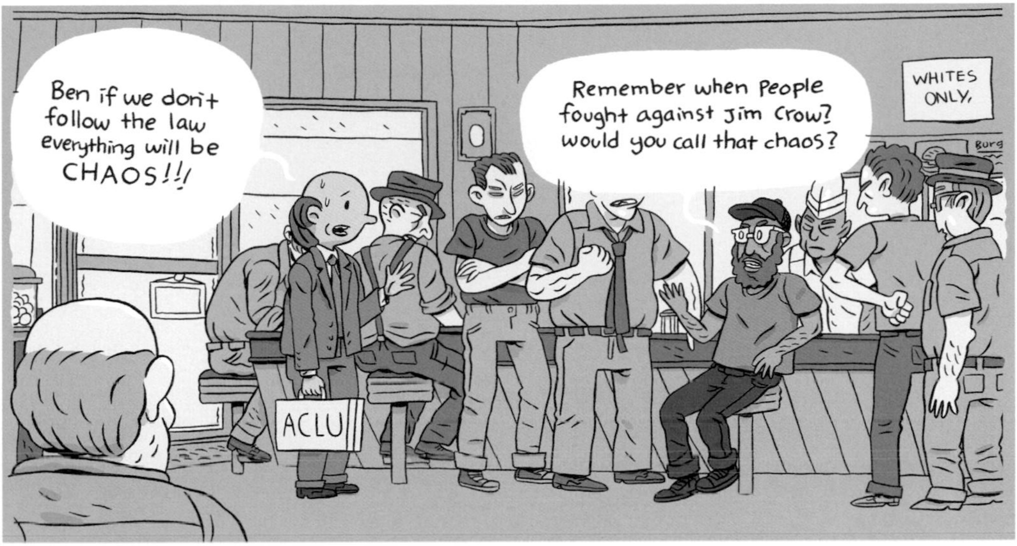
Ben if we don't follow the law everything will be CHAOS!!!
Remember when people fought against Jim Crow? would you call that chaos?
WHITES ONLY.
ACLU

Has BLM joined all other establishment lefty groups in becoming part of the scenery of society's social structure, satisfied with lobbying, running for office, and pod-casting? You'll probably tell me that that's the realistic path way toward change.

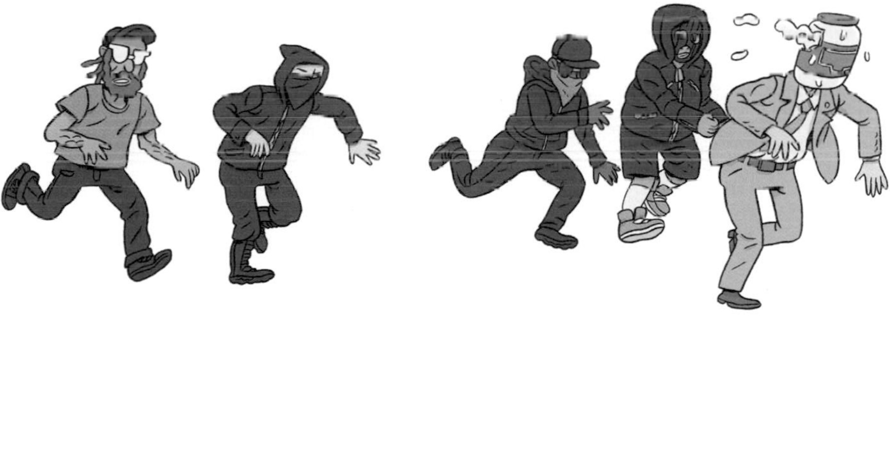

I'd like to think many stratgies can exist at the same time. Clearly for things to improve we have to do more than debate. "Freedom of Speech" isn't worth much if it facilitates inactivity. Which brings me back to everyone's favorite spencher punchers; Antifa.

I was surprised to see Antifa groups crop-up as the Alt-Right, fascist, and white supremacy groups started to rally around Trump in a big way. I associated Antifa with a bygone era that only some of the older punks I knew had been a part of.

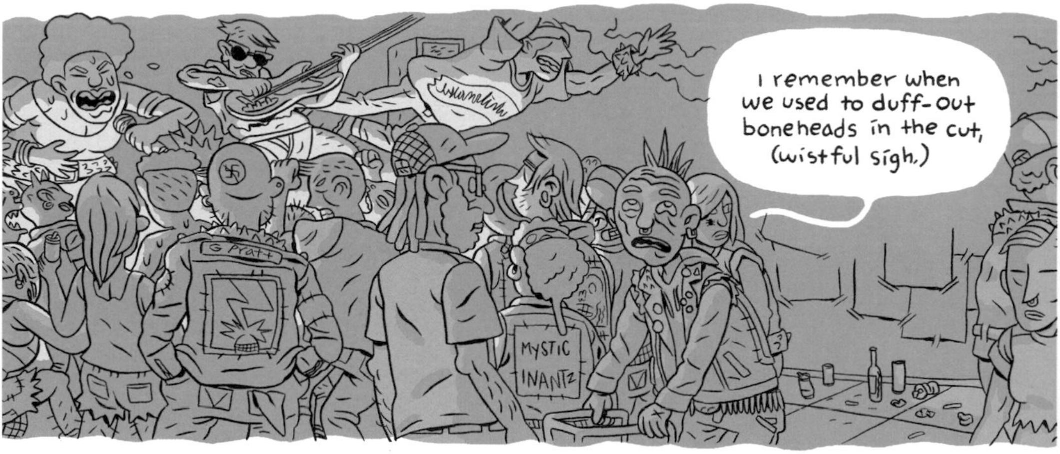
I remember when we used to duff-out boneheads in the cut, (wistful sigh.)

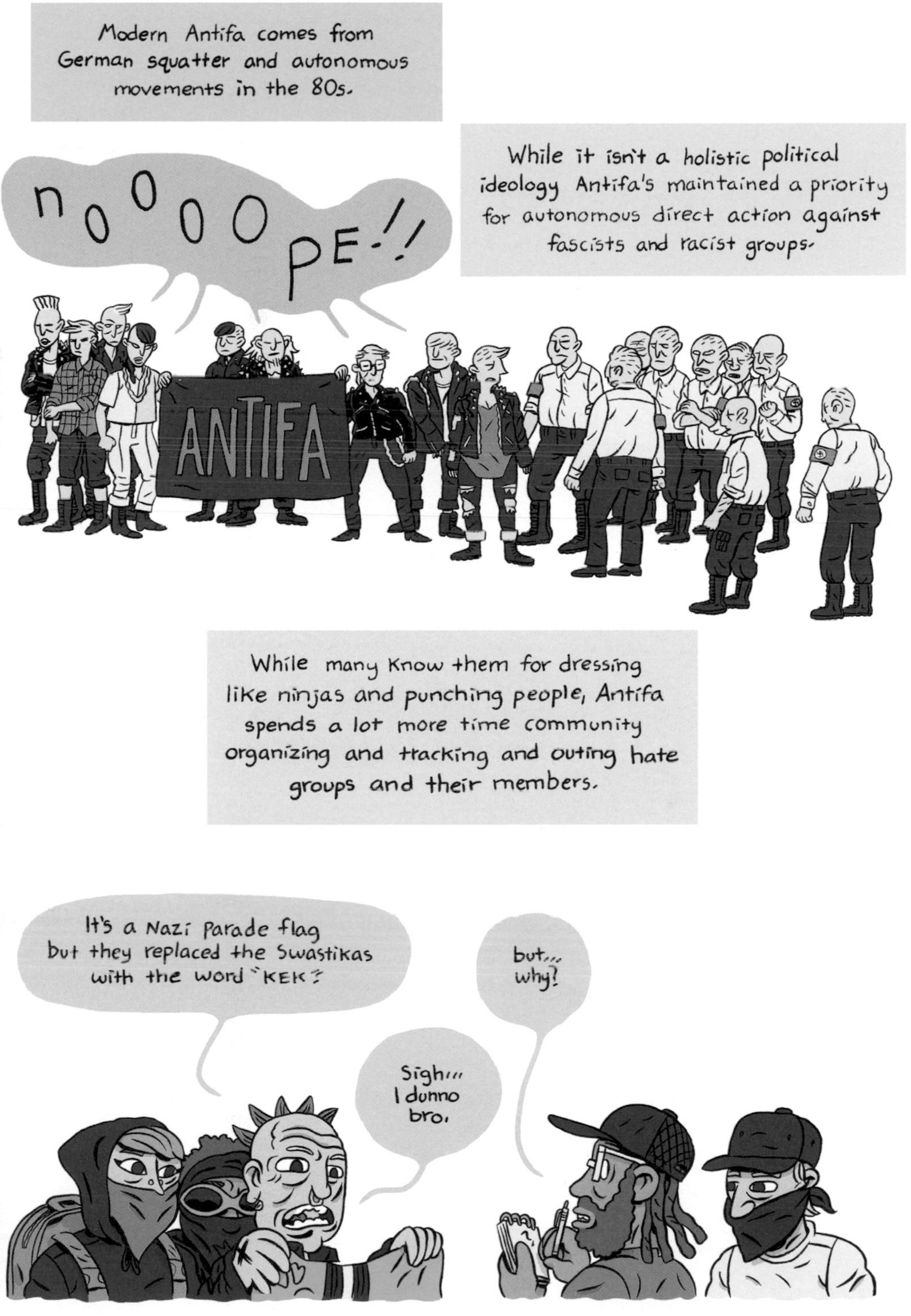
Modern Antifa comes from German squatter and autonomous movements in the 80s.
noooooPE!!
While it isn't a holistic political ideology Antifa's maintained a priority for autonomous direct action against fascists and racist groups.
ANTIFA
While many know them for dressing like ninjas and punching people, Antifa spends a lot more time community organizing and tracking and outing hate groups and their members.
It's a Nazi Parade flag but they replaced the Swastikas with the word "KEK?"
but... why?
Sigh... I dunno bro.

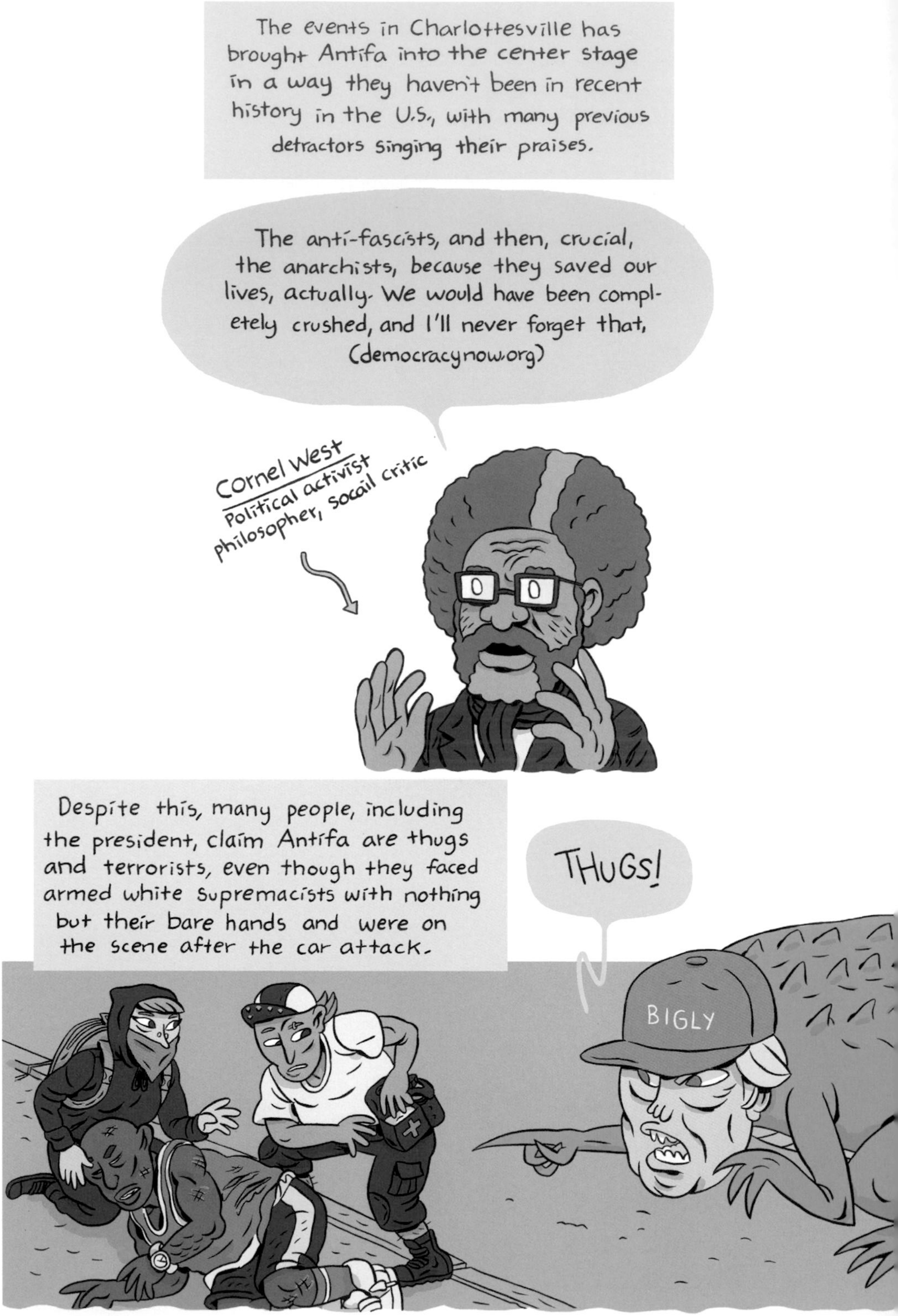
The events in Charlottesville has brought Antifa into the center stage in a way they haven't been in recent history in the U.S., with many previous detractors singing their praises.
The anti-fascists, and then, crucial, the anarchists, because they saved our lives, actually. We would have been completely crushed, and I'll never forget that, (democracynow.org)
Cornel West
Political activist philosopher, socail critic
Despite this, many people, including the president, claim Antifa are thugs and terrorists, even though they faced armed white supremacists with nothing but their bare hands and were on the scene after the car attack.
THUGS!
BIGLY

After Charlottesville, tons of Confederate monuments have come down around the country--but we still have the largest monument to white-supremacy in the country: the presidency of Donald Trump. If the fight to remove racists made out of stone and metal is any indication, we will have to use just as diverse tactics to overcome the real ones.

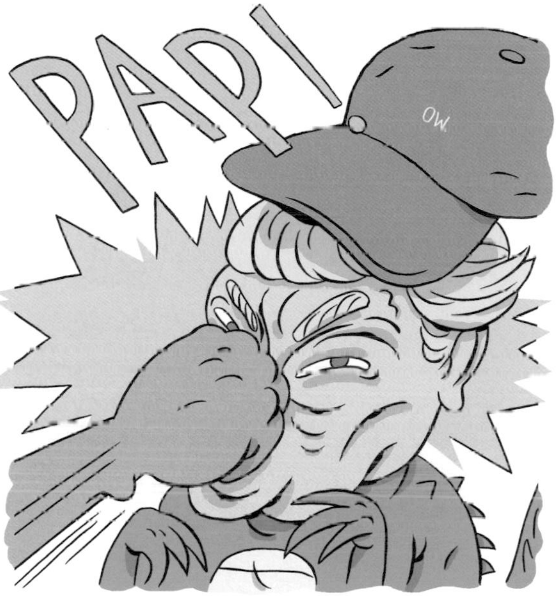
PAP!
OW.

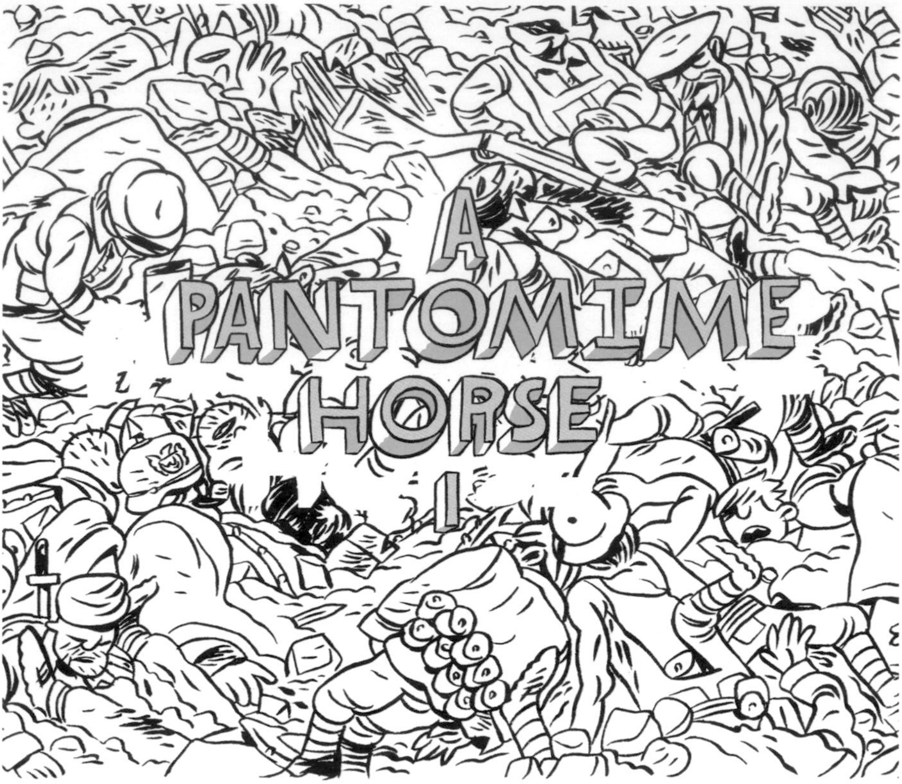
A PANTOMIME HORSE
1

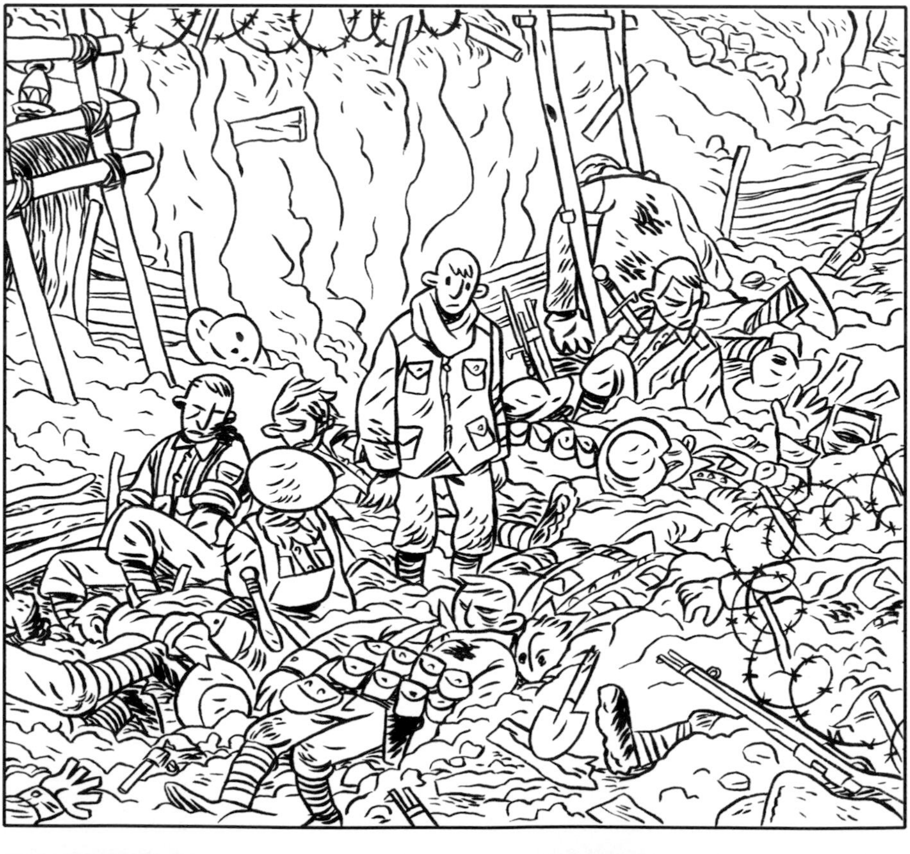

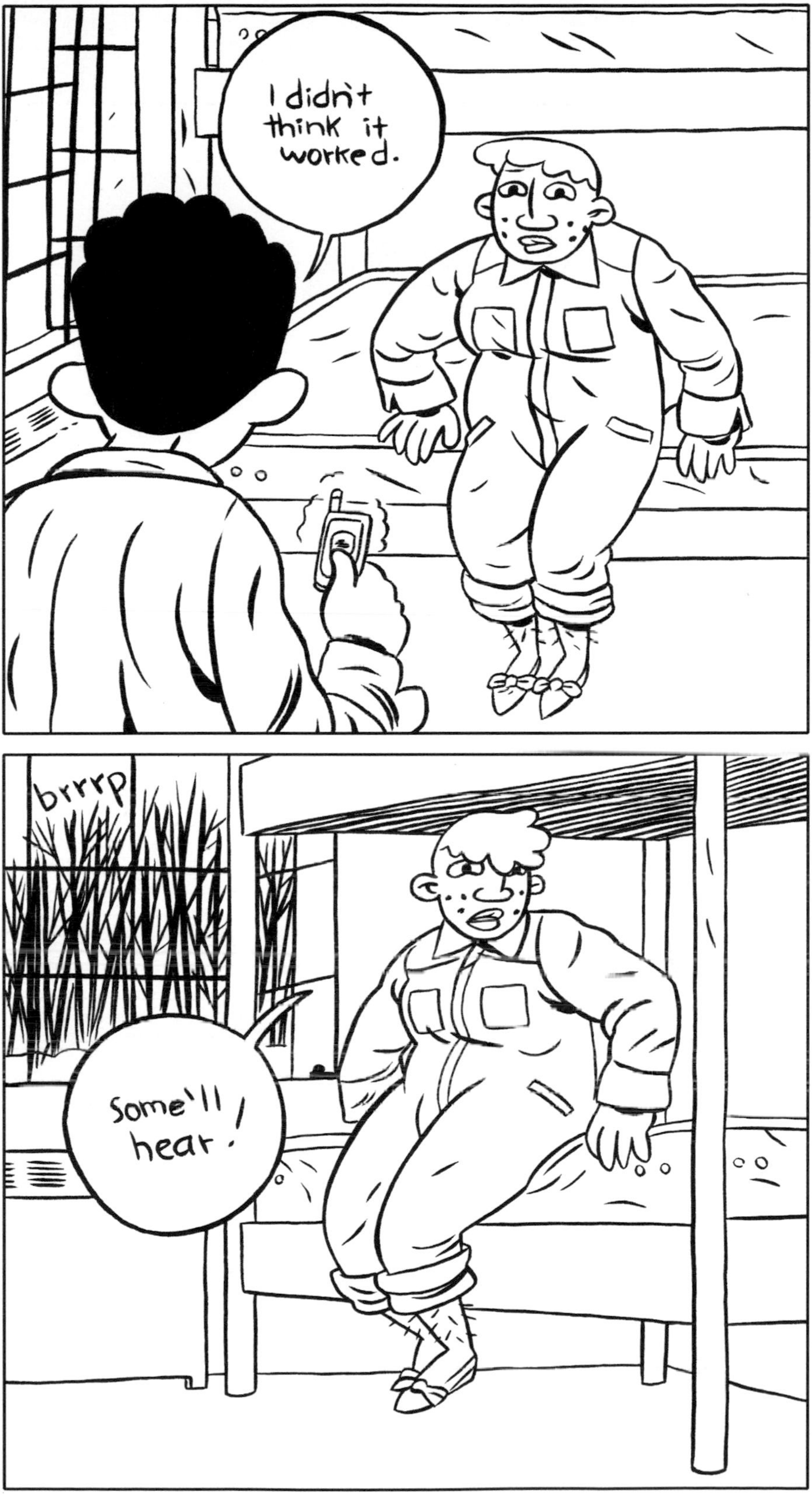
I didn't think it worked.
brrrp
Some'll hear!

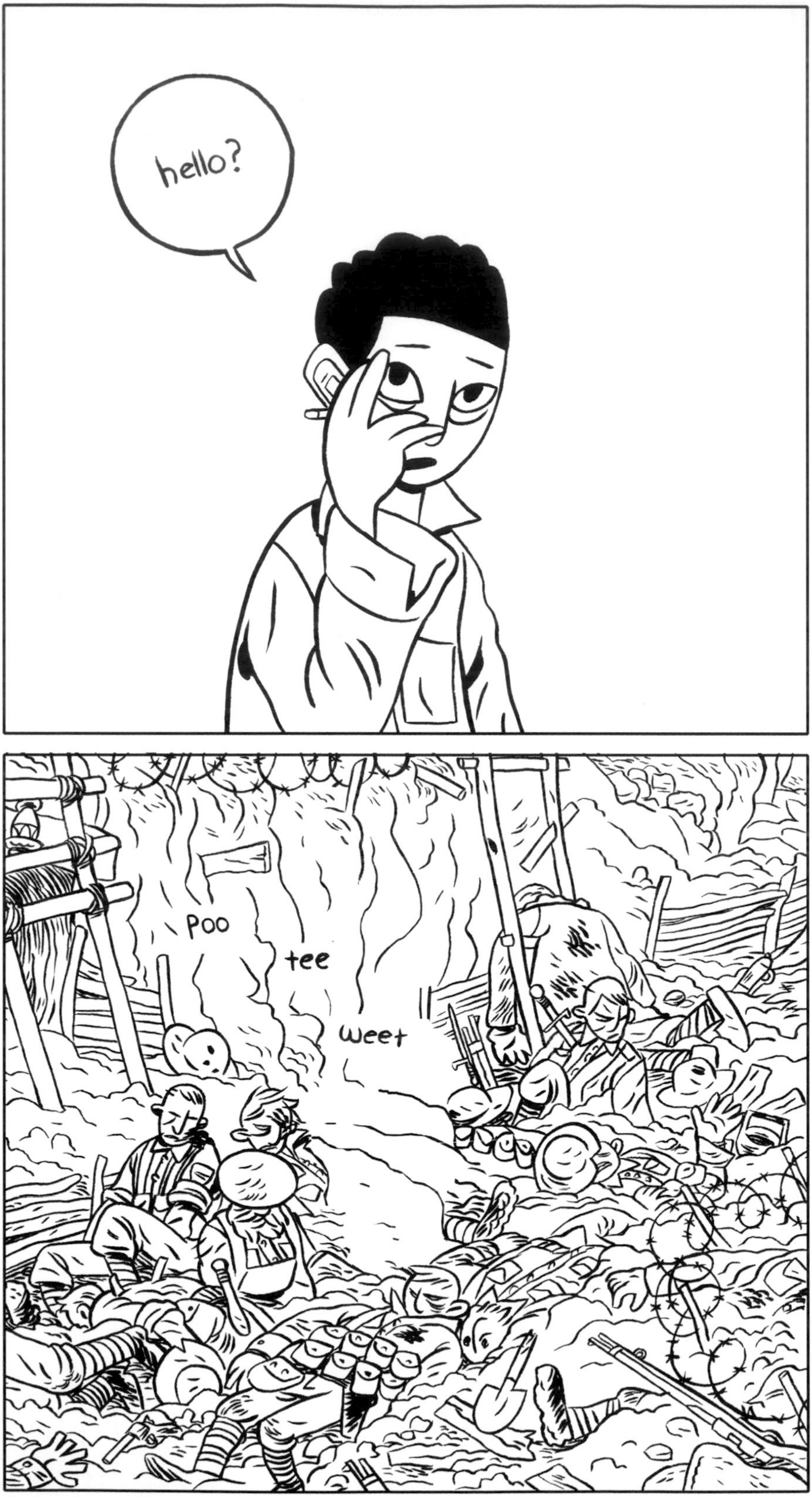
hello?
Poo
tee
weet

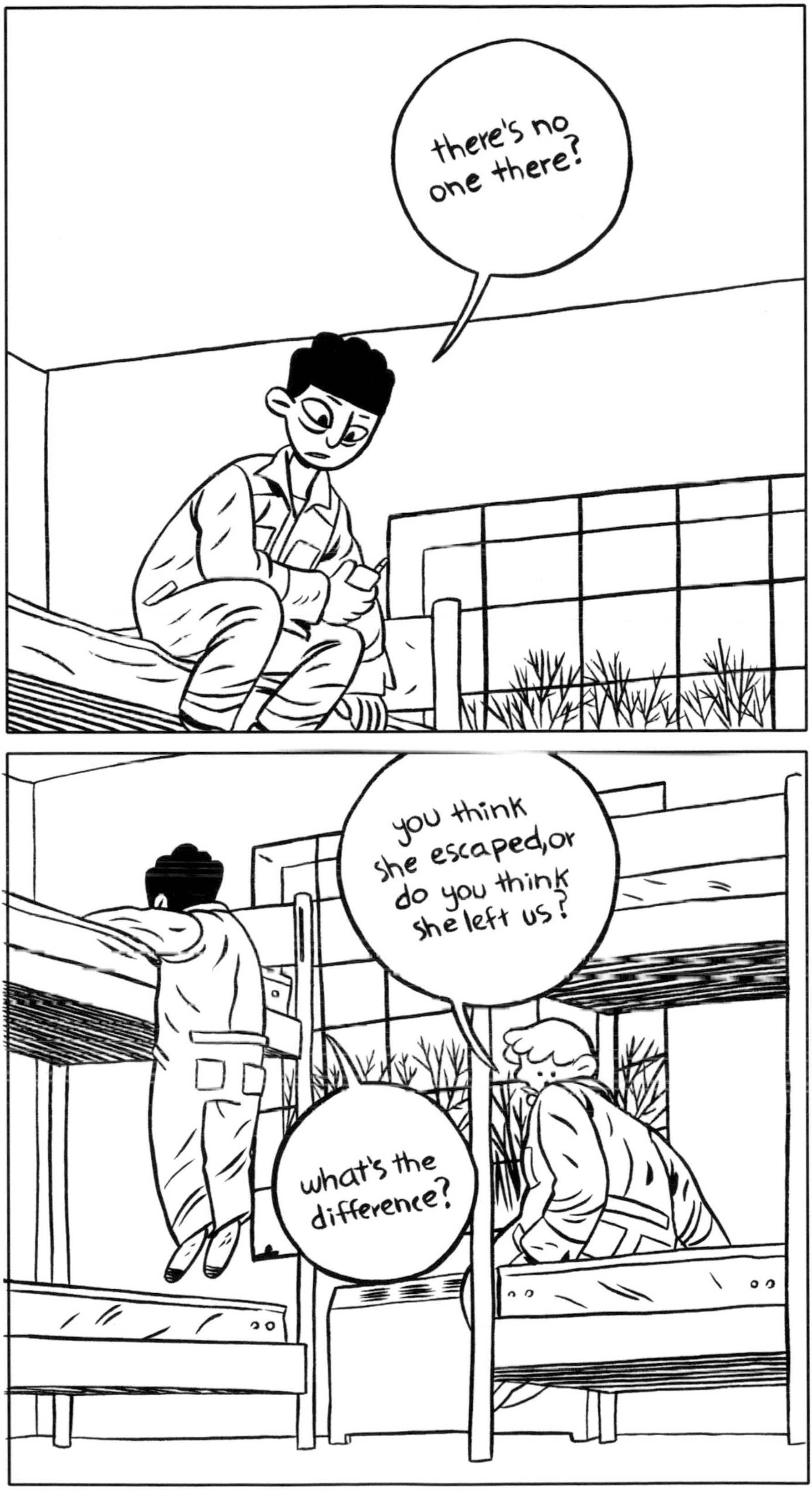
there's no one there?
you think she escaped, or do you think she left us?
what's the difference?

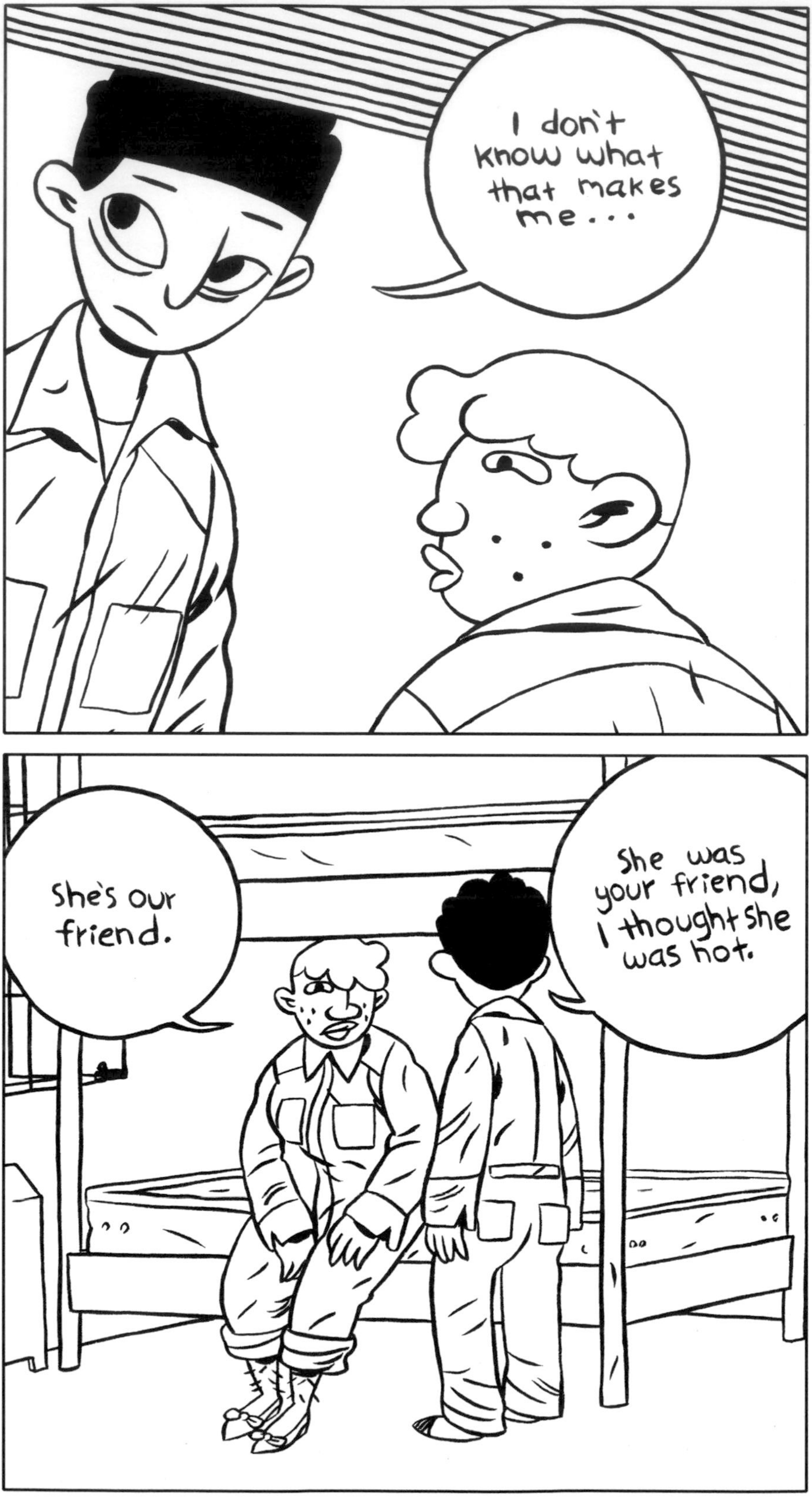
I don't know what that makes me...
She's our friend.
She was your friend, I thought she was hot.

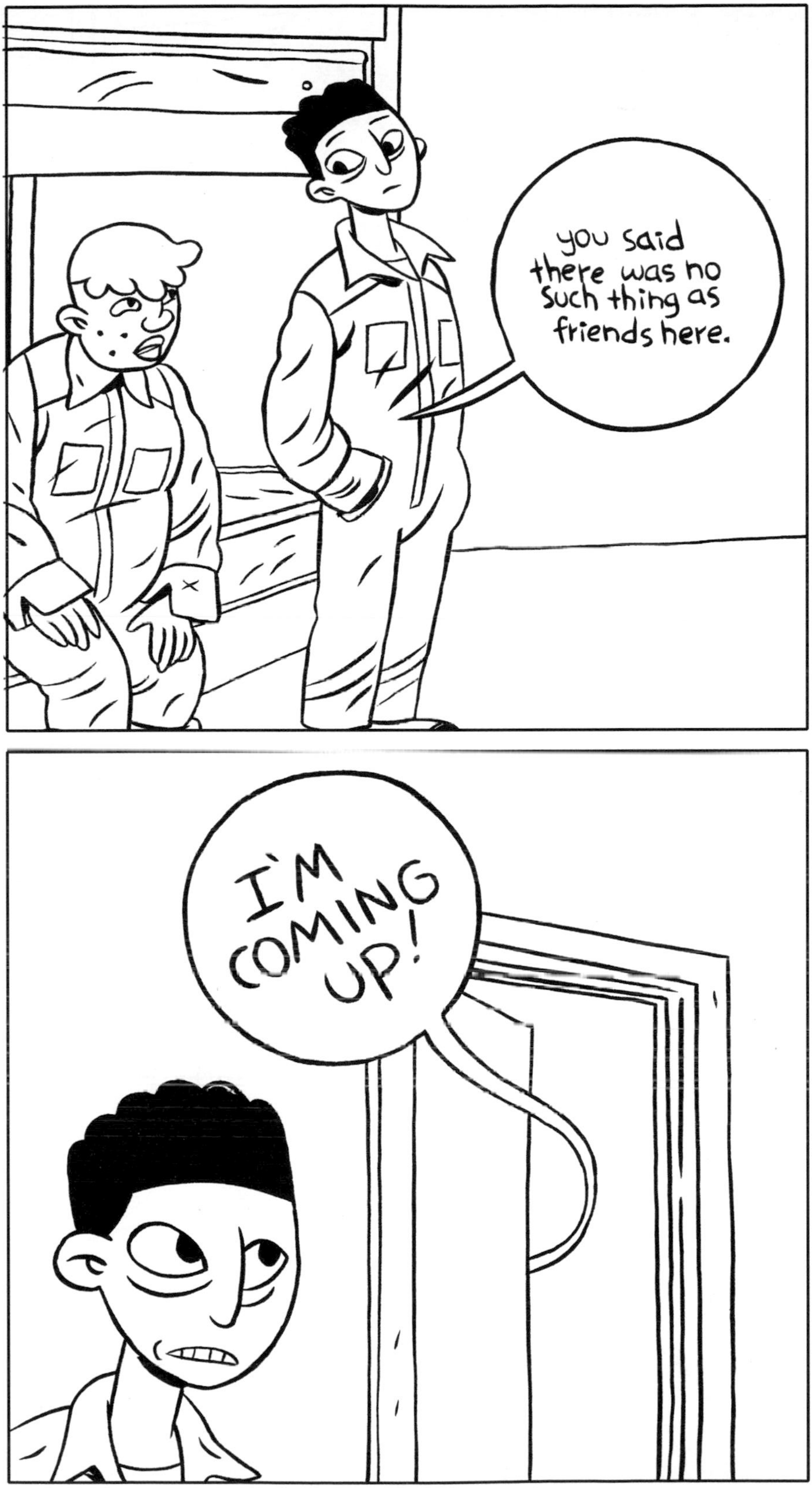
you said there was no such thing as friends here.
I'M COMING UP!

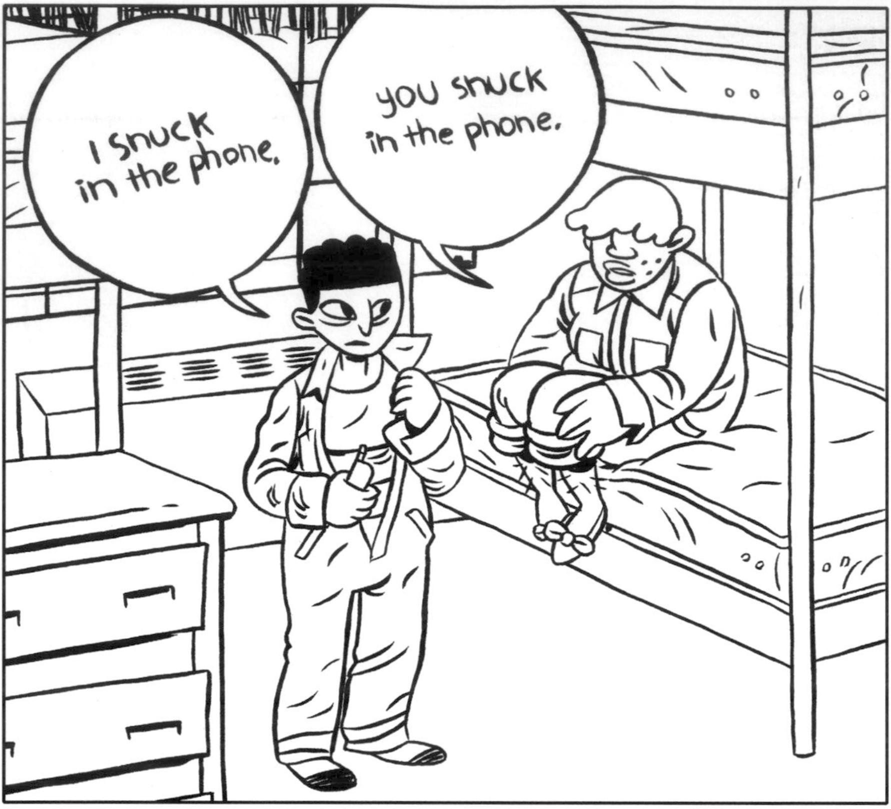
I snuck in the phone.
you snuck in the phone.

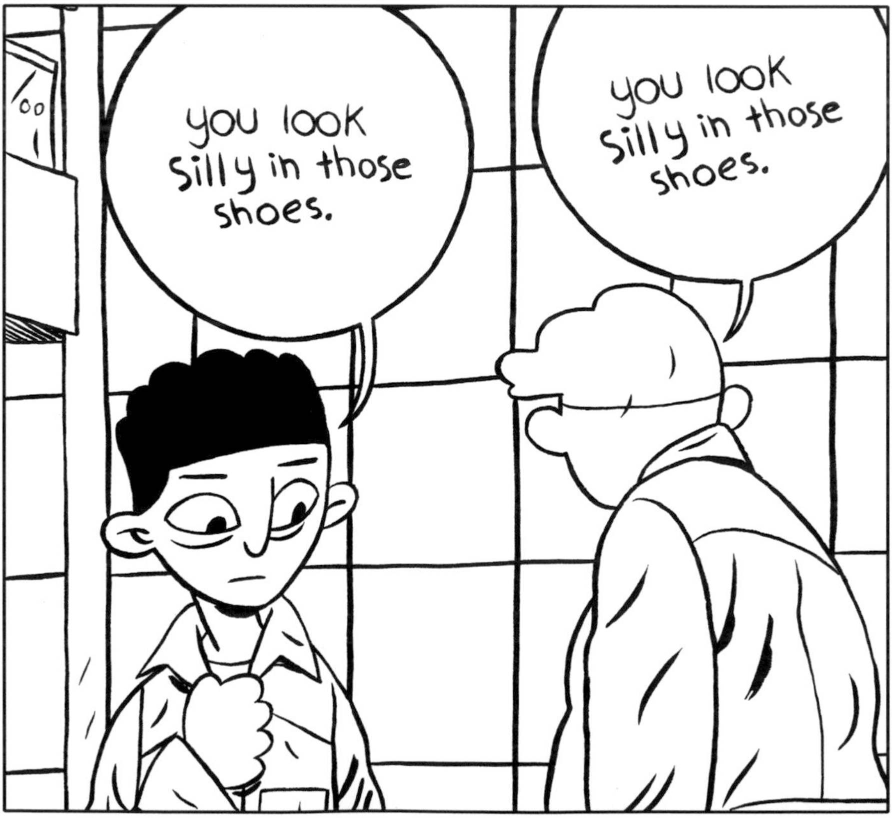
you look silly in those shoes.
you look silly in those shoes.

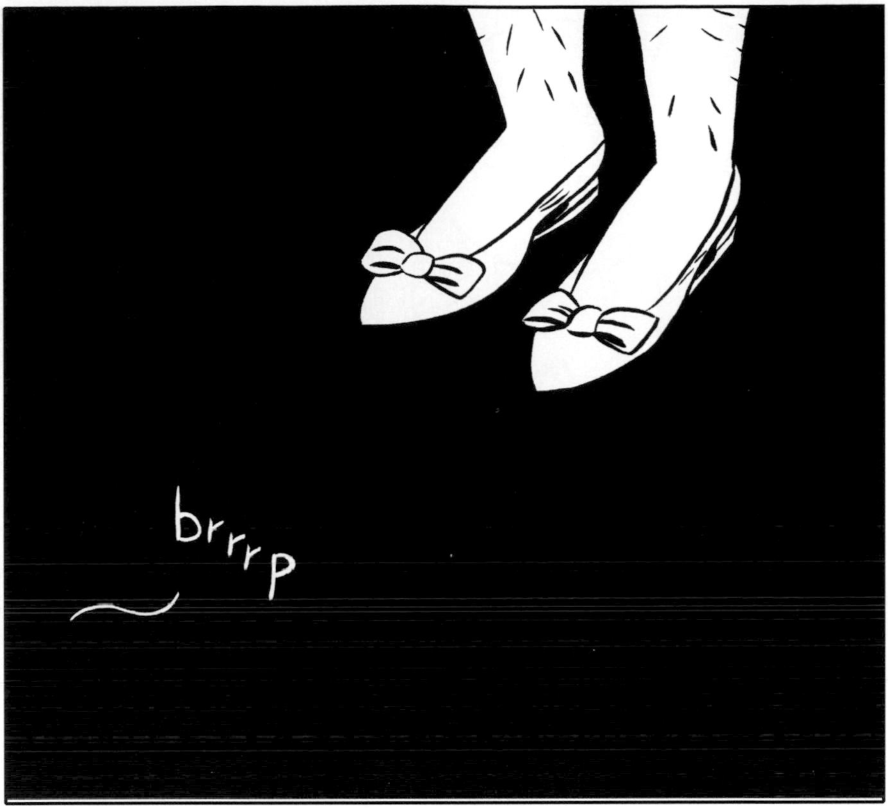
brrrp

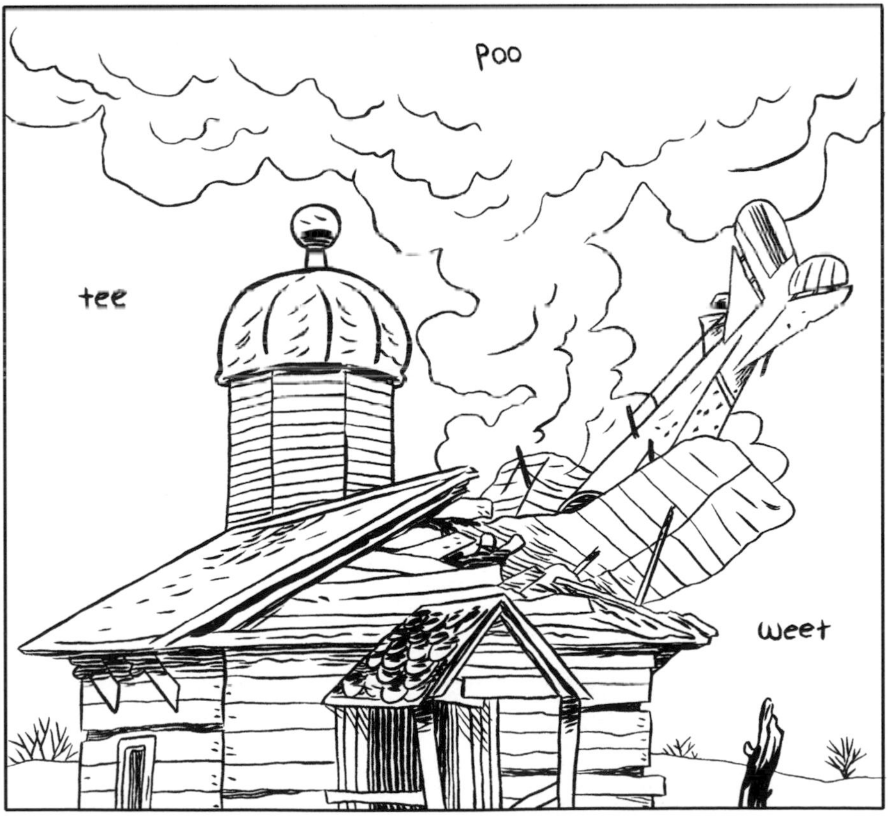
poo
tee
weet

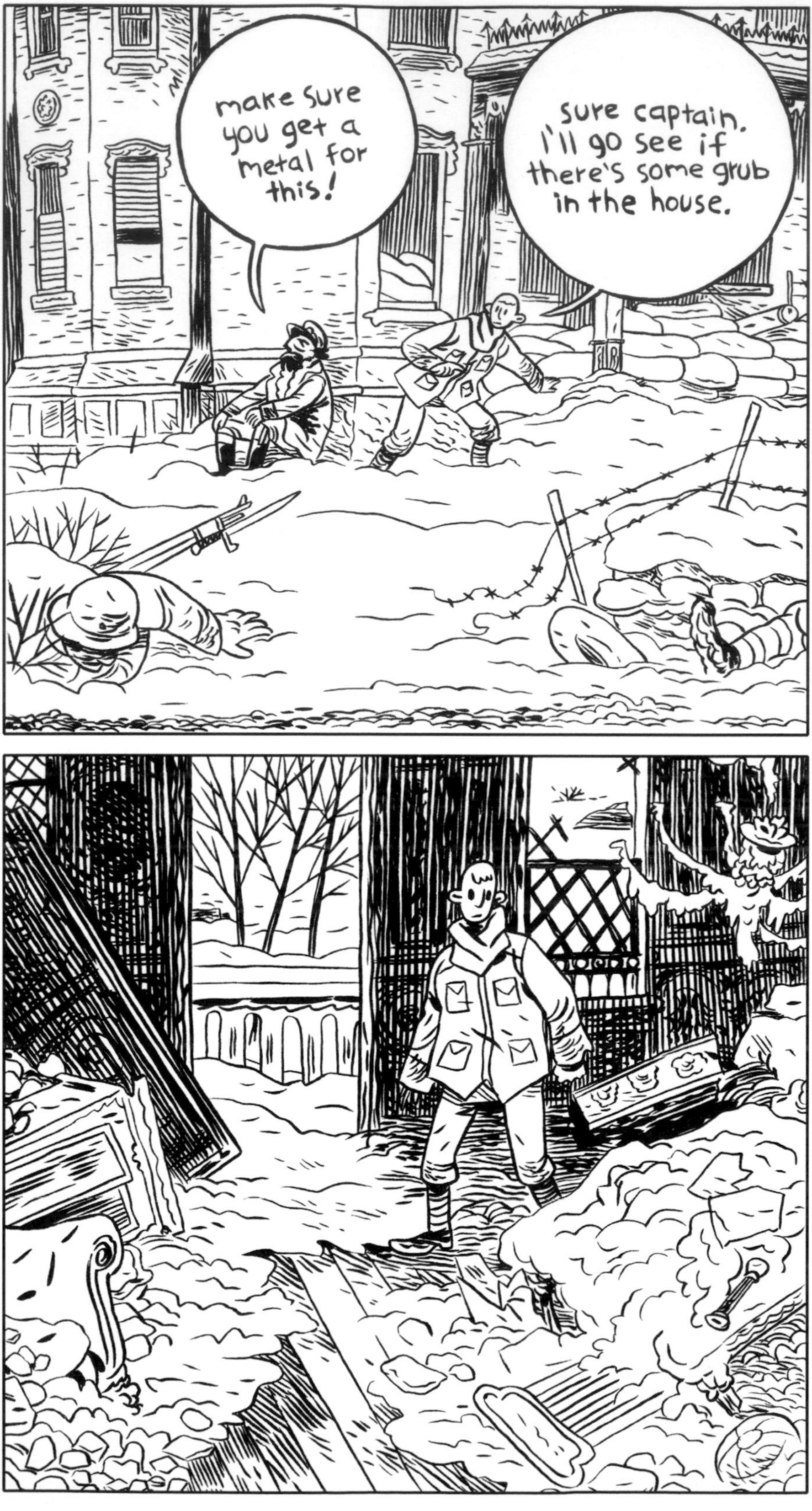
make sure you get a metal for this!
sure captain. I'll go see if there's some grub in the house.

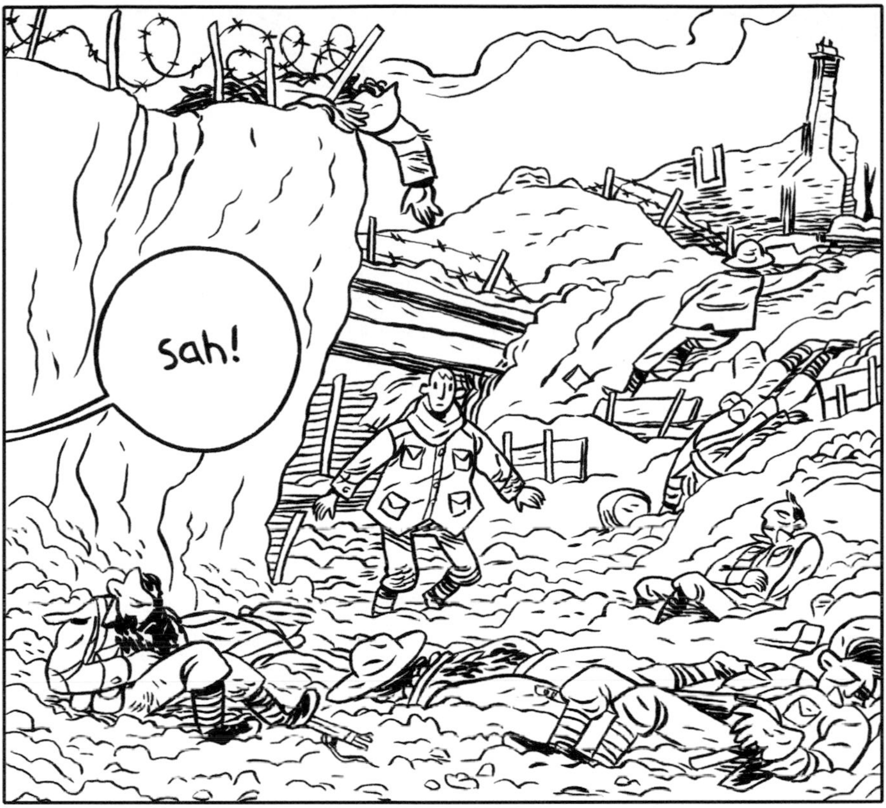
sah!

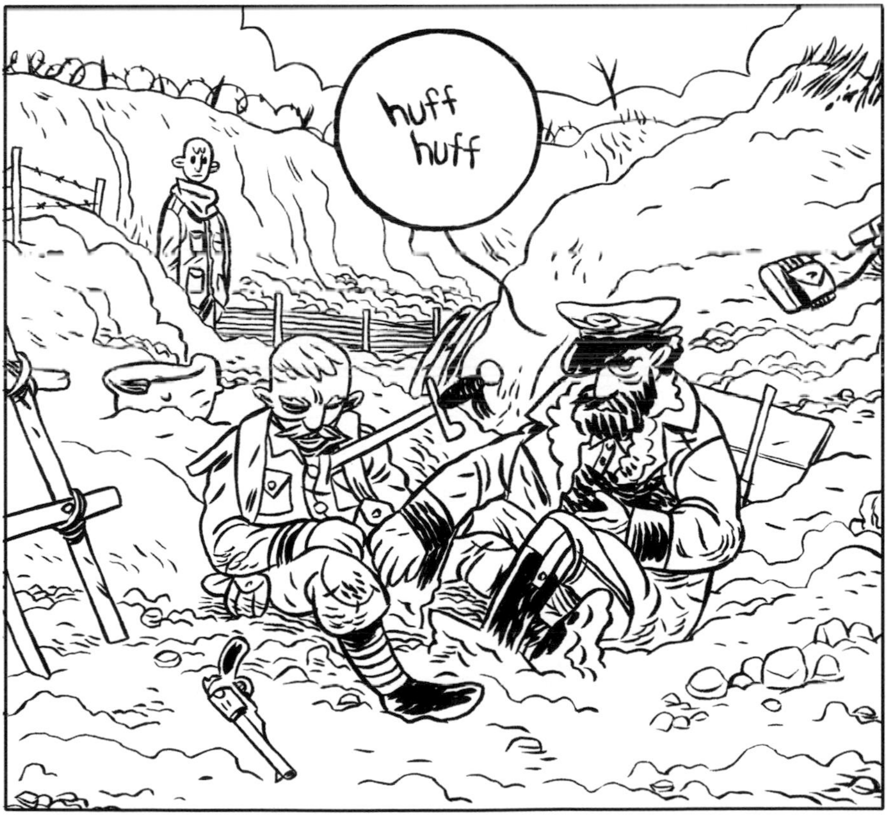
huff
huff

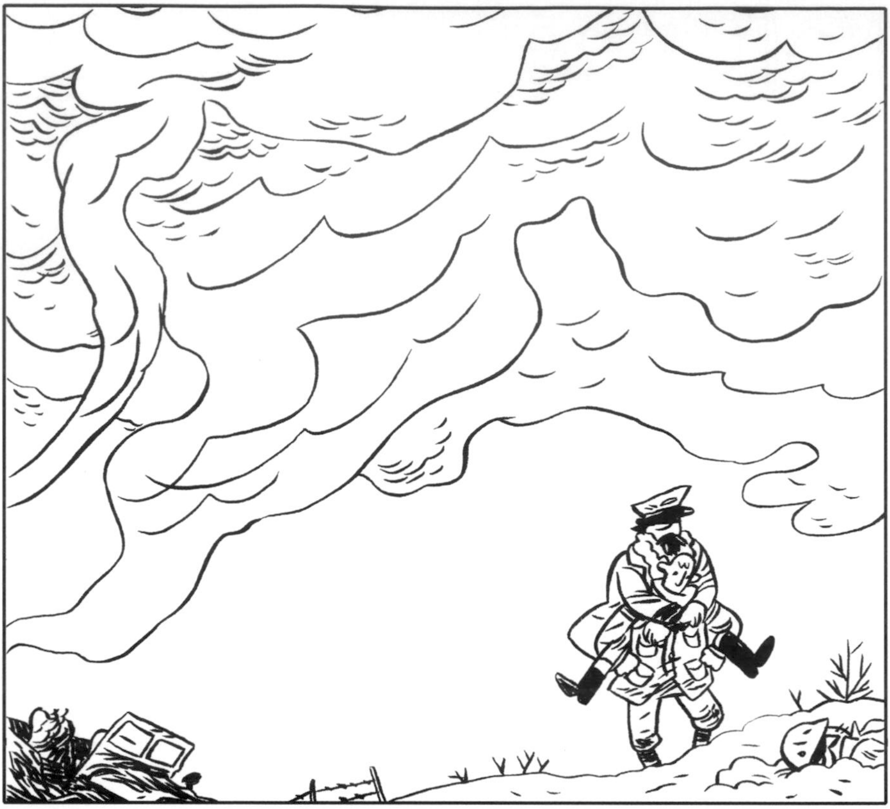

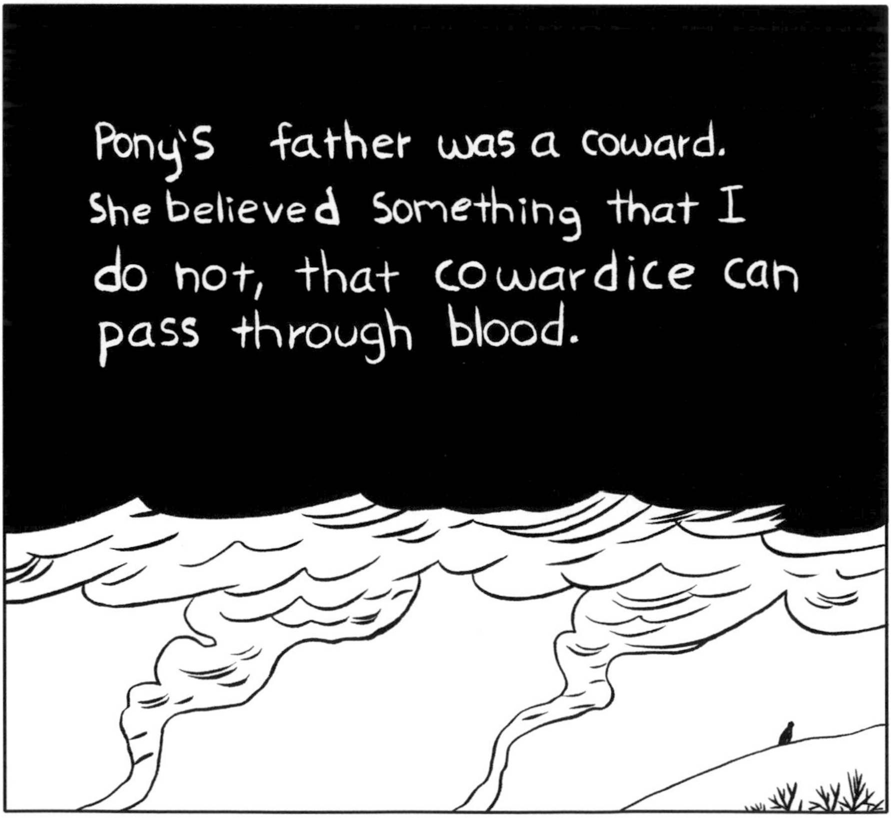
Pony's father was a coward. She believed something that I do not, that cowardice can pass through blood.

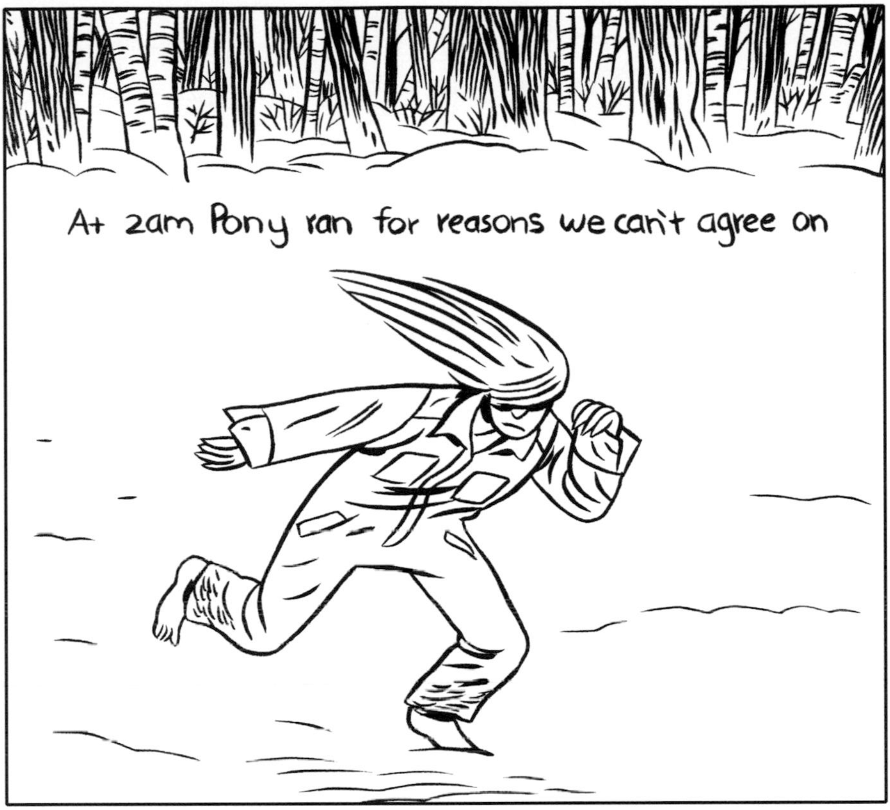
At 2am Pony ran for reasons we can't agree on

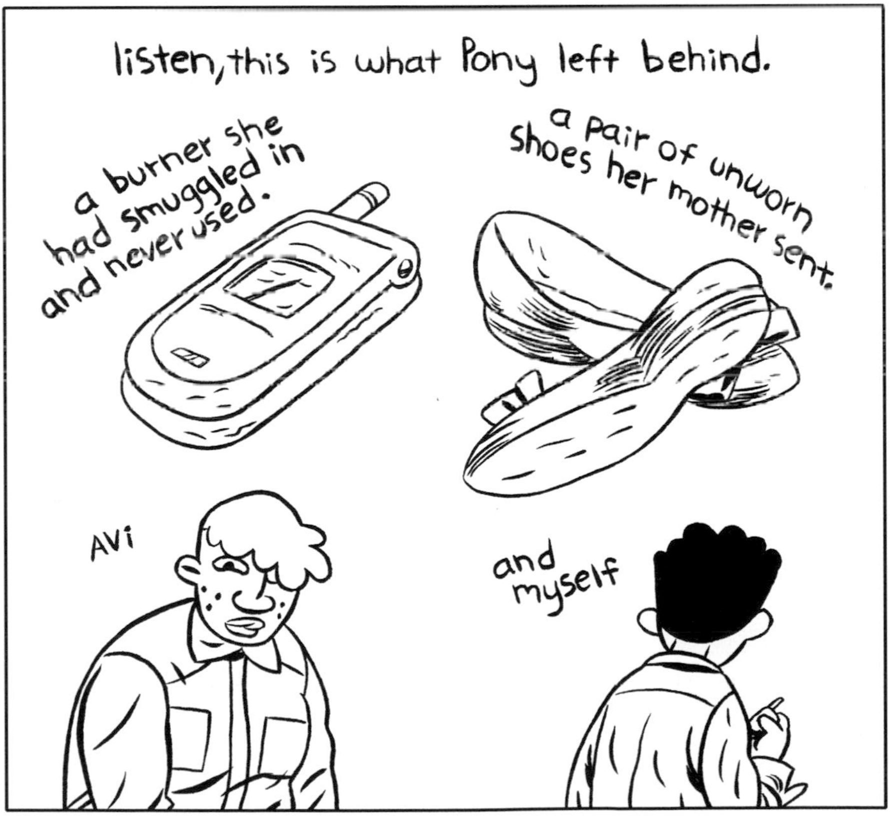
listen, this is what Pony left behind.
a burner she had smuggled in and never used.
a pair of unworn shoes her mother sent.
AVi
and myself

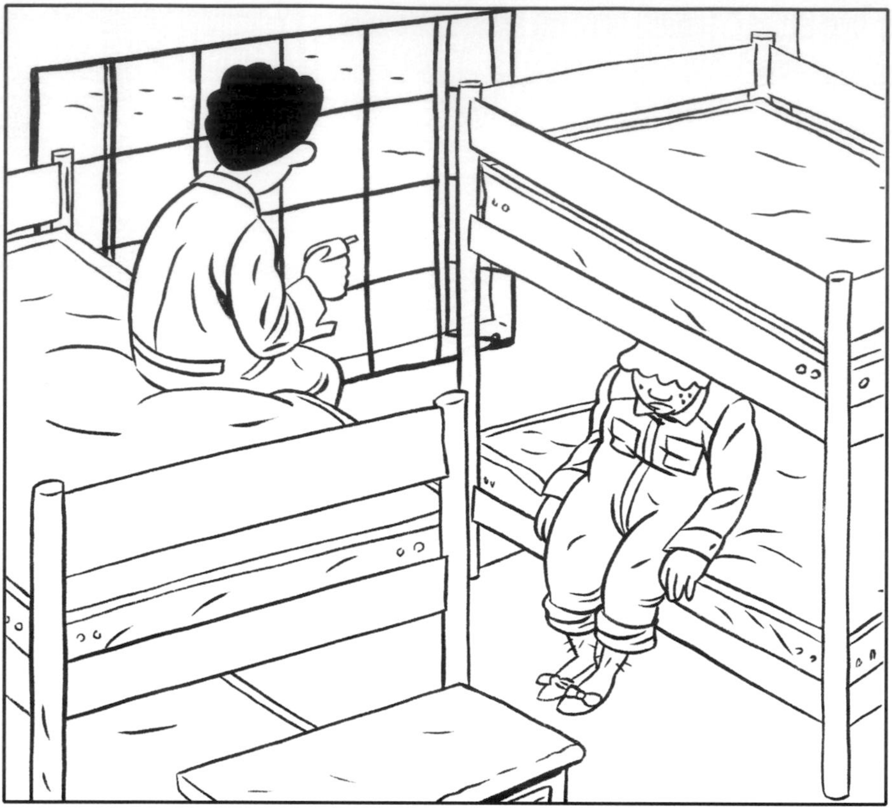

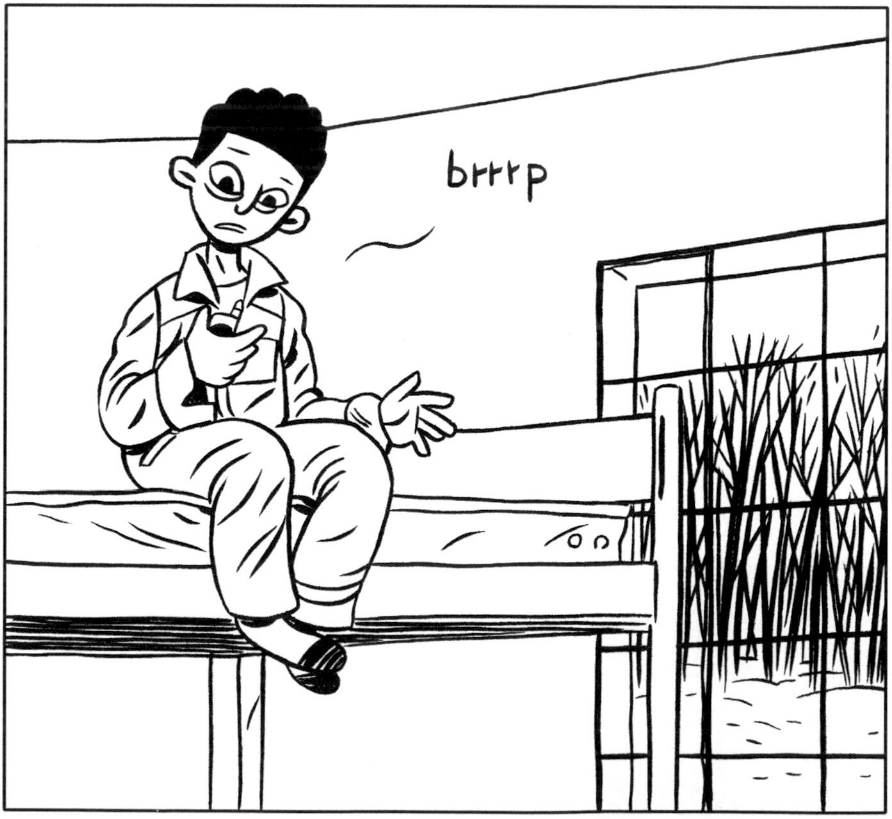
brrrp

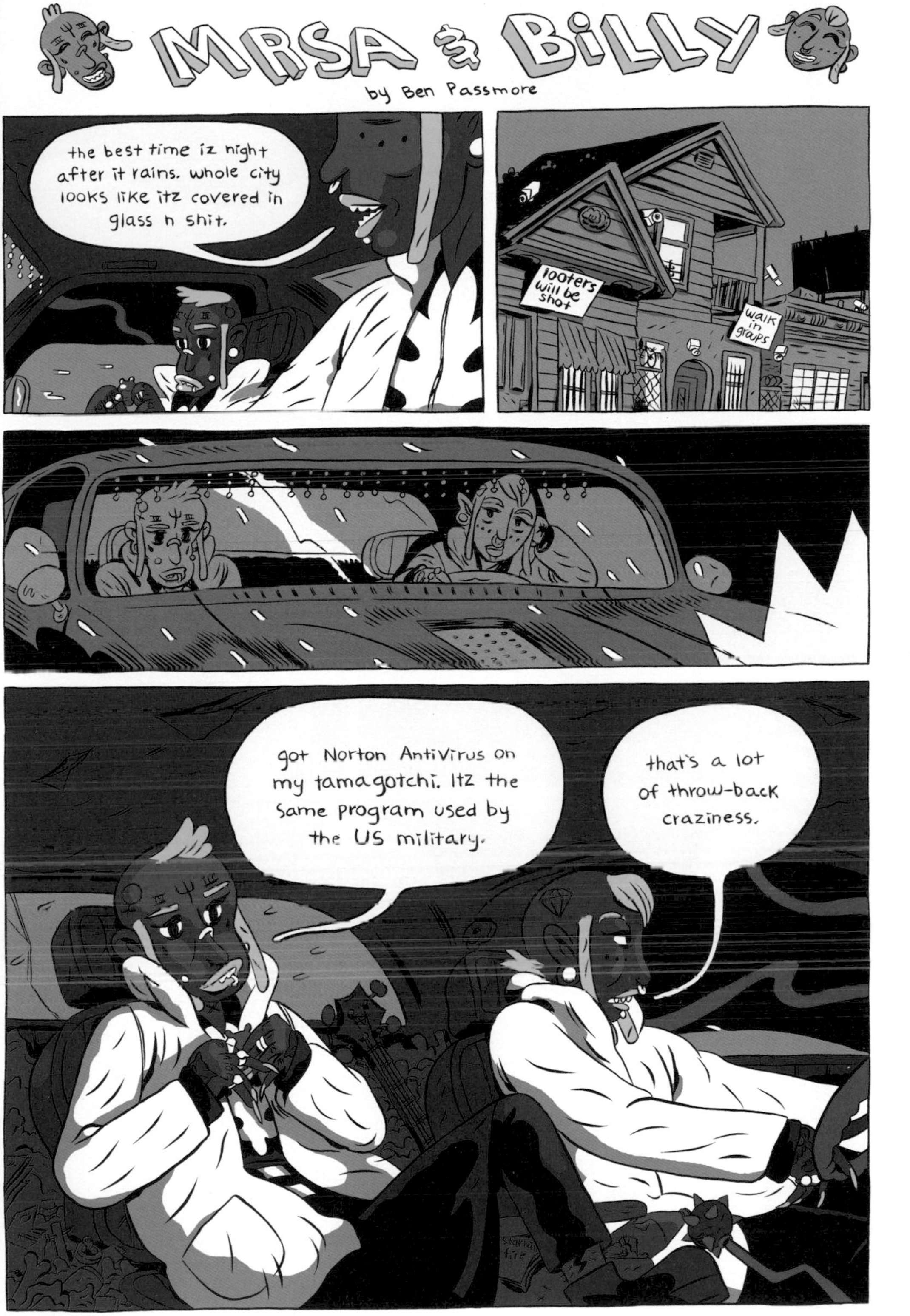
MRSA & BiLLY
by Ben Passmore
the best time iz night after it rains. whole city looks like itz covered in glass n shit.
looters will be shot
walk in groups
got Norton AntiVirus on my tamagotchi. Itz the same program used by the US military.
that's a lot of throw-back craziness.

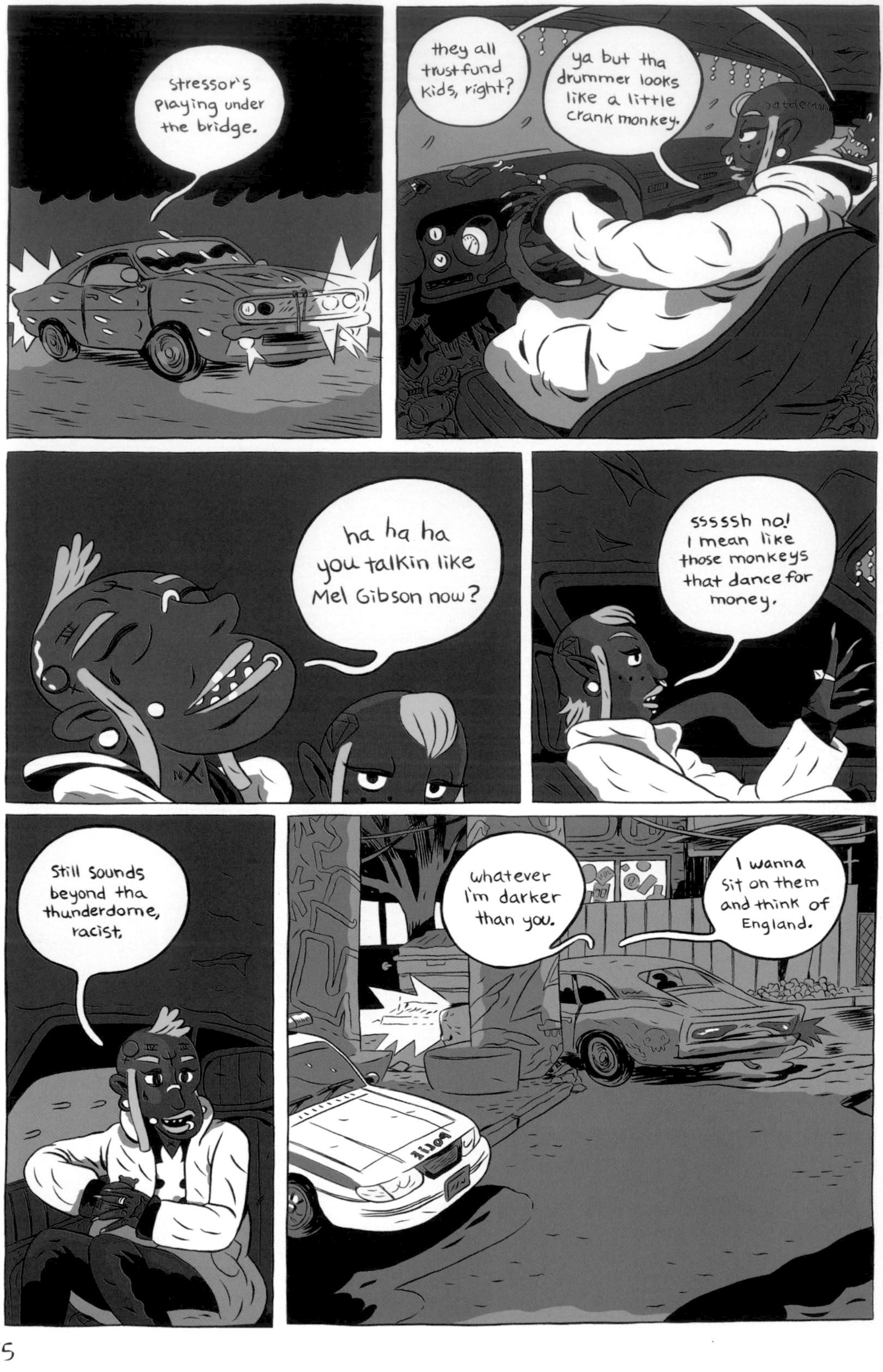
stressor's playing under the bridge.
they all trust-fund kids, right?
ya but tha drummer looks like a little crank monkey.
ha ha ha you talkin like Mel Gibson now?
ssssh no! I mean like those monkeys that dance for money.
Still sounds beyond tha thunderdome, racist.
whatever I'm darker than you.
I wanna sit on them and think of England.

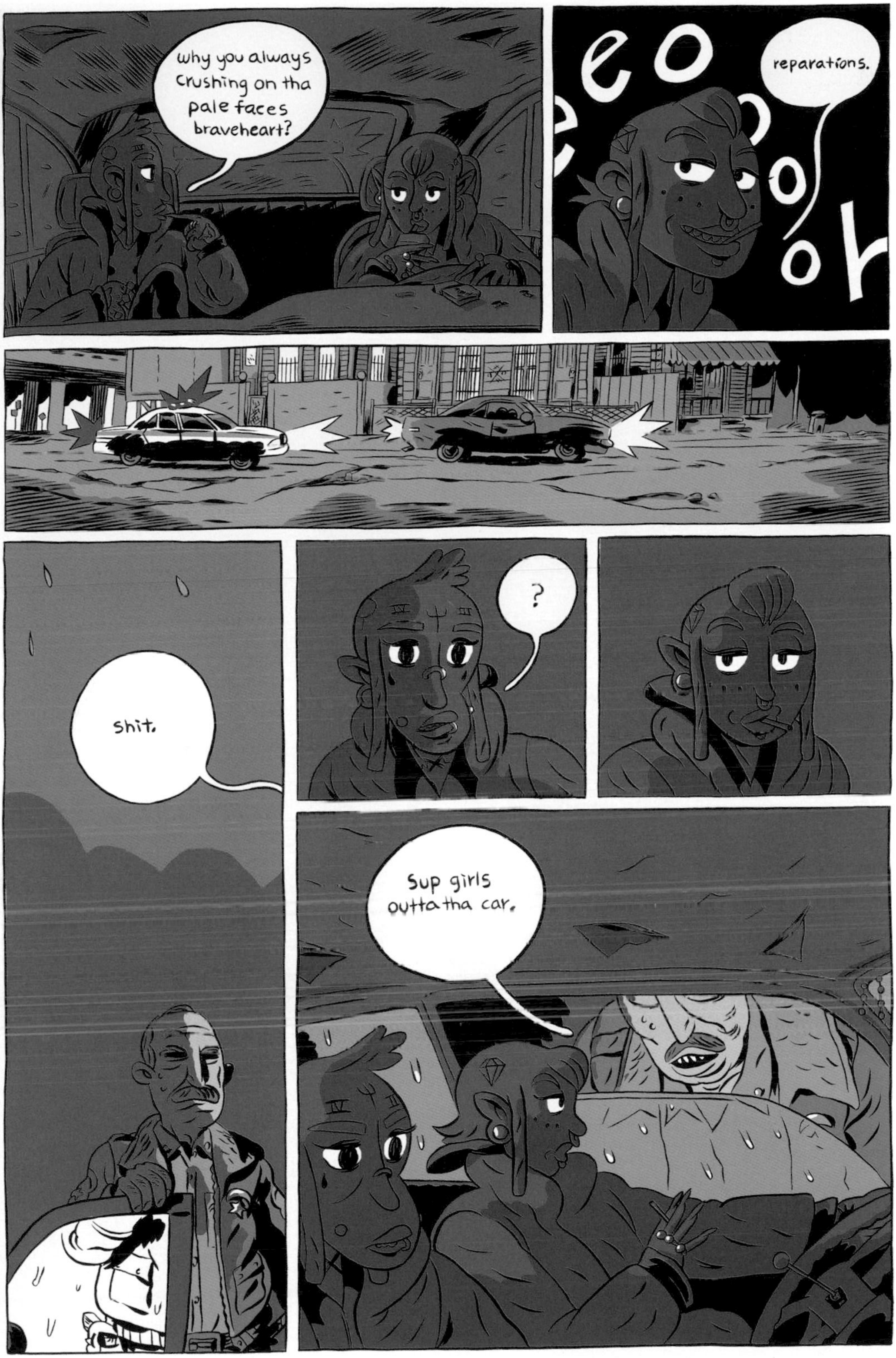
why you always crushing on tha pale faces braveheart?
eeoooooh
reparations.
shit.
?
Sup girls outtatha car.

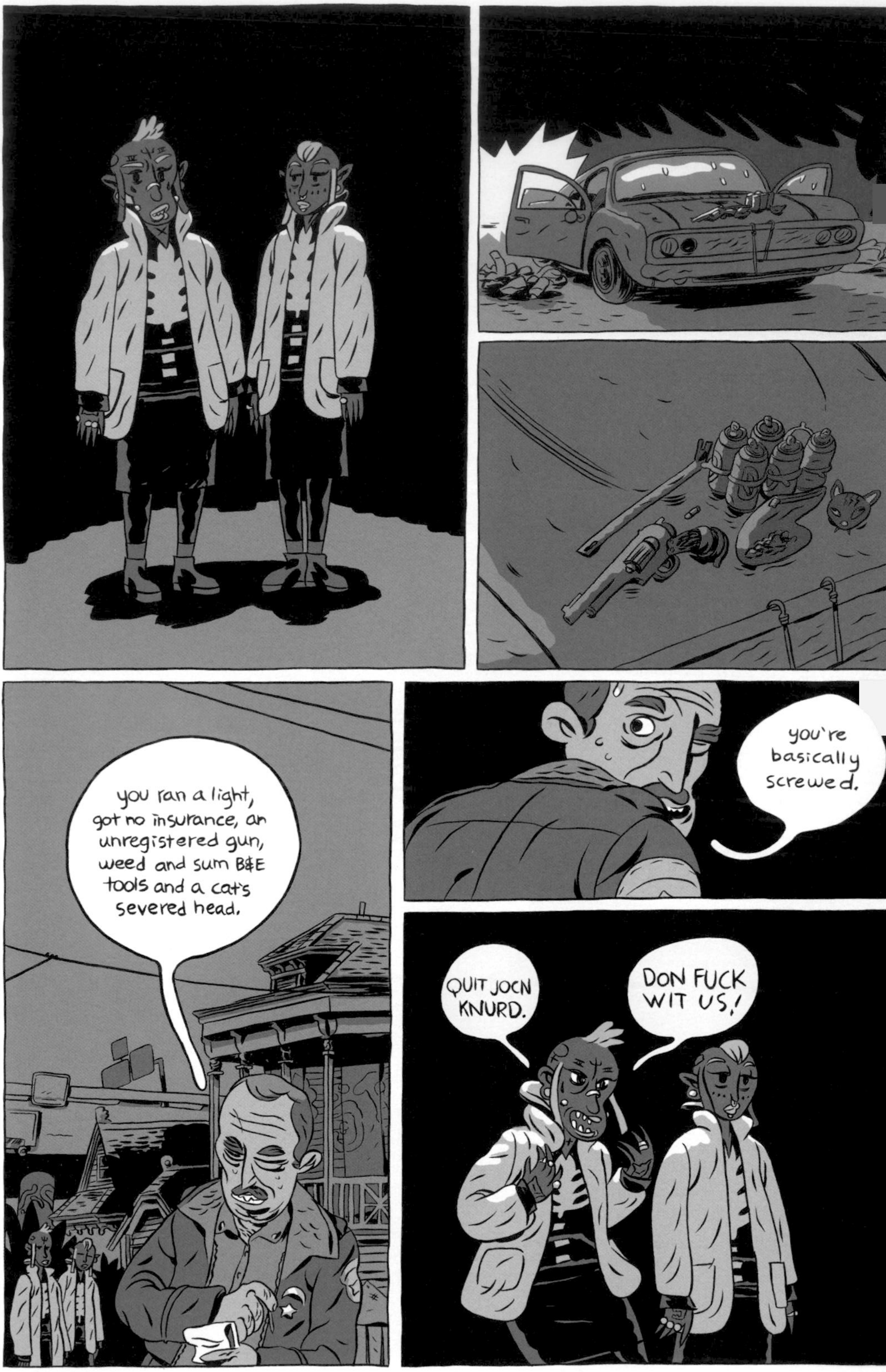
you ran a light, got no insurance, an unregistered gun, weed and sum B&E tools and a cat's severed head.
you're basically screwed.
QUIT JOCN KNURD.
DON FUCK WIT US.!

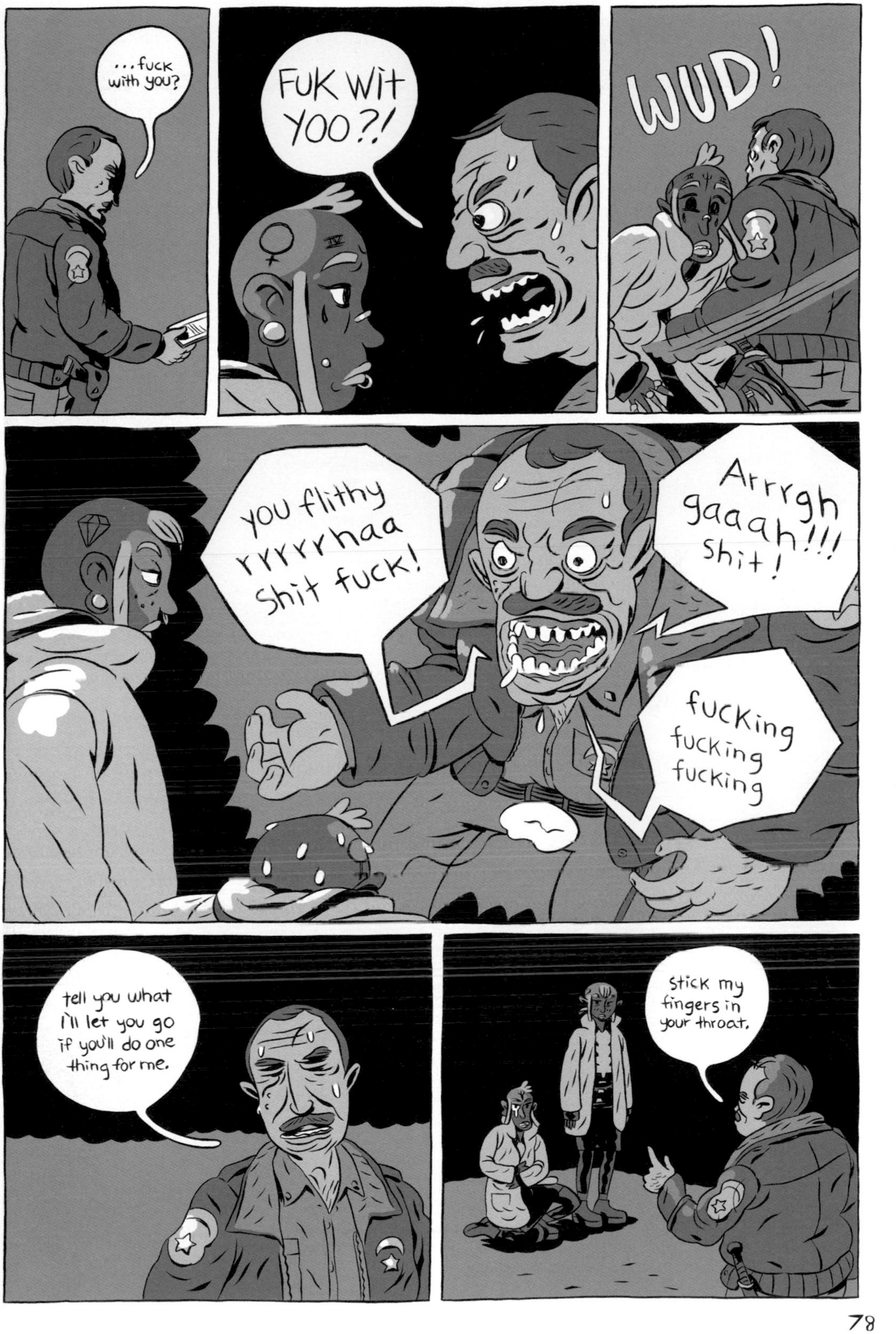
...fuck with you?
FUK WIT YOO?!
WUD!
you flithy rrrrrhaa Shit fuck!
Arrrgh gaaah!!! shit!
fucking fucking fucking
tell you what I'll let you go if you'll do one thing for me.
stick my fingers in your throat.

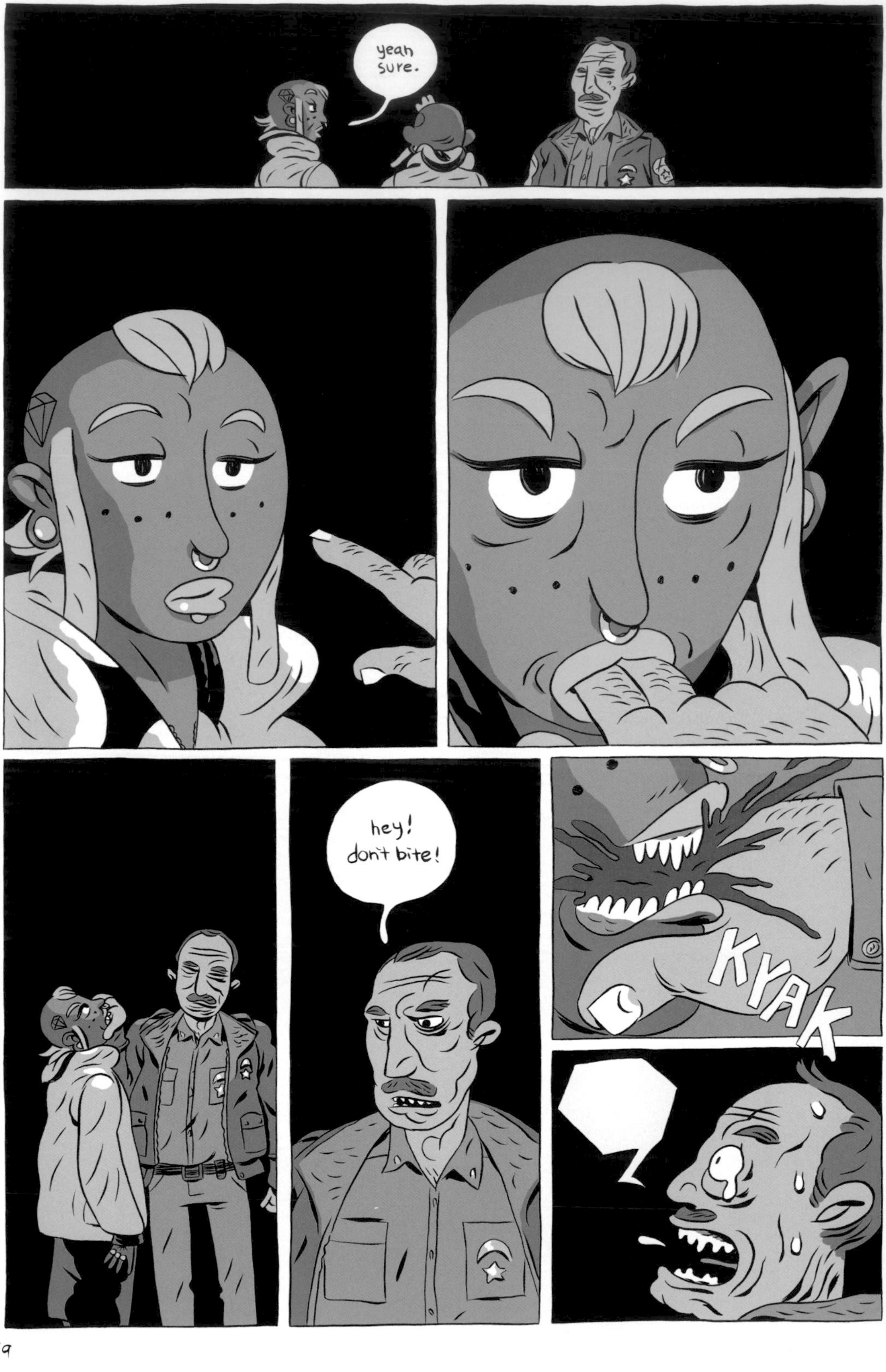
yeah sure.
hey! don't bite!
KYAK

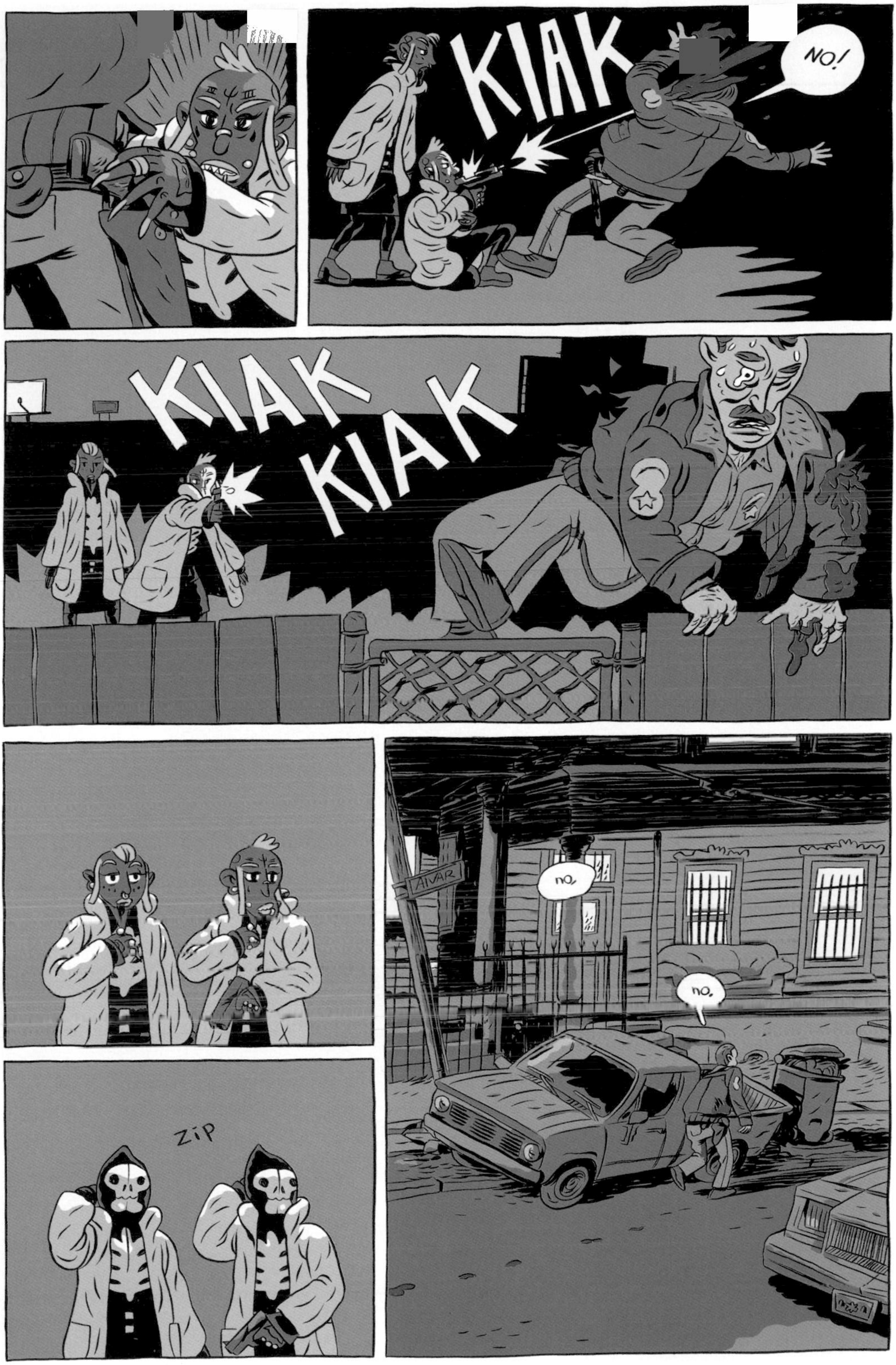
KIAK
NO!
KIAK
KIAK
KIAK
AIVAR
no,
no,
ZIP

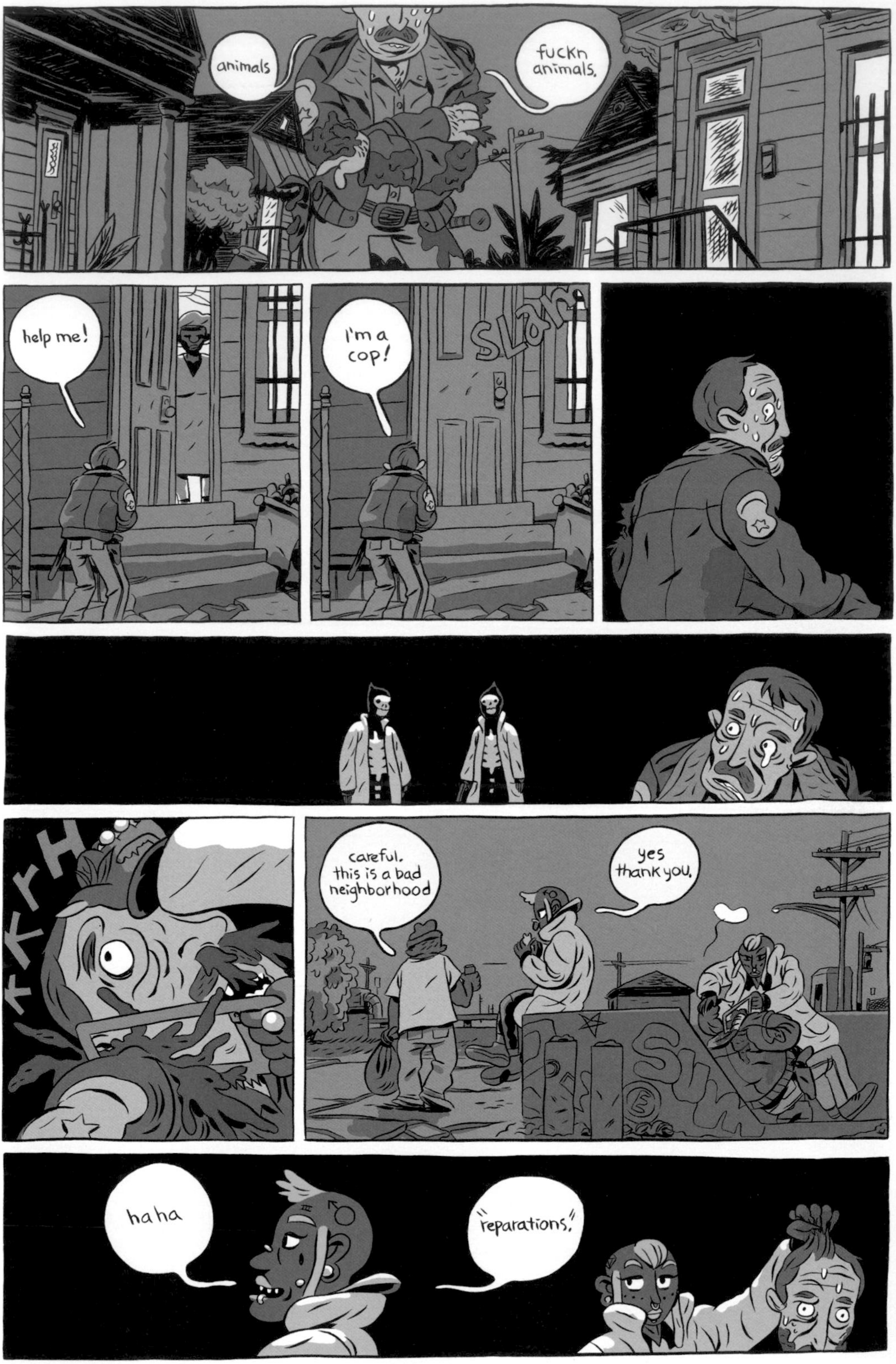
animals
fuckn animals.
help me!
I'm a cop!
SLAM
careful. this is a bad neighborhood
yes thank you.
ha ha
"reparations."

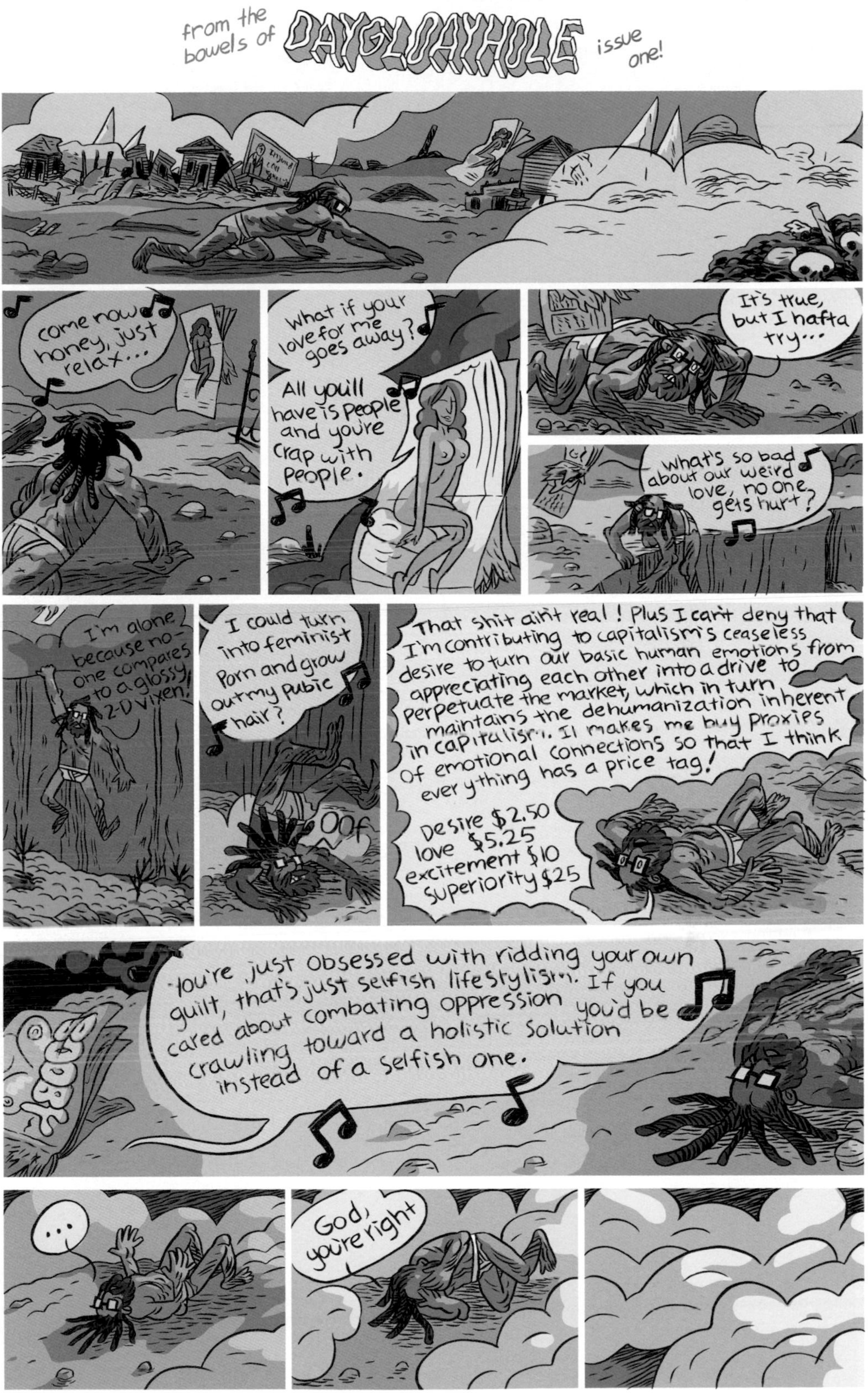
from the bowels of DAYGLOAYHOLE issue one!
come now honey, just relax...
What if your love for me goes away?
All you'll have is people and you're crap with people.
It's true, but I hafta try...
what's so bad about our weird love, no one gets hurt?
I'm alone because no-one compares to a glossy 2-D vixen!
I could turn into feminist Porn and grow out my pubic hair?
OOF
That shit ain't real! Plus I can't deny that I'm contributing to capitalism's ceaseless desire to turn our basic human emotions from appreciating each other into a drive to perpetuate the market, which in turn maintains the dehumanization inherent in capitalism. It makes me buy proxies of emotional connections so that I think everything has a price tag!
Desire $2.50
love $5.25
excitement $10
Superiority $25
You're just obsessed with ridding your own guilt, that's just selfish lifestylism. If you cared about combating oppression you'd be crawling toward a holistic solution instead of a selfish one.
...
God, you're right

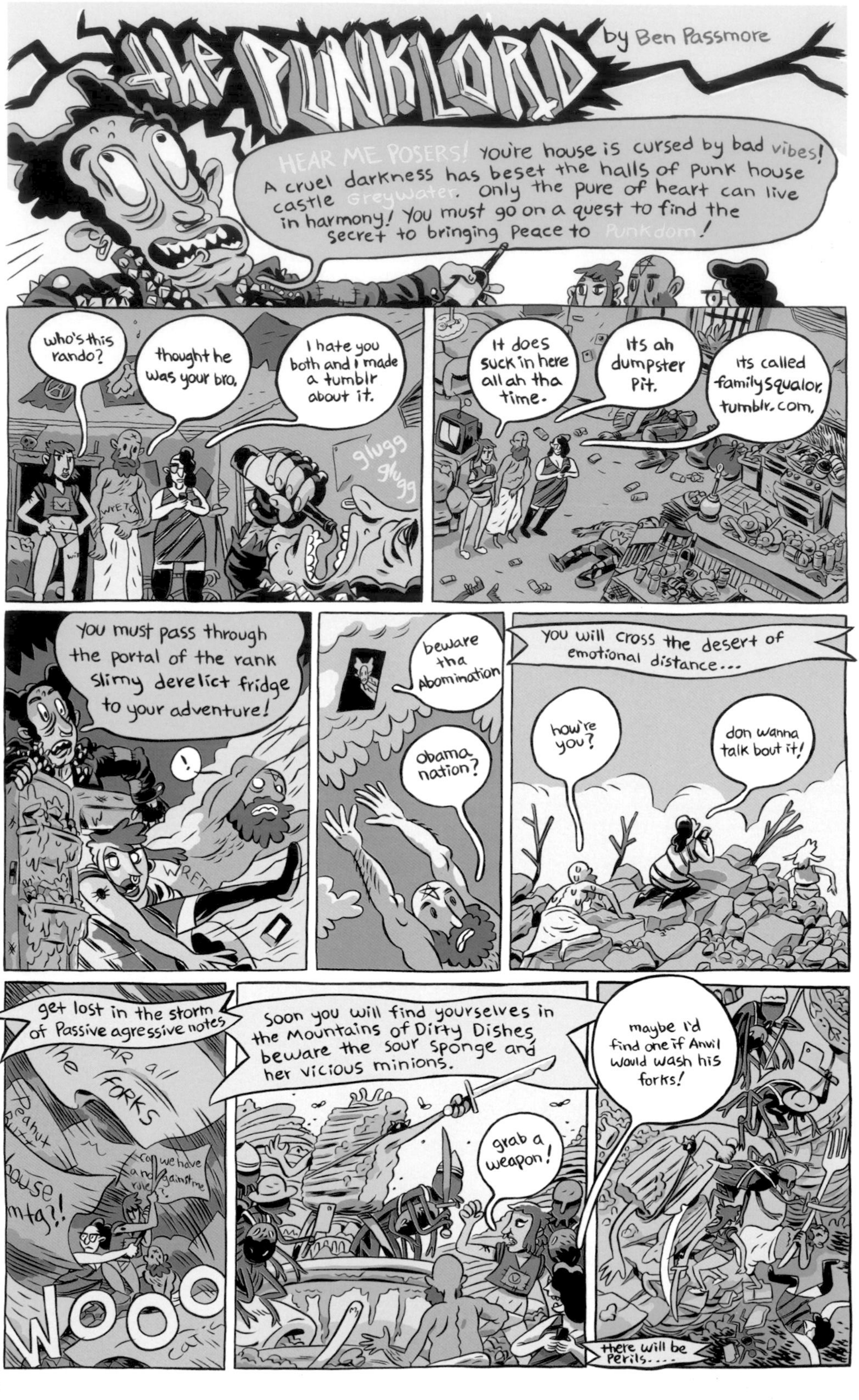

the PUNKLORD
by Ben Passmore
HEAR ME POSERS! You're house is cursed by bad vibes! A cruel darkness has beset the halls of punk house castle Greywater. Only the pure of heart can live in harmony! You must go on a quest to find the secret to bringing peace to Punkdom!
who's this rando?
thought he was your bro,
I hate you both and I made a tumblr about it.
glugg glugg
It does suck in here all ah tha time.
Its ah dumpster Pit.
Its called familysqualor. tumblr.com,
You must pass through the portal of the rank slimy derelict fridge to your adventure!
!
beware tha Abomination
obama nation?
You will cross the desert of emotional distance...
how're you?
don wanna talk bout it!
get lost in the storm of Passive agressive notes
FORKS
WOOO
Soon you will find yourselves in the Mountains of Dirty Dishes beware the sour sponge and her vicious minions.
grab a weapon!
maybe I'd find one if Anvil would wash his forks!
there will be Perils....

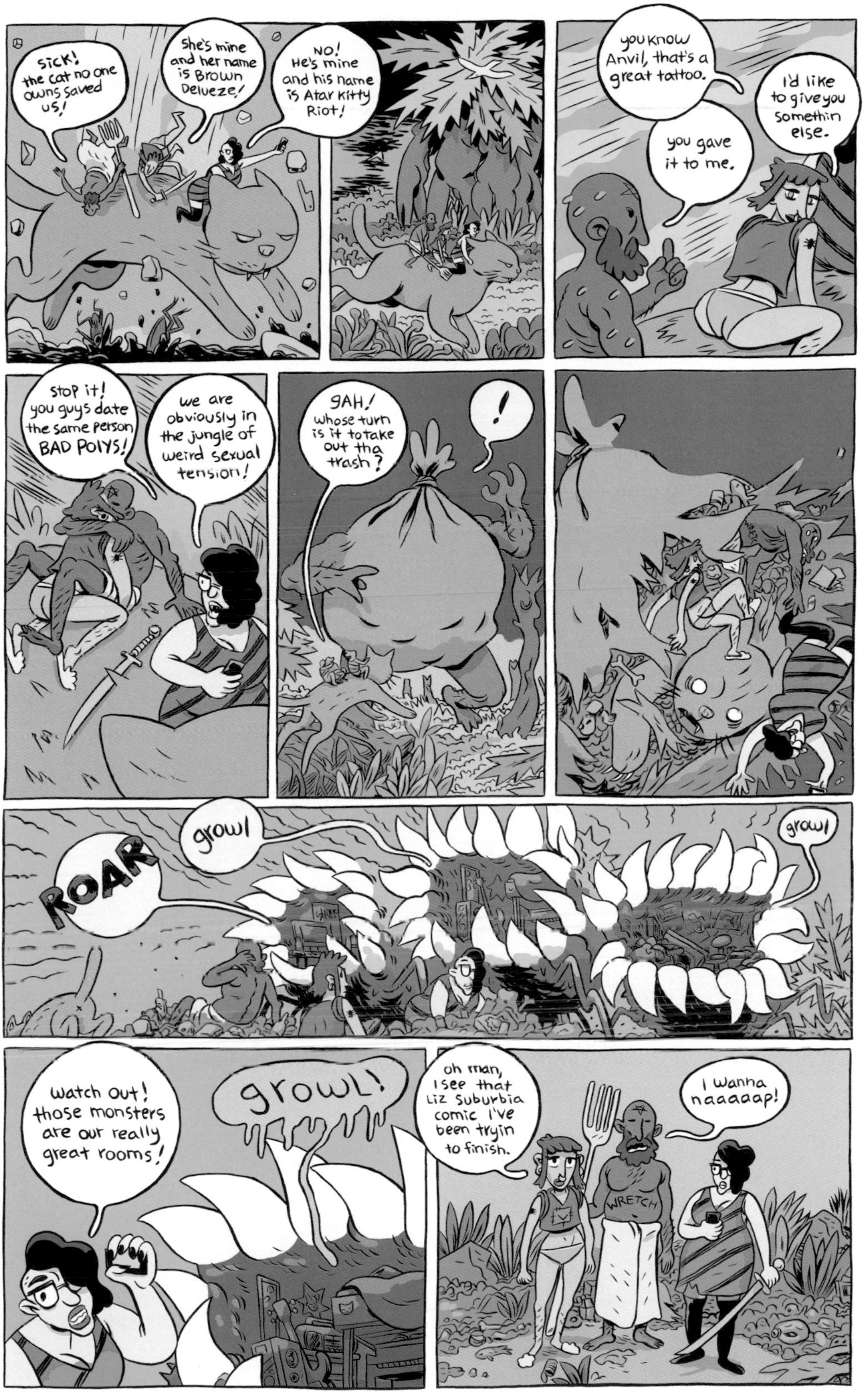

Sick! the cat no one owns saved us!
She's mine and her name is Brown Delueze!
No! He's mine and his name is Atar Kitty Riot!
you know Anvil, that's a great tattoo.
you gave it to me.
I'd like to give you somethin else.
Stop it! you guys date the same person BAD POLYS!
we are obviously in the jungle of weird sexual tension!
gAH! whose turn is it to take out tha trash?
!
growl
ROAR
growl
watch out! those monsters are our really great rooms!
growl!
oh man, I see that Liz Suburbia comic I've been tryin to finish.
I wanna naaaaap!
WRETCH

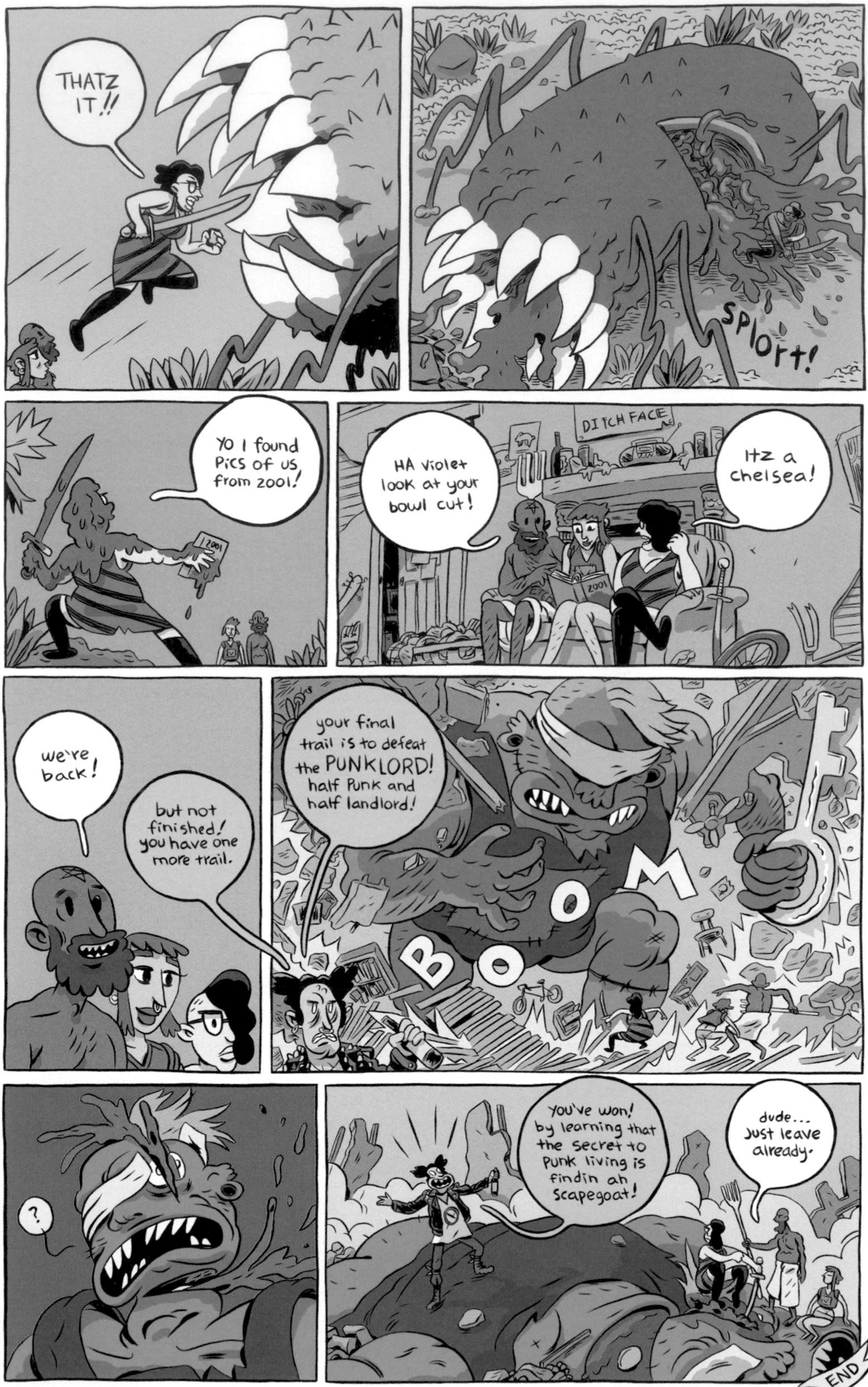
THATZ IT!!
Splort!
YO I found Pics of us from 2001!
2001
HA violet look at your bowl cut!
DITCH FACE
Itz a chelsea!
2001
we're back!
but not finished! you have one more trail.
your final trail is to defeat the PUNKLORD! half Punk and half landlord!
BOOM
?
you've won! by learning that the secret to Punk living is findin ah Scapegoat!
dude... Just leave already.
END

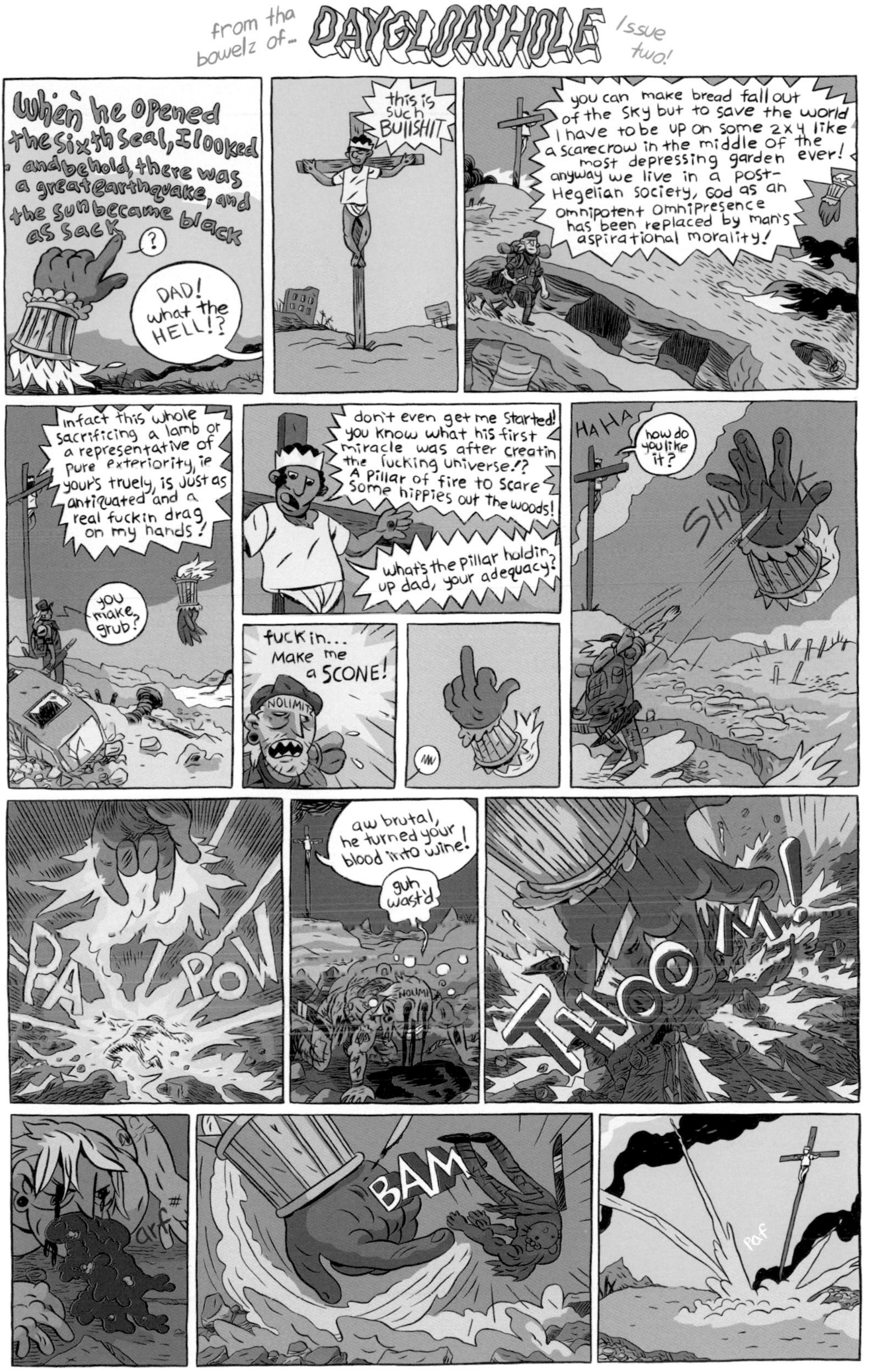

from tha bowelz of... DAYGLOAYHOLE Issue two!
When he opened the sixth seal, I looked and behold, there was a great earthquake, and the sun became black as sack
?
DAD! what the HELL!?
this is such BULLSHIT
you can make bread fall out of the sky but to save the world I have to be up on some 2x4 like a scarecrow in the middle of the most depressing garden ever! anyway we live in a post-Hegelian society, God as an omnipotent omnipresence has been replaced by man's aspirational morality!
infact this whole sacrificing a lamb or a representative of pure exteriority, ie your's truely, is just as antiquated and a real fuckin drag on my hands!
you make grub?
don't even get me started! you know what his first miracle was after creatin the fucking universe!? A pillar of fire to scare some hippies out the woods!
what's the pillar holdin up dad, your adequacy?
HA HA
how do you like it?
fuckin... make me a SCONE!
NOLIMIT
aw brutal, he turned your blood into wine!
guh wast'd
PA POW
THOOM!
arf
BAM
paf

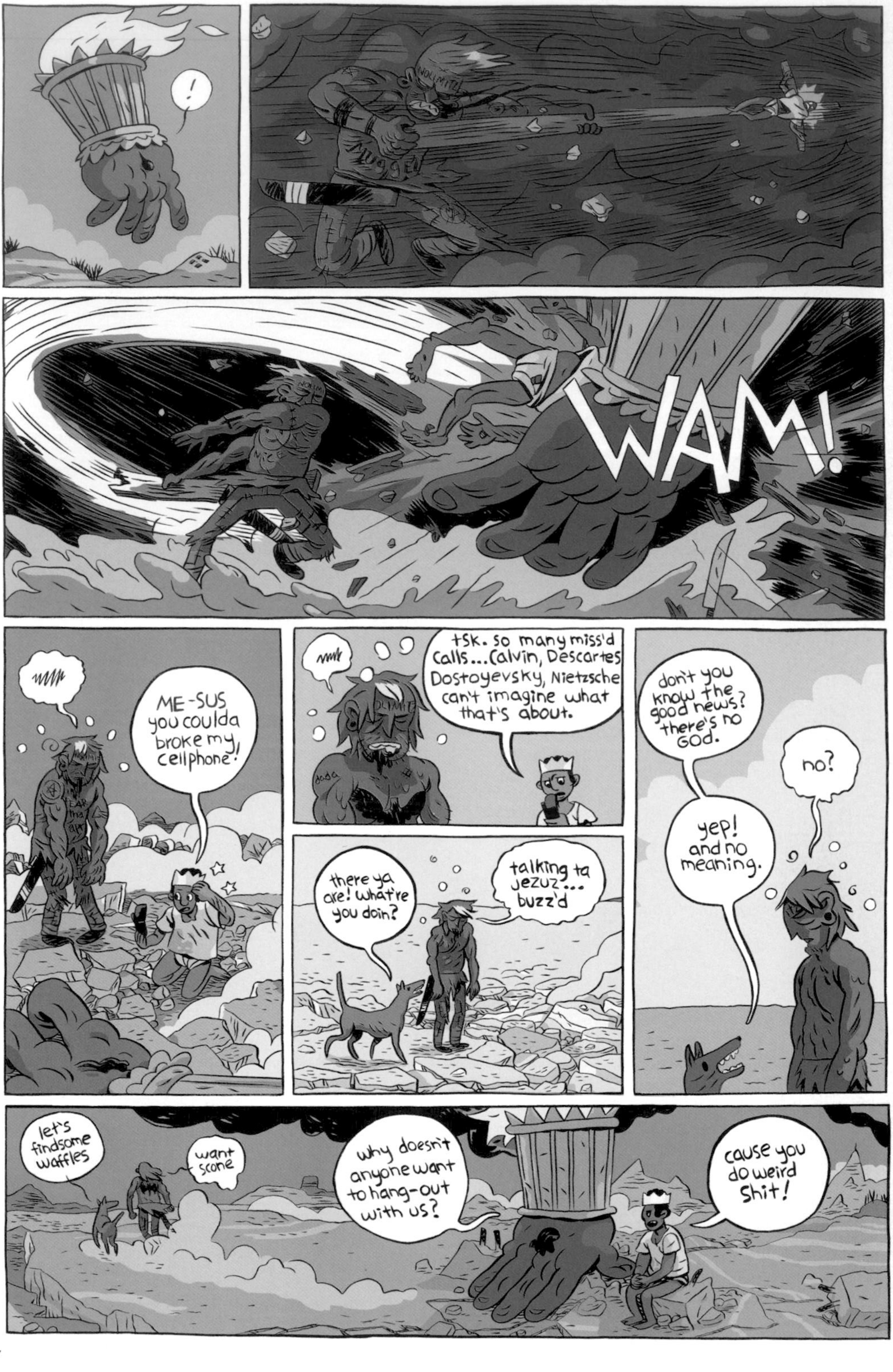
!
WAM!
ME-SUS you coulda broke my cellphone!
tsk. so many miss'd calls... Calvin, Descartes Dostoyevsky, Nietzsche can't imagine what that's about.
there ya are! what're you doin?
talking ta jezuz... buzz'd
don't you know the good news? there's no GOD.
no?
yep! and no meaning.
let's findsome waffles
want scone
why doesn't anyone want to hang-out with us?
cause you do weird Shit!

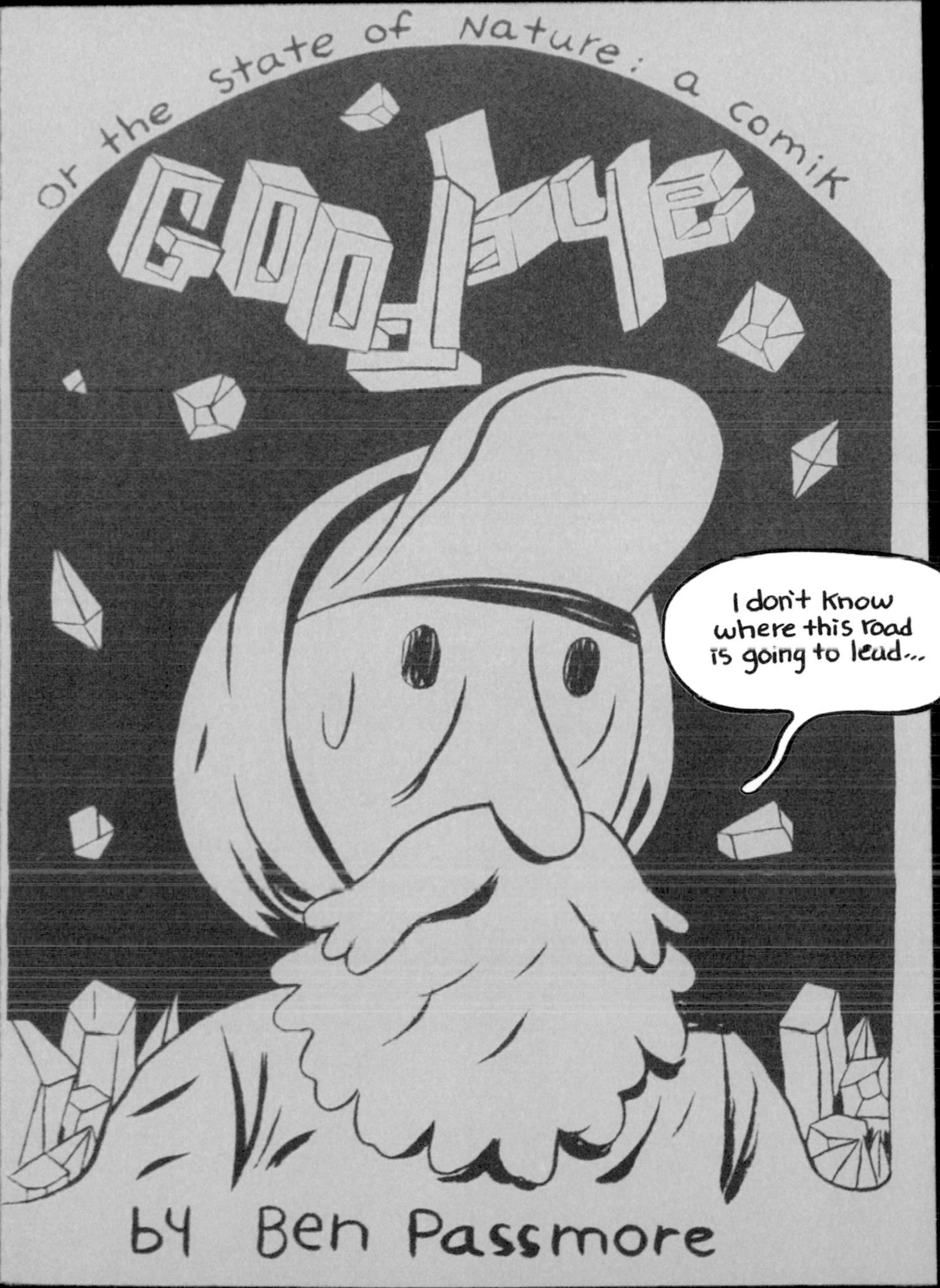
or the State of Nature: a comik
GOODBYE
I don't know where this road is going to lead...
by Ben Passmore

goodbye

I hope you stay dangerous reader, and even though things don't look so hot I hope we can build something out of all our garbage.

Ben

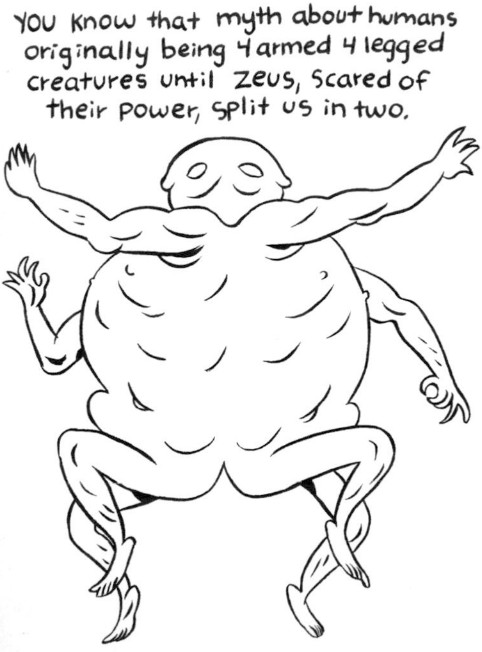
YOU KNOW that myth about humans originally being 4 armed 4 legged creatures until ZEUS, Scared of their power, split us in two.

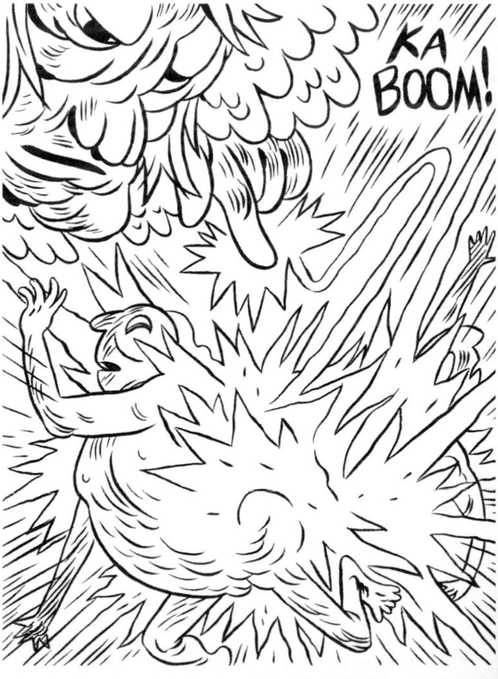
KA BOOM!

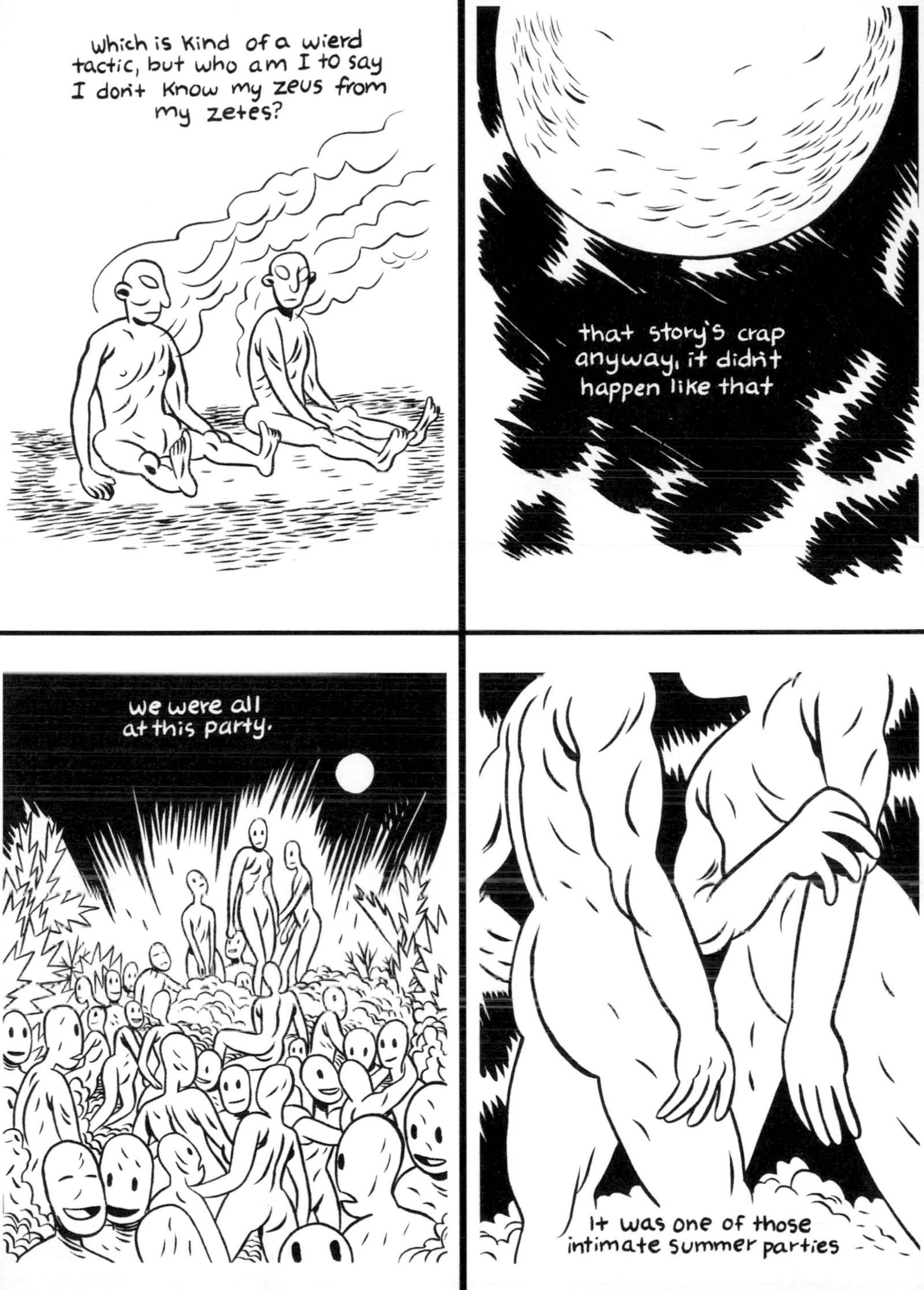
which is Kind of a wierd tactic, but who am I to say I don't Know my zeus from my zetes?
that story's crap anyway, it didn't happen like that
we were all at this party.
It was one of those intimate summer parties

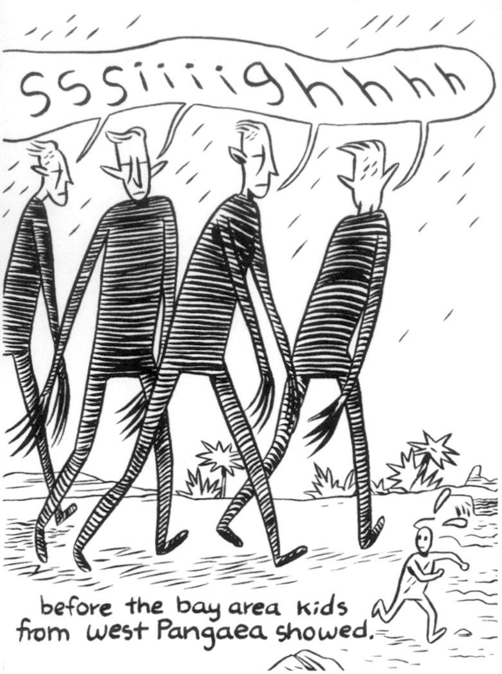
sssiiiiighhhhh
before the bay area kids
from west Pangaea showed.

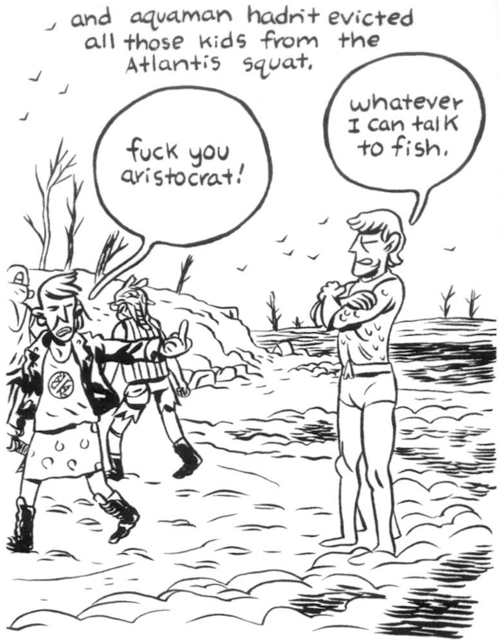
and aquaman hadn't evicted
all those kids from the
Atlantis squat.
fuck you aristocrat!
whatever I can talk to fish.

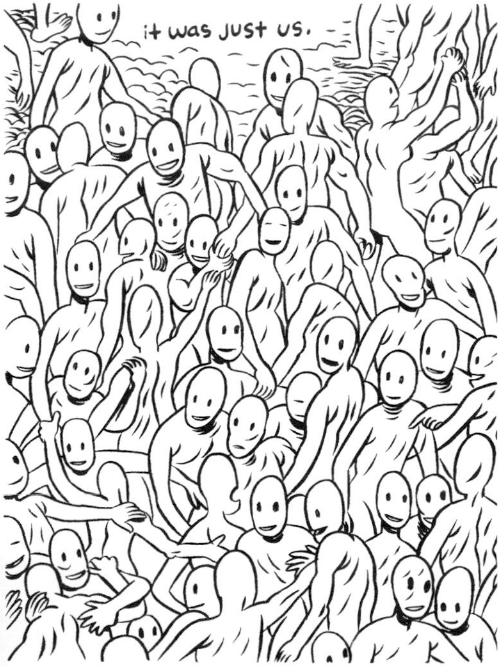
it was just us.

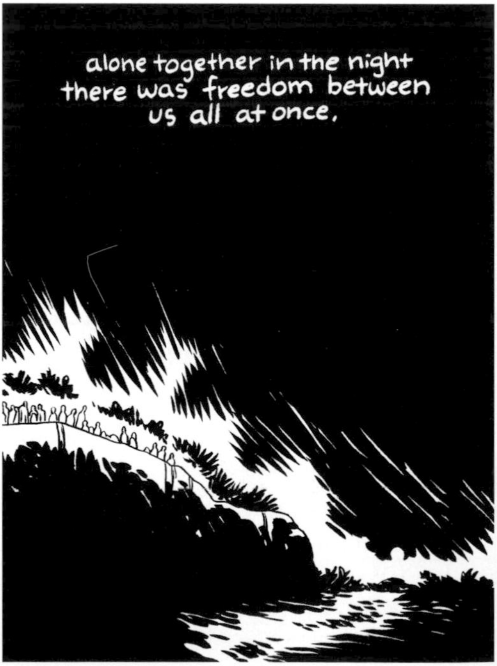
alone together in the night
there was freedom between
us all at once.

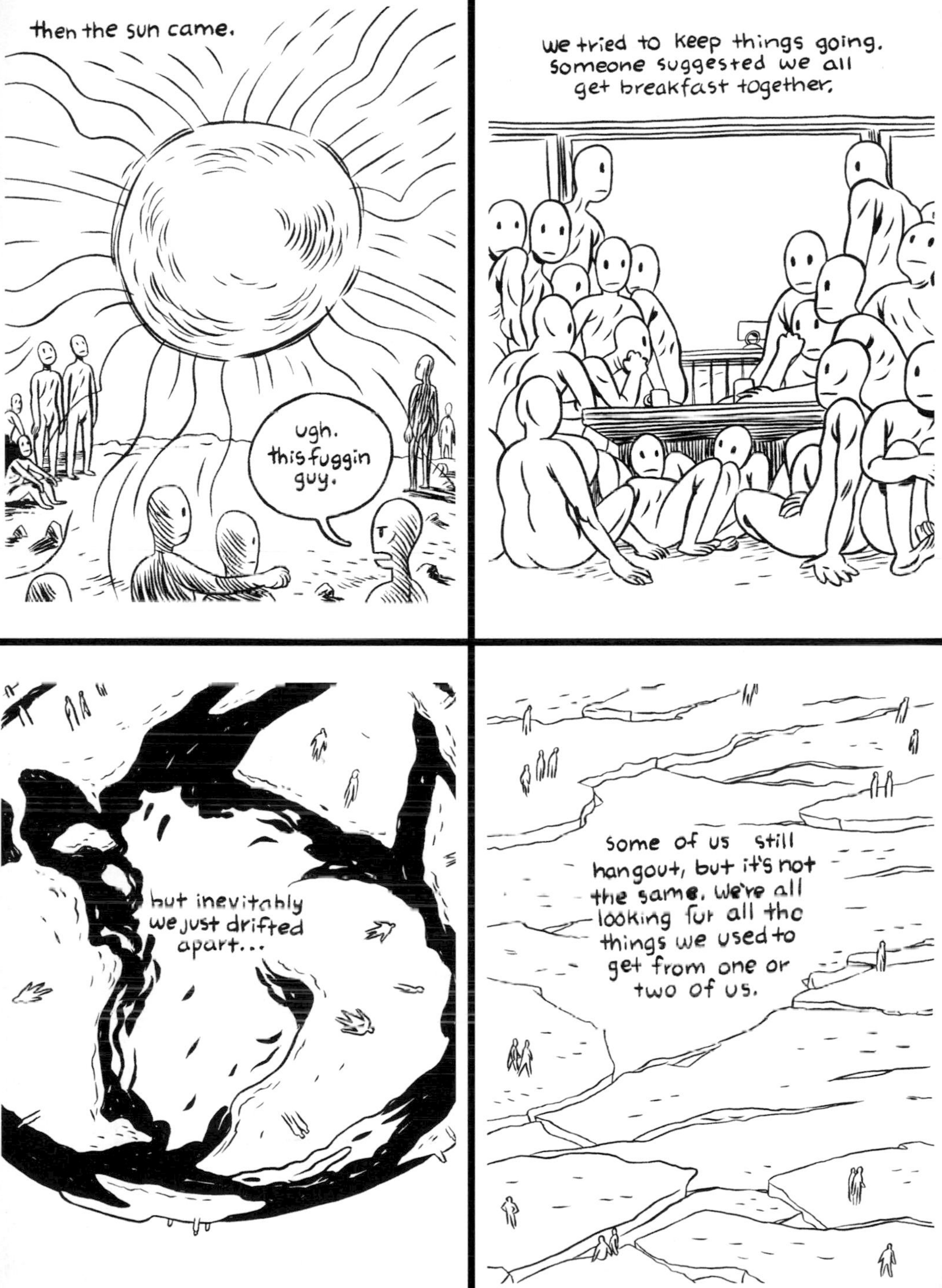
then the sun came.
ugh. this fuggin guy.
we tried to keep things going. someone suggested we all get breakfast together.
but inevitably we just drifted apart...
some of us still hangout, but it's not the same. we're all looking for all the things we used to get from one or two of us.

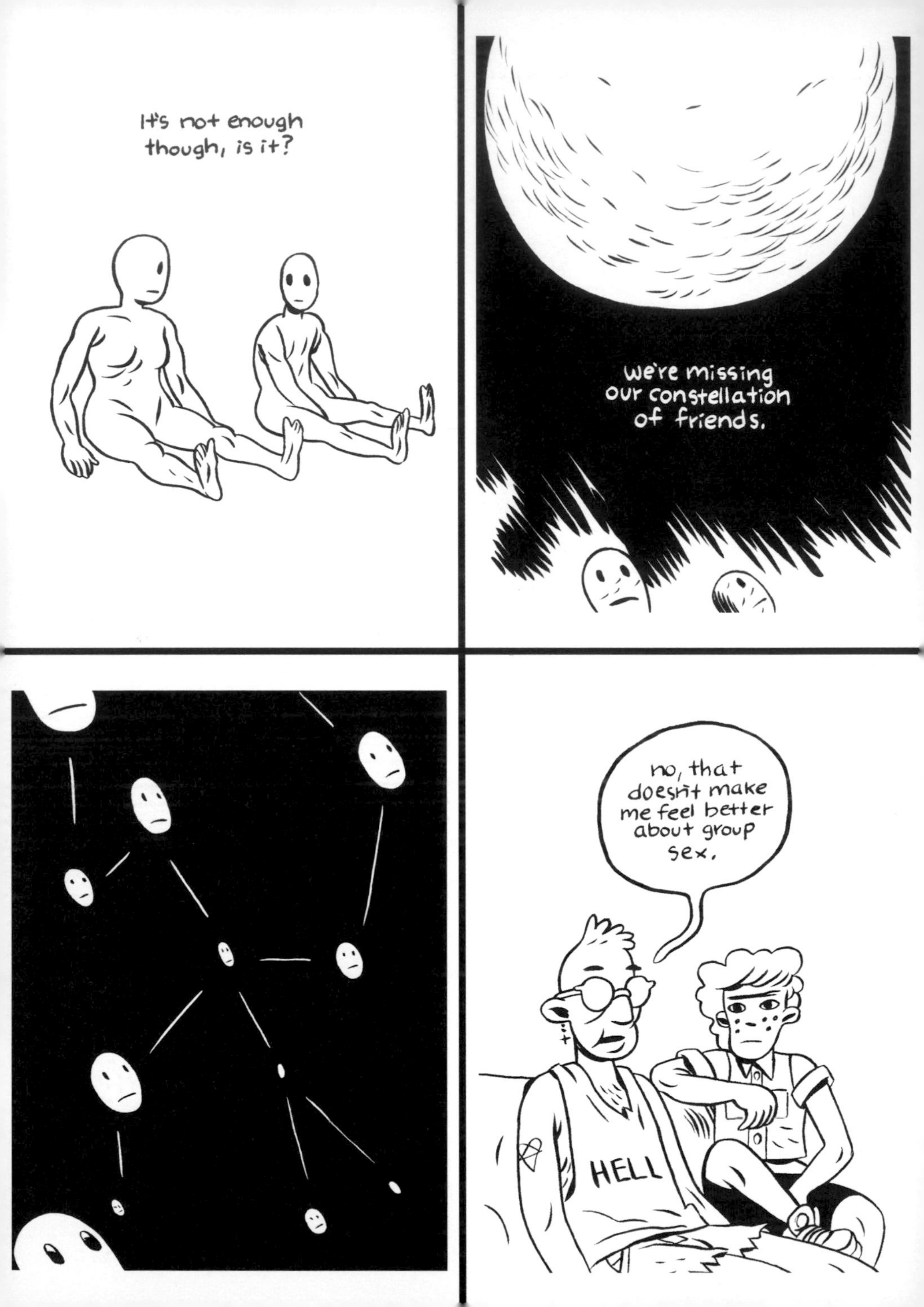
It's not enough though, is it?
we're missing our constellation of friends.
no, that doesn't make me feel better about group sex.
HELL

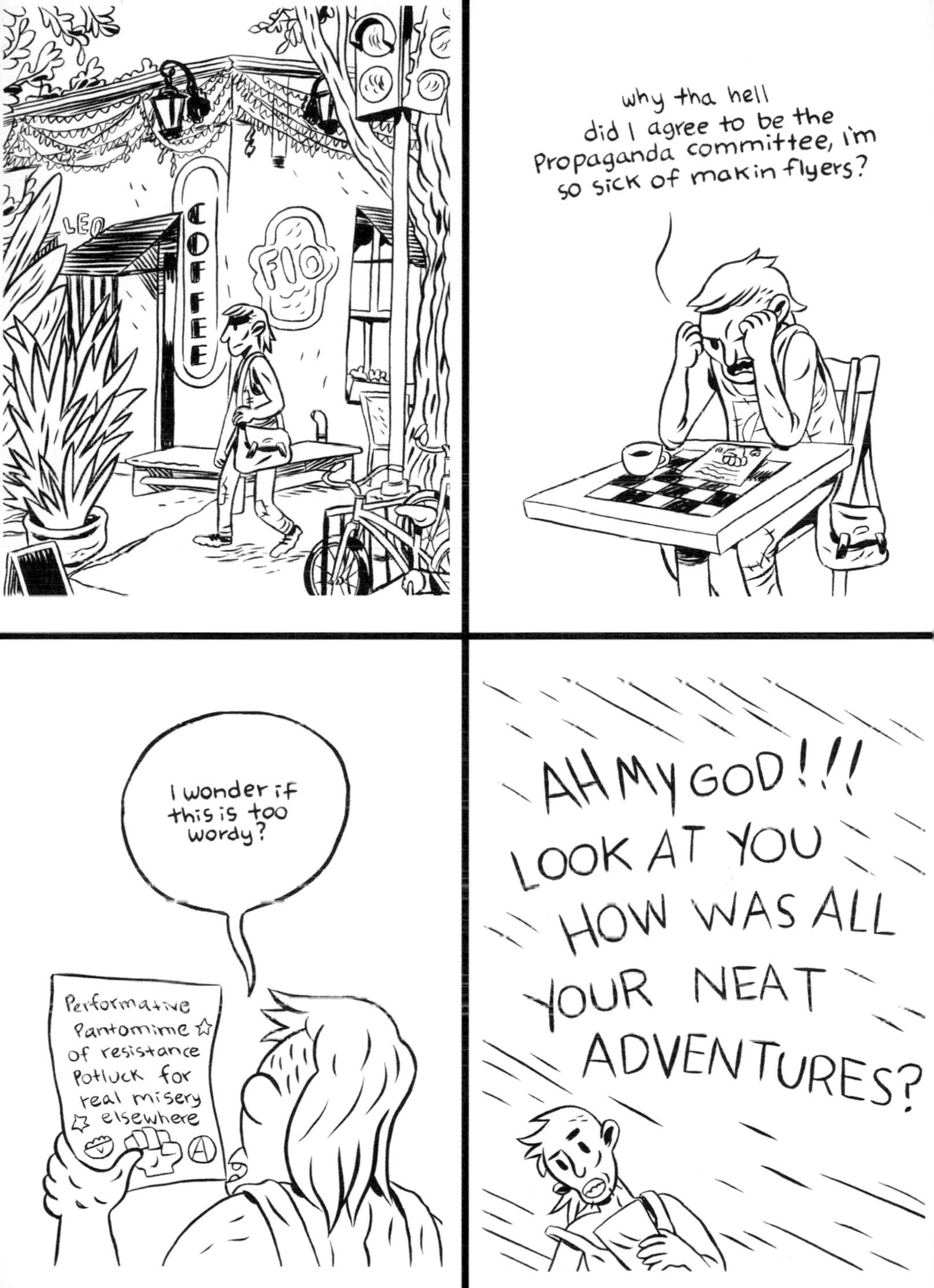
LEO
COFFEE
FIO
why tha hell did I agree to be the Propaganda committee, i'm so sick of makin flyers?
I wonder if this is too wordy?
Performative Pantomime of resistance Potluck for real misery elsewhere
AH MY GOD!!! LOOK AT YOU HOW WAS ALL YOUR NEAT ADVENTURES?

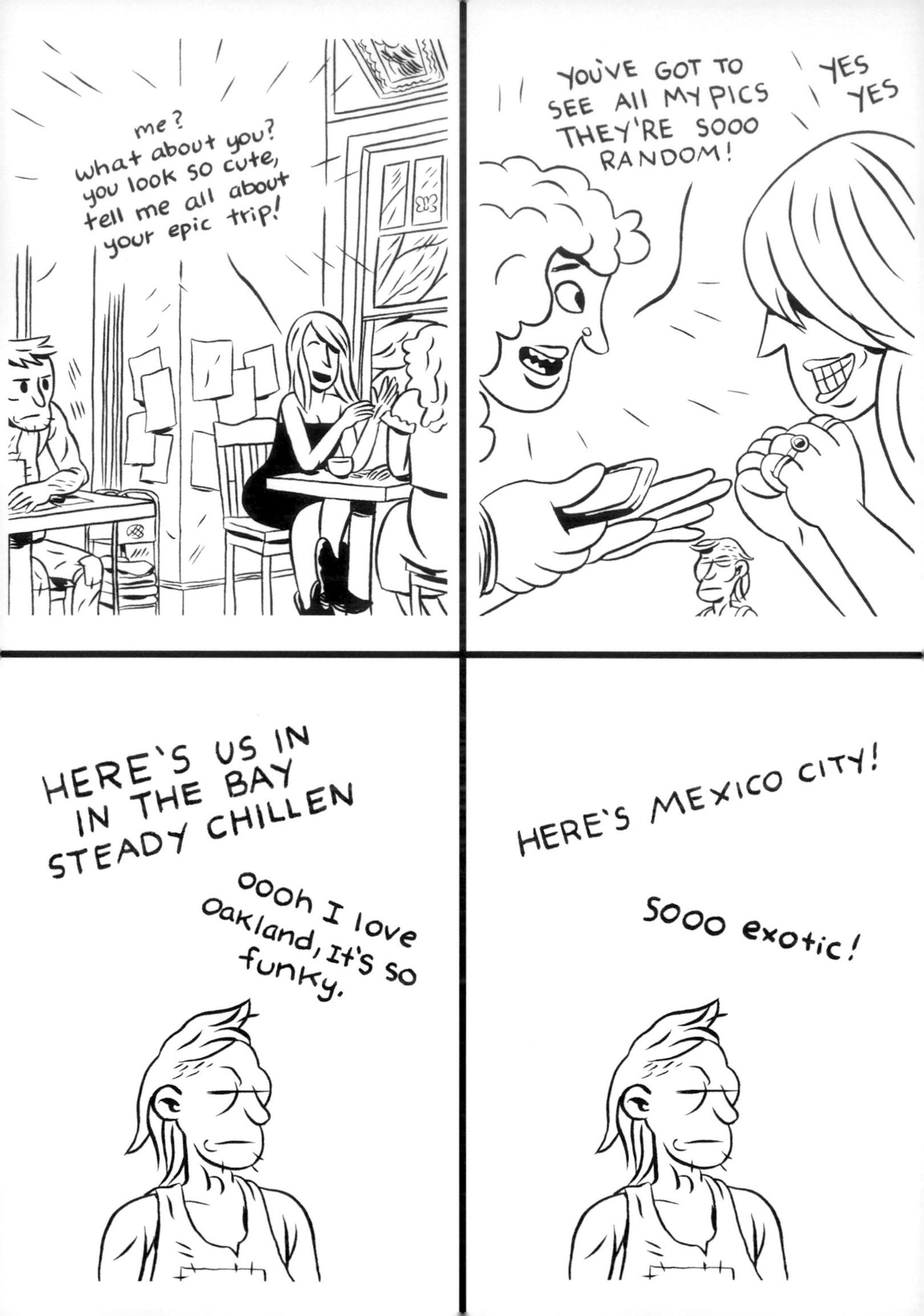
me? what about you? you look so cute, tell me all about your epic trip!
YOU'VE GOT TO SEE All MY PICS THEY'RE SOOO RANDOM!
YES YES
HERE'S US IN IN THE BAY STEADY CHILLEN
oooh I love Oakland, It's so funky.
HERE'S MEXICO CITY!
Sooo exotic!

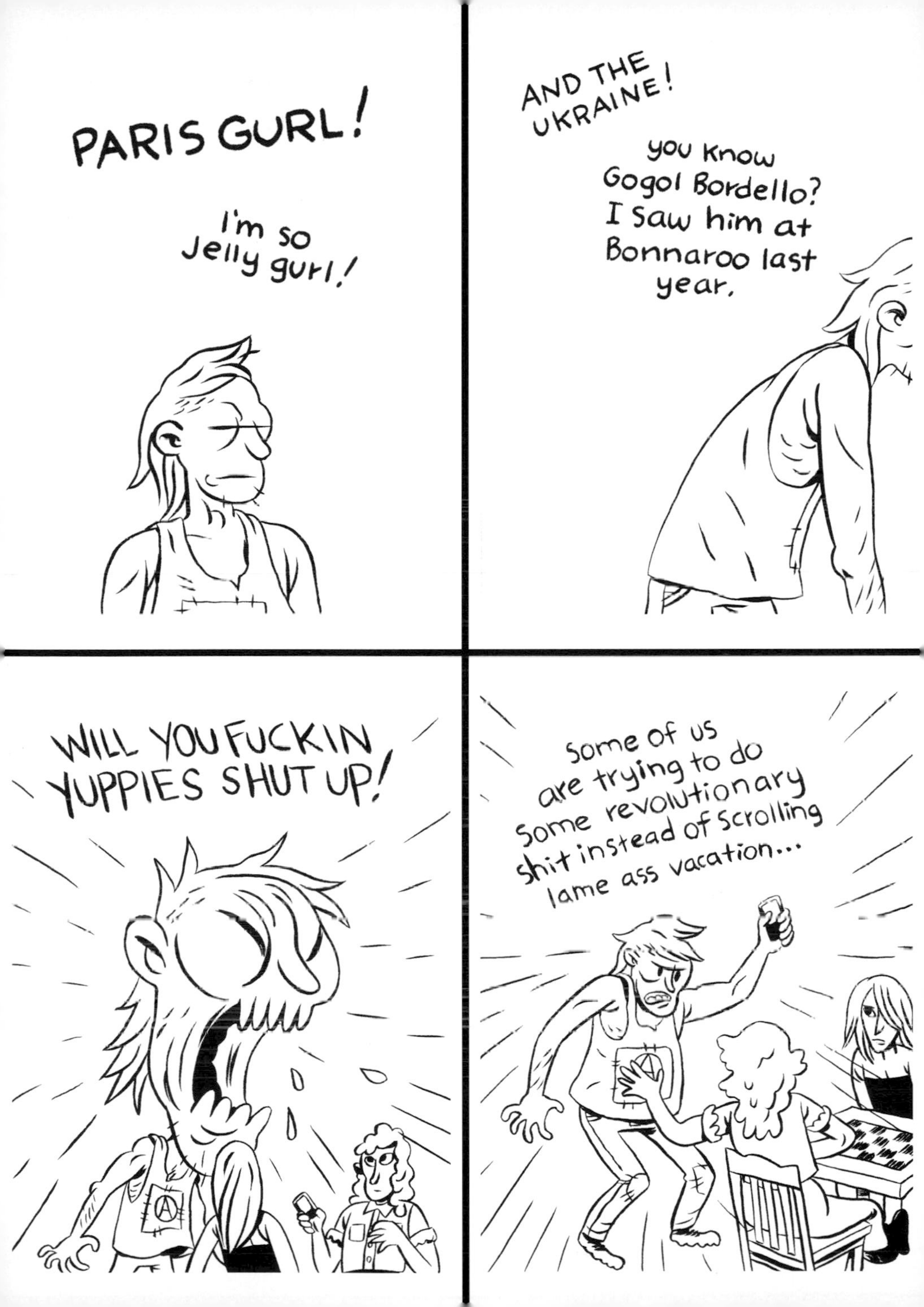
PARIS GURL!
I'm so Jelly gurl!
AND THE UKRAINE!
you know Gogol Bordello? I saw him at Bonnaroo last year.
WILL YOU FUCKIN YUPPIES SHUT UP!
Some of us are trying to do some revolutionary shit instead of scrolling lame ass vacation...

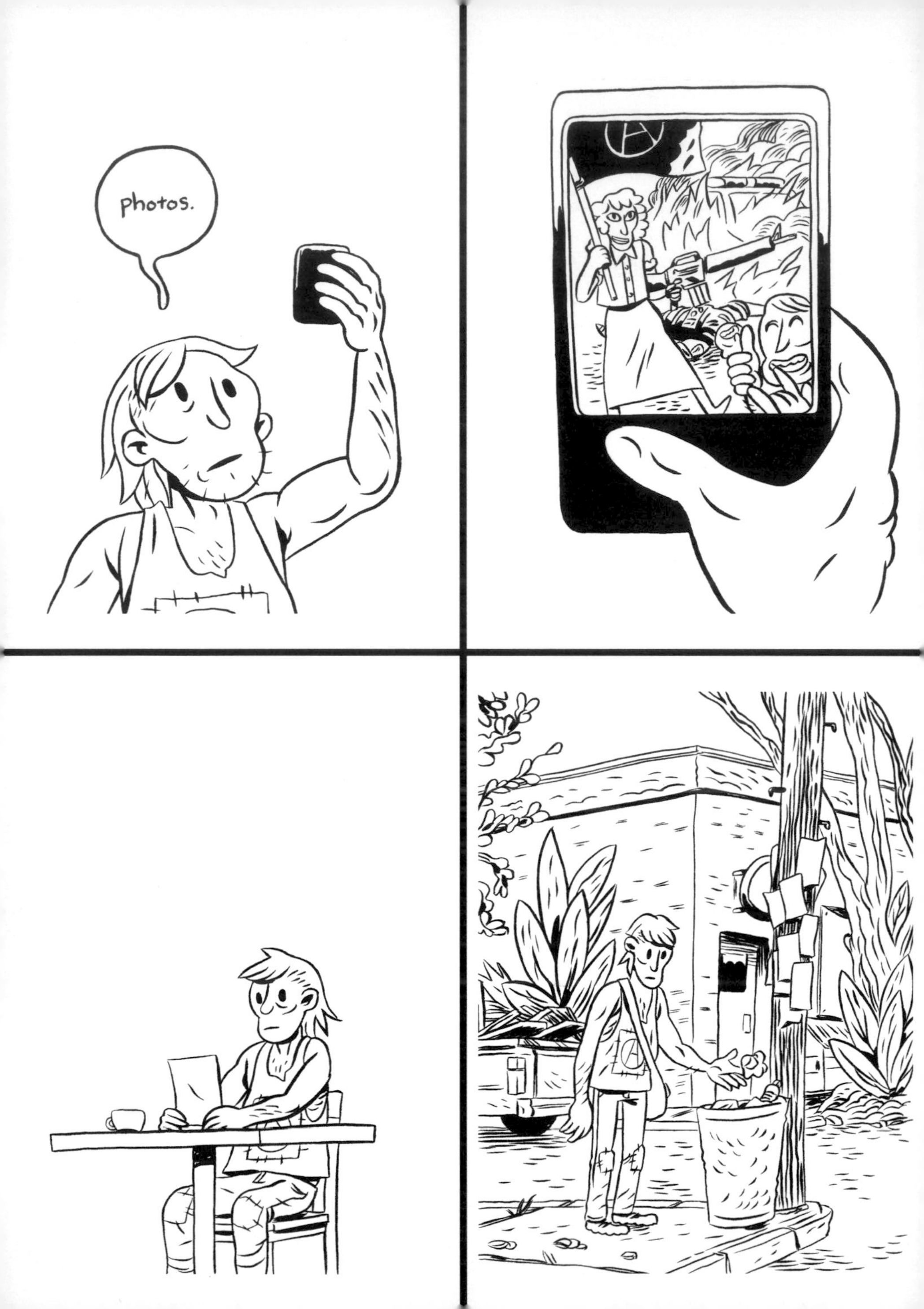
photos.

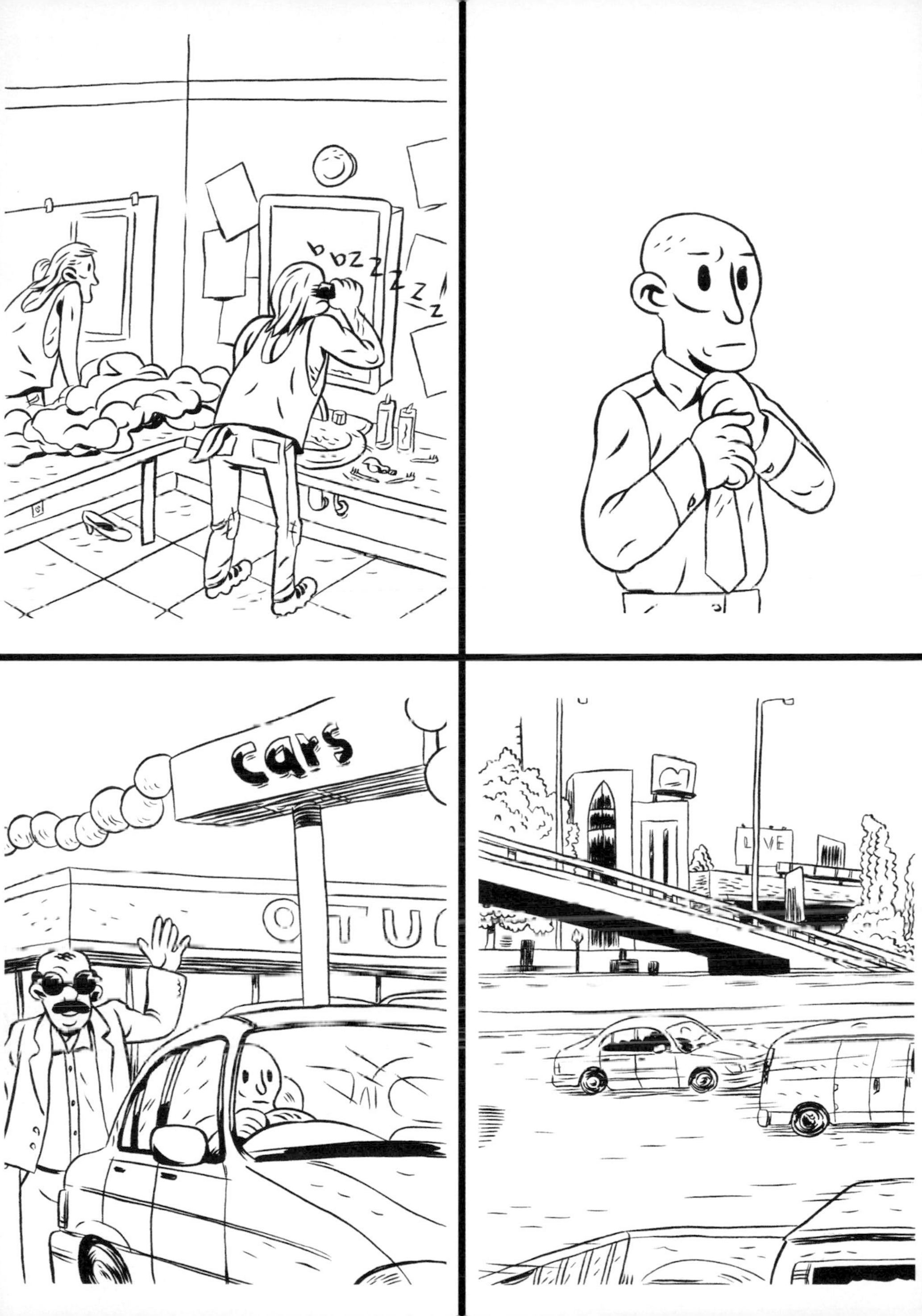
Cars

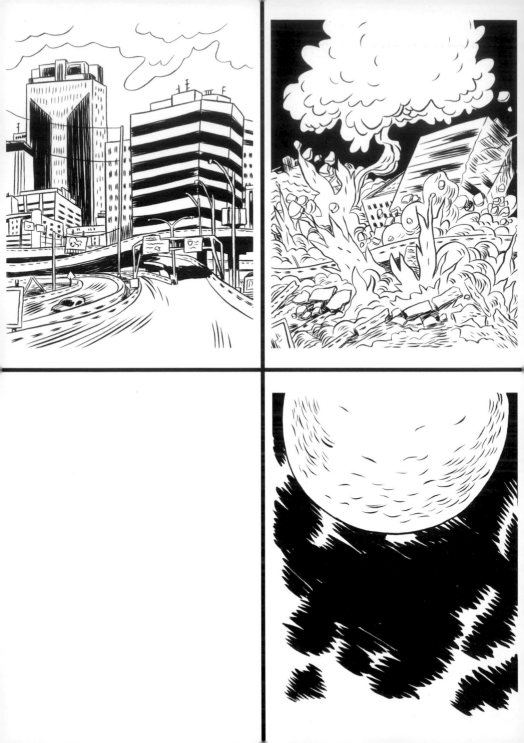

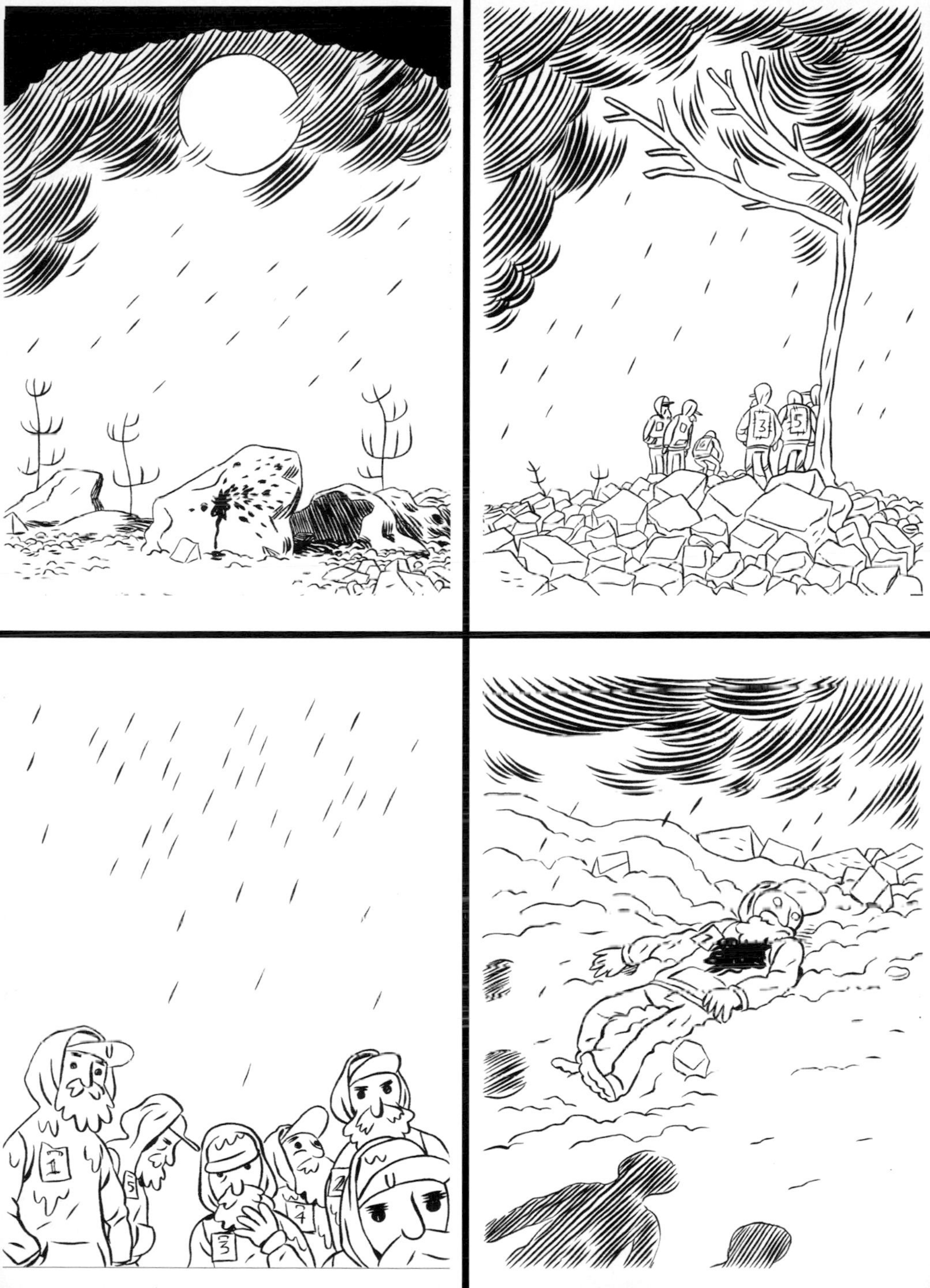

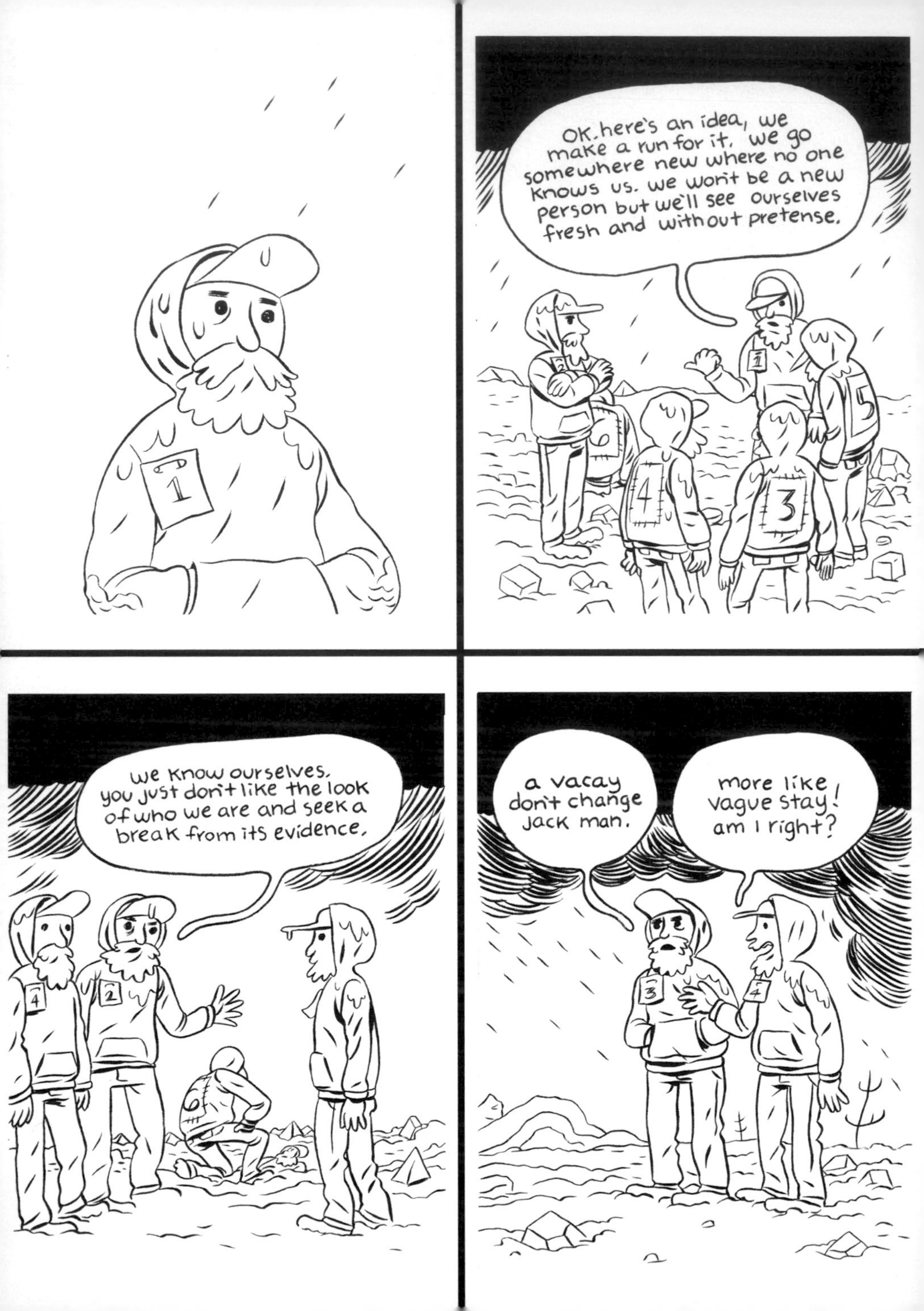
OK. here's an idea, we make a run for it, we go somewhere new where no one knows us. we won't be a new person but we'll see ourselves fresh and without pretense.
we know ourselves. you just don't like the look of who we are and seek a break from its evidence.
a vacay don't change jack man.
more like vague stay! am I right?

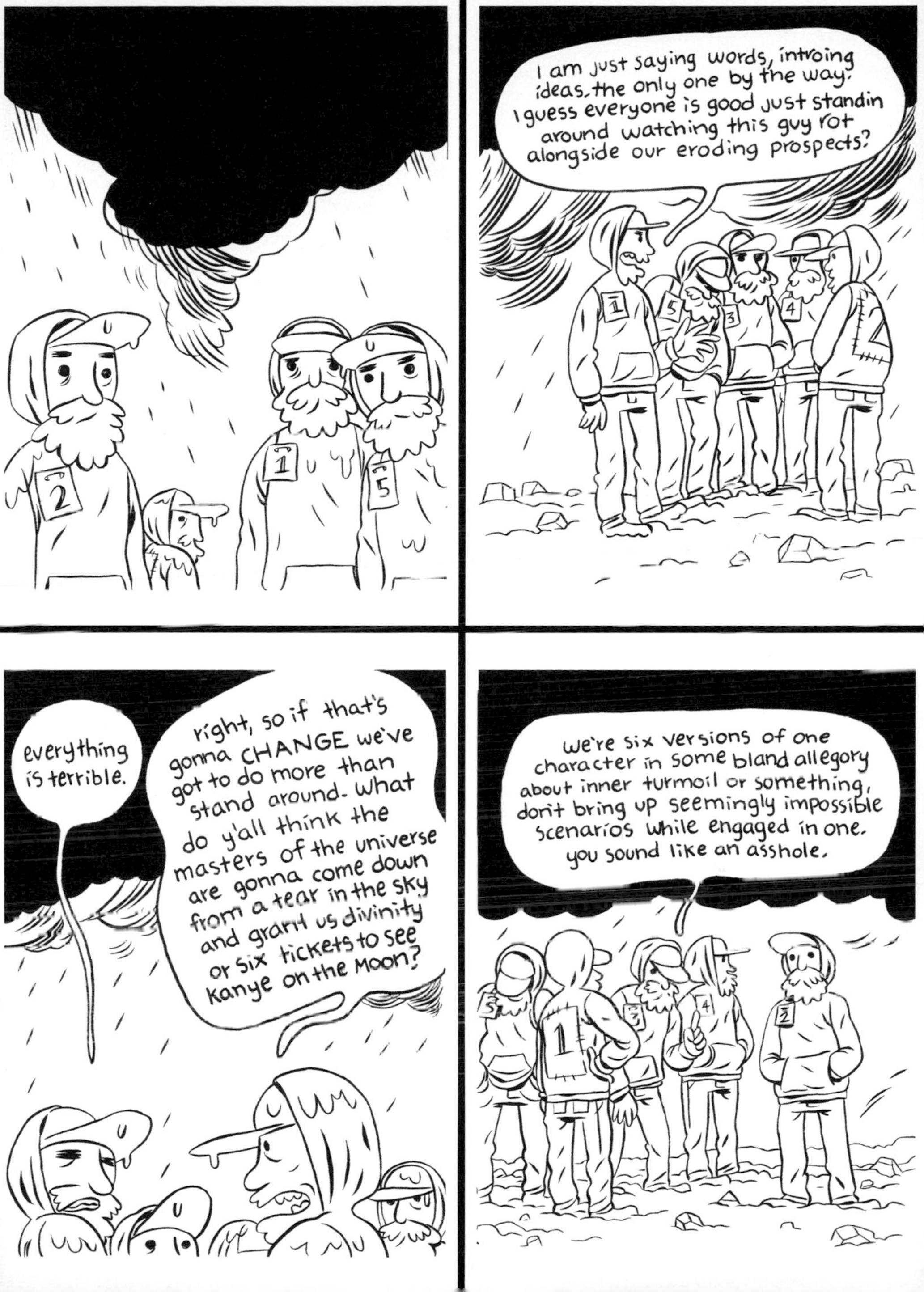
I am just saying words, introing ideas, the only one by the way. I guess everyone is good just standin around watching this guy rot alongside our eroding prospects?
everything is terrible.
right, so if that's gonna CHANGE we've got to do more than stand around. what do y'all think the masters of the universe are gonna come down from a tear in the sky and grant us divinity or six tickets to see Kanye on the moon?
we're six versions of one character in some bland allegory about inner turmoil or something, don't bring up seemingly impossible scenarios while engaged in one. you sound like an asshole.

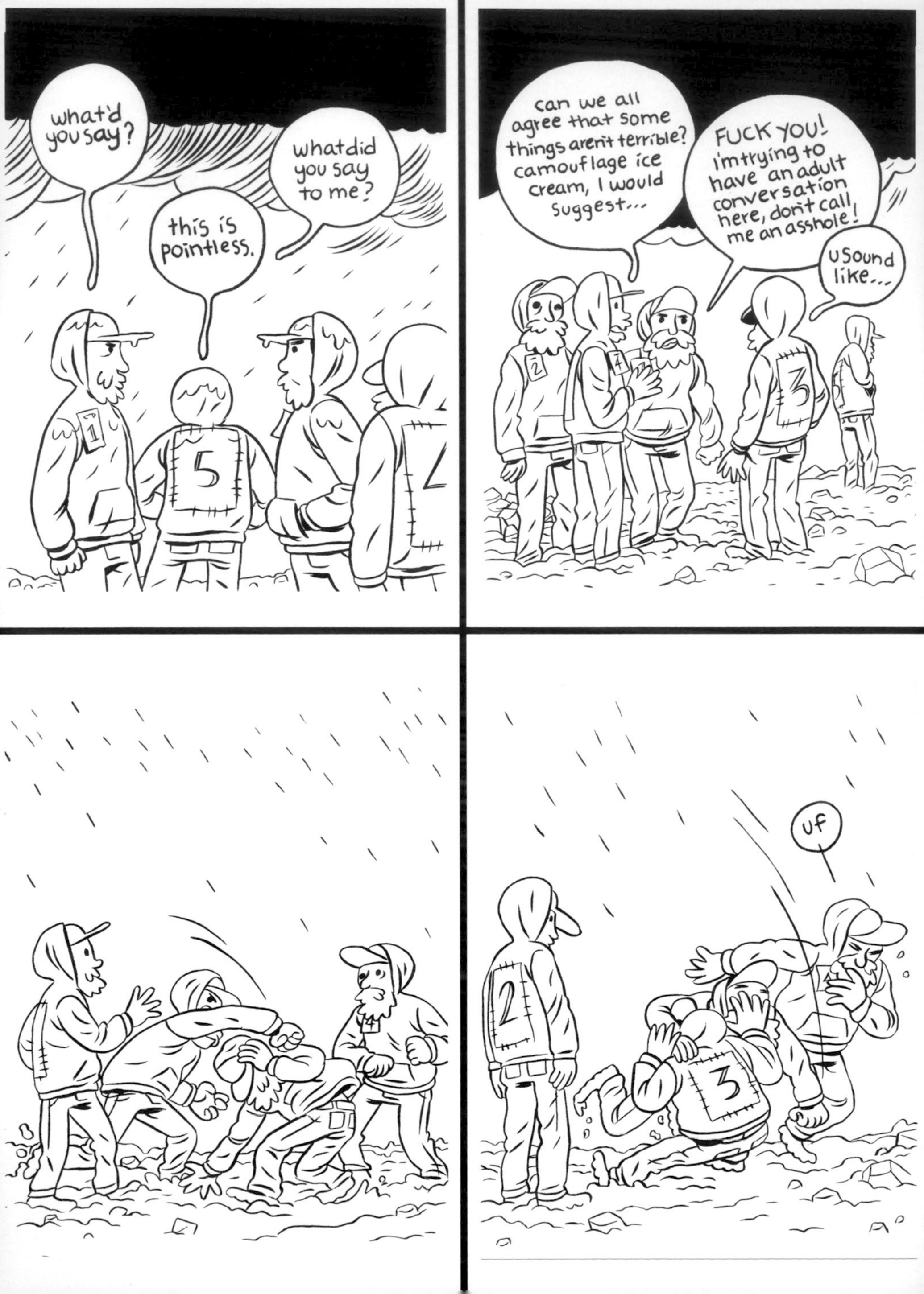
what'd you say?
whatdid you say to me?
this is pointless.
can we all agree that some things aren't terrible? camouflage ice cream, I would suggest...
FUCK YOU! I'm trying to have an adult conversation here, don't call me an asshole!
U sound like...
uf

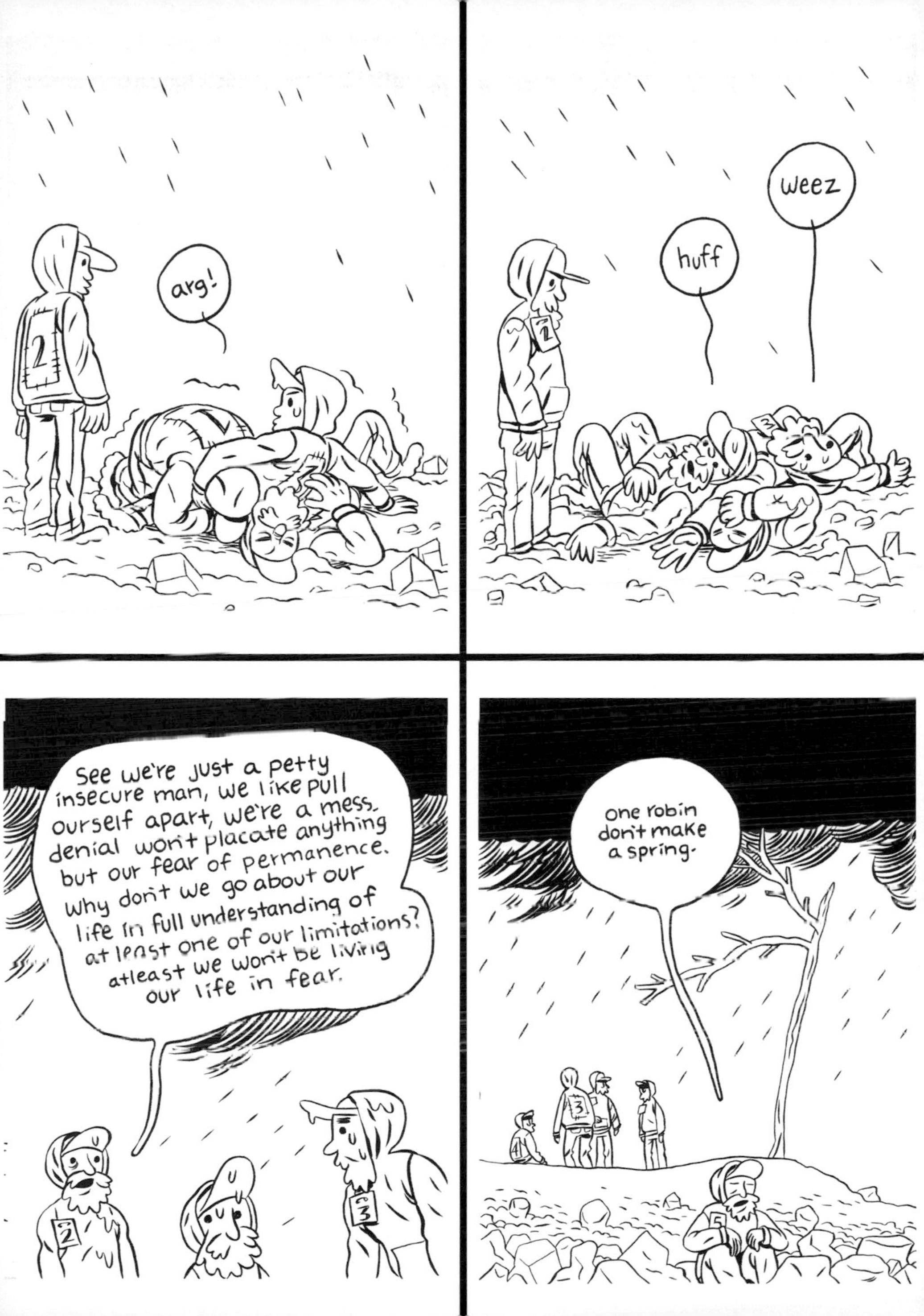
arg!
huff
weez
See we're just a petty insecure man, we like pull ourself apart, we're a mess. denial won't placate anything but our fear of permanence. why don't we go about our life in full understanding of at least one of our limitations? atleast we won't be living our life in fear.
one robin don't make a spring.

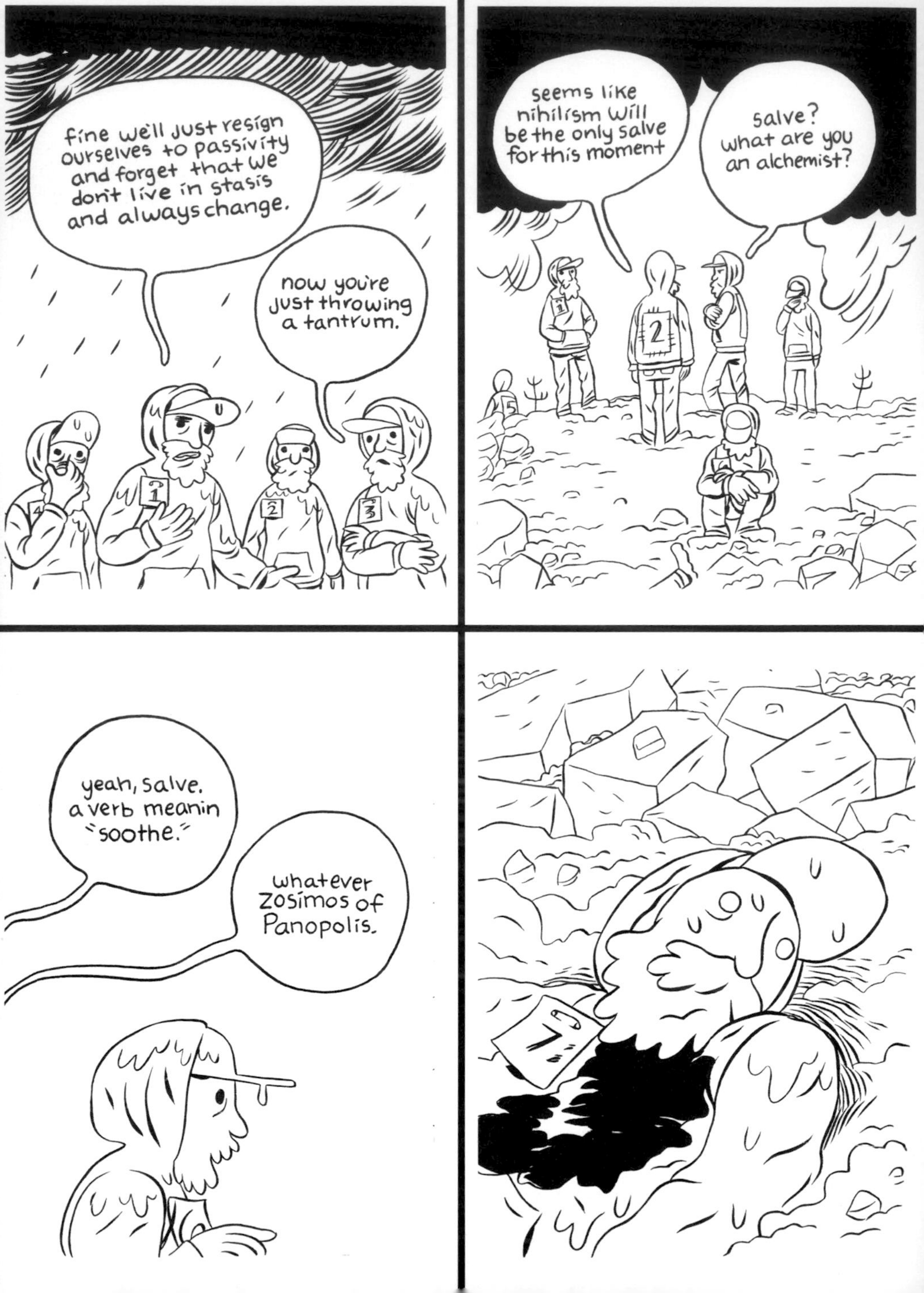
fine we'll just resign ourselves to passivity and forget that we don't live in stasis and always change.
now you're just throwing a tantrum.
seems like nihilism will be the only salve for this moment
salve? what are you an alchemist?
yeah, salve. a verb meanin soothe.
whatever Zosimos of Panopolis.

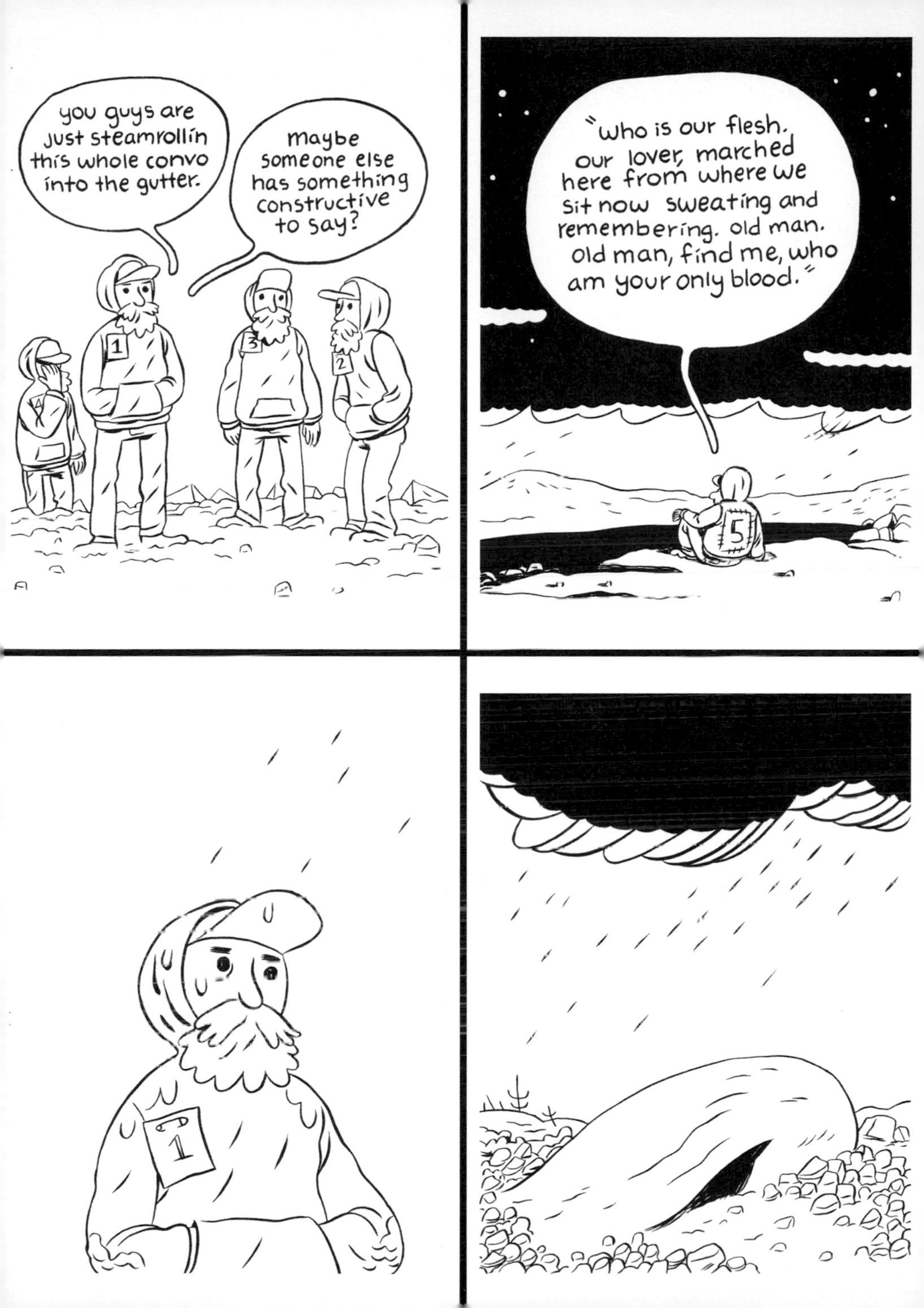
you guys are just steamrollin this whole convo into the gutter.
maybe someone else has something constructive to say?
"who is our flesh. our lover, marched here from where we sit now sweating and remembering. old man. old man, find me, who am your only blood."

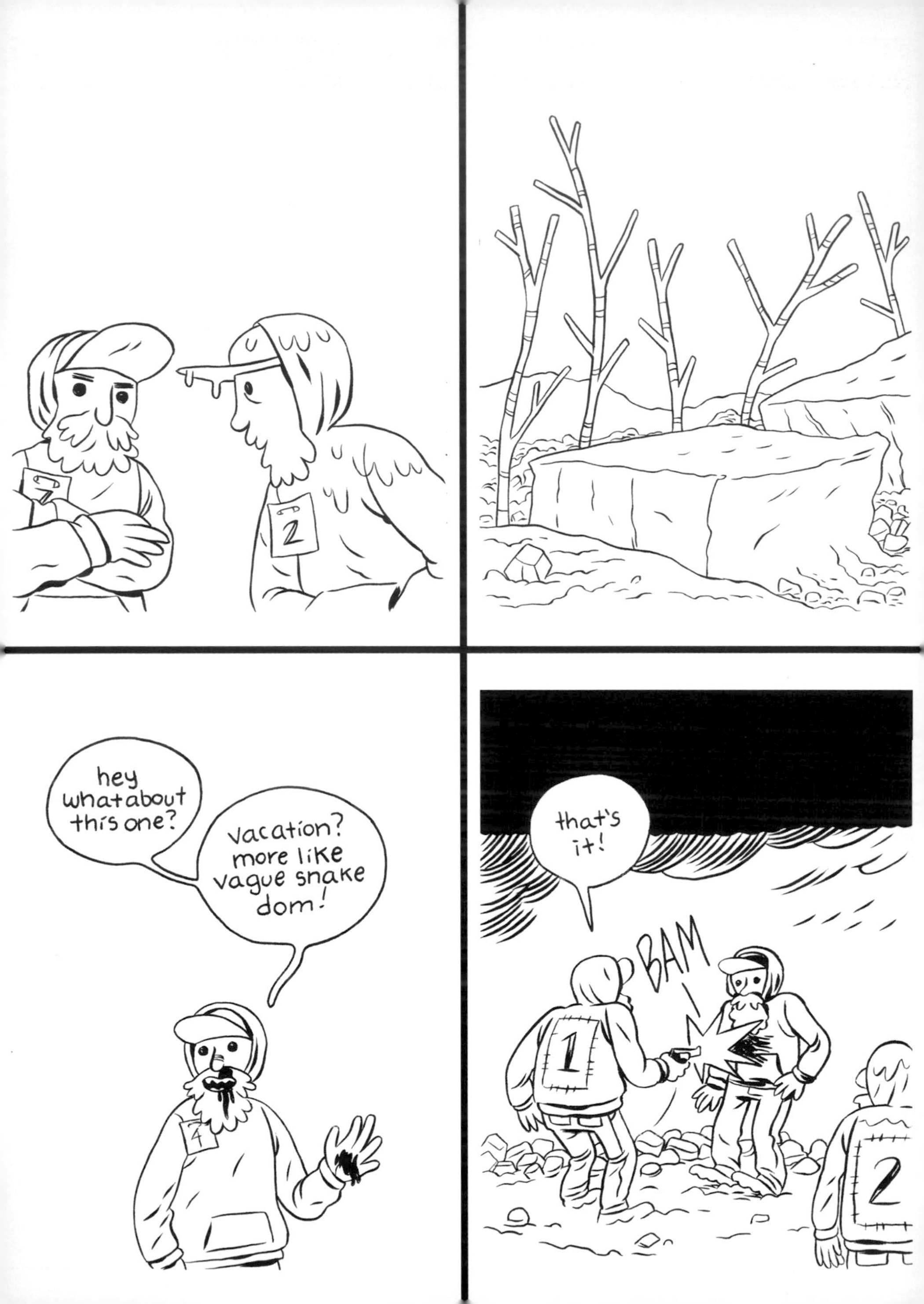
hey whatabout this one?
vacation? more like vague snake dom!
that's it!
BAM

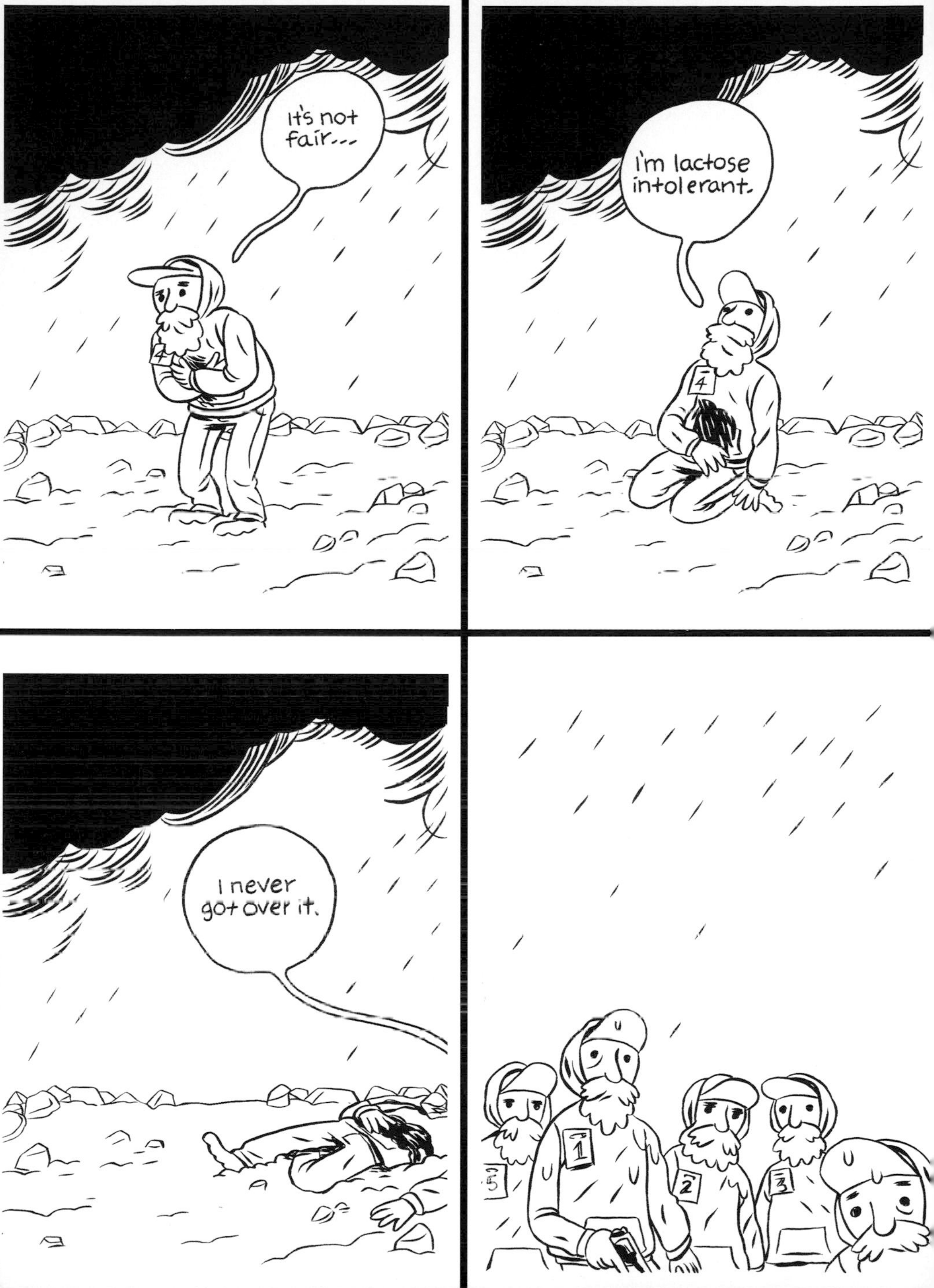
It's not fair...
I'm lactose intolerant.
I never got over it.
4
4
1
2
3
5

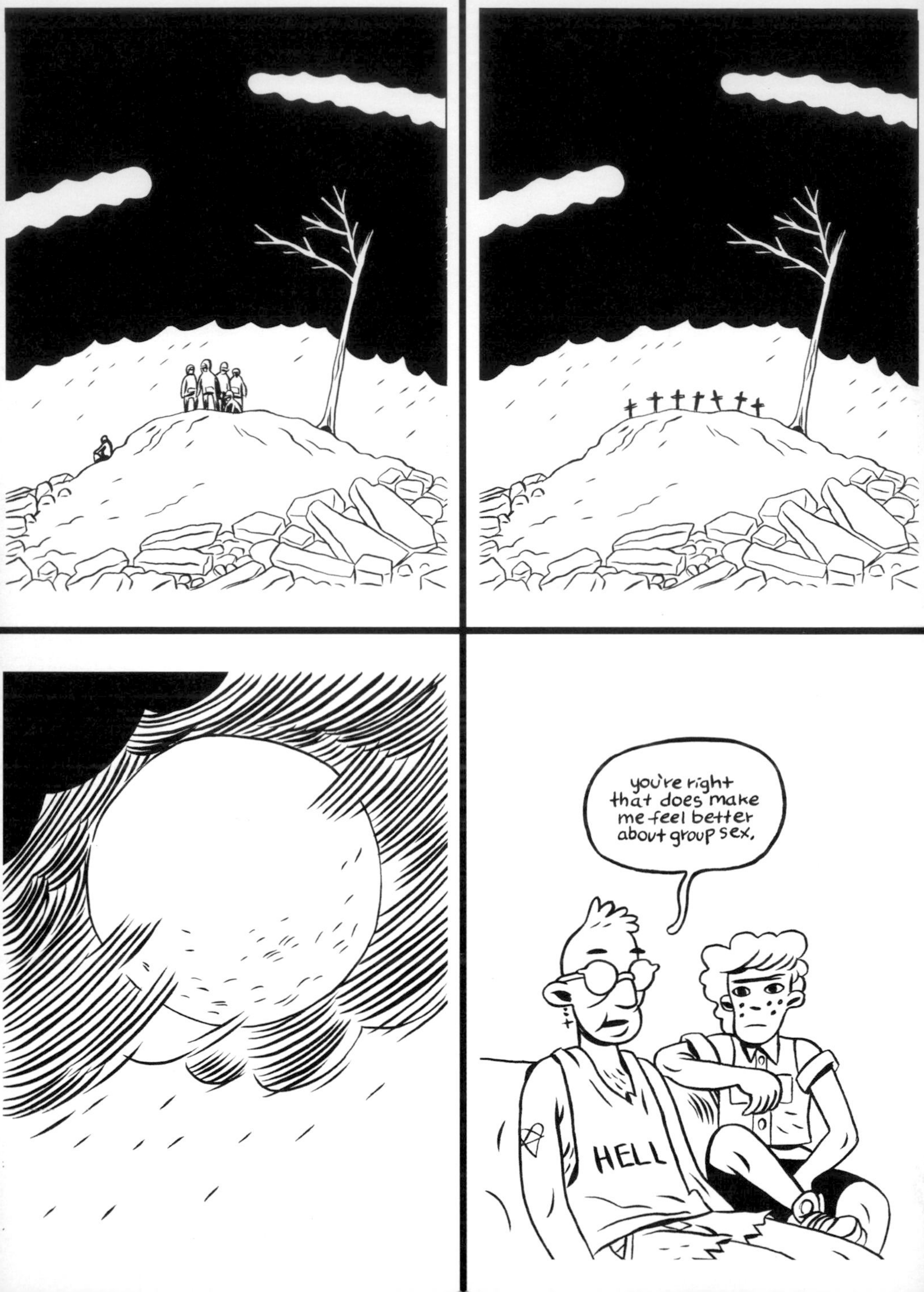
you're right that does make me feel better about group sex.
HELL

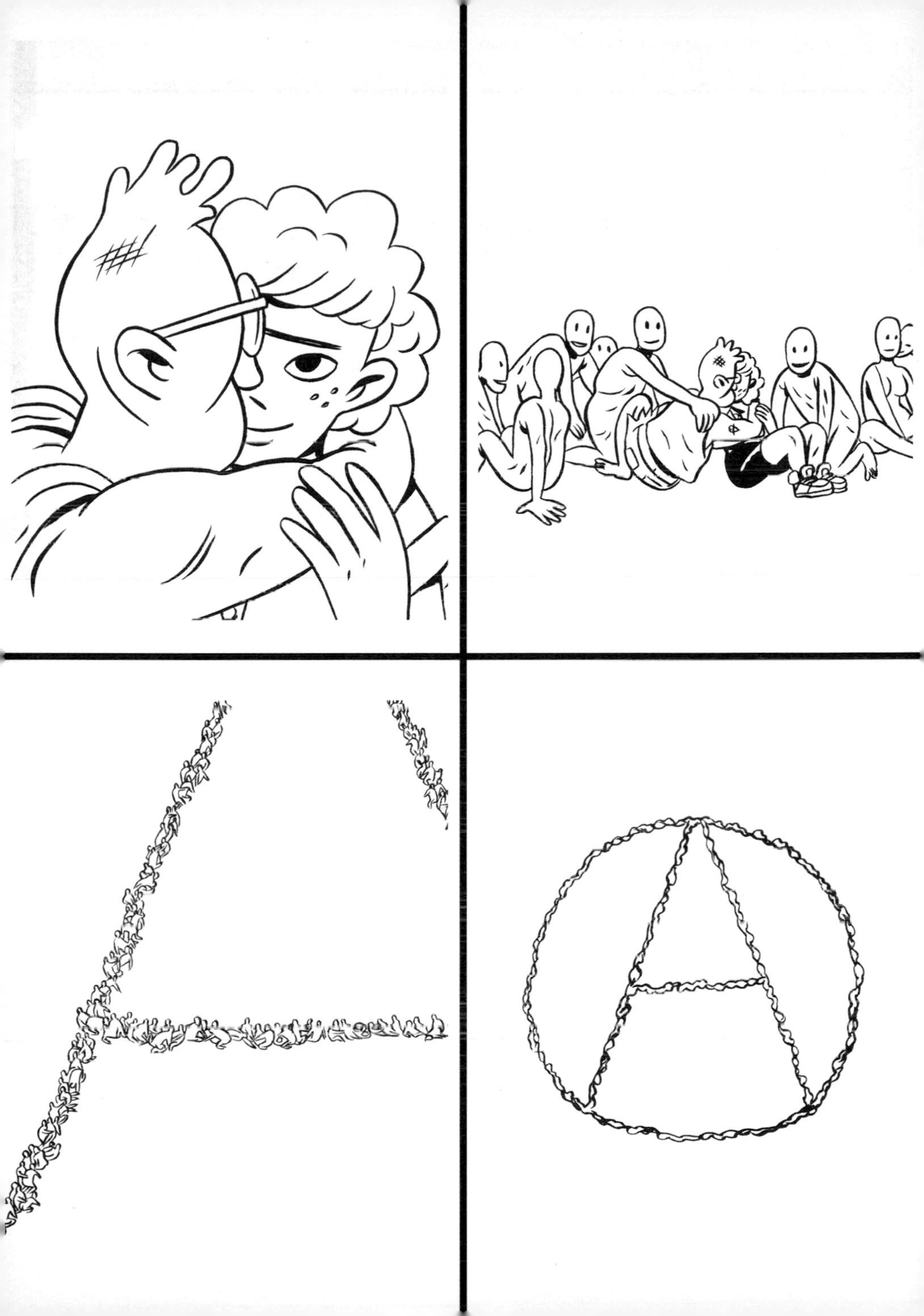

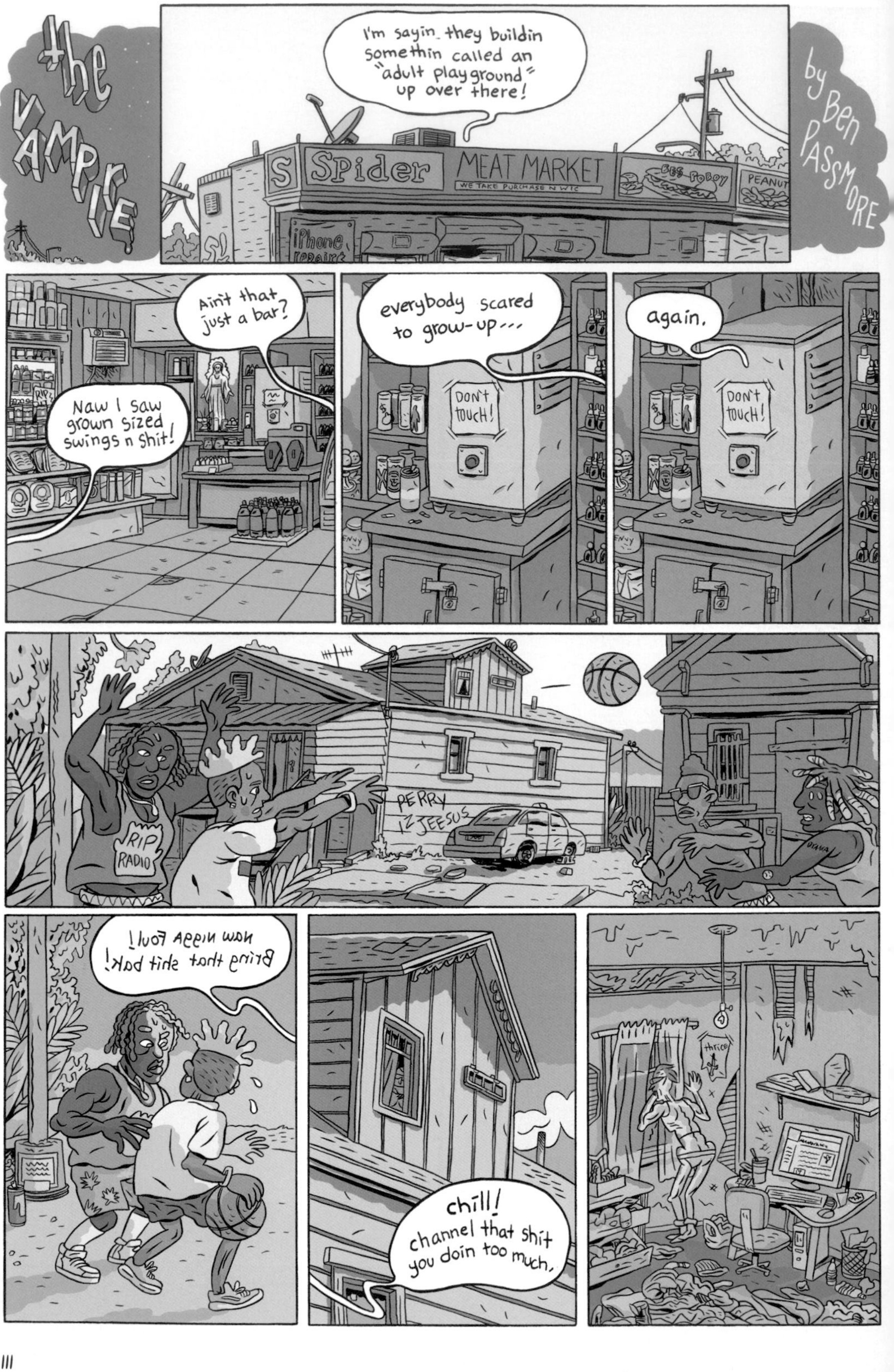
the VAMPIRE
by Ben Passmore
I'm sayin they buildin somethin called an "adult playground" up over there!
Spider
MEAT MARKET
WE TAKE PURCHASE N WIC
PEANUT
Ain't that just a bar?
Naw I saw grown sized swings n shit!
everybody scared to grow-up...
DON'T TOUCH!
again.
DON'T TOUCH!
RIP RADIO
PERRY IZ JEESUS
naw nigga Foul! Bring that shit bak!
chill! channel that shit you doin too much.
thrice

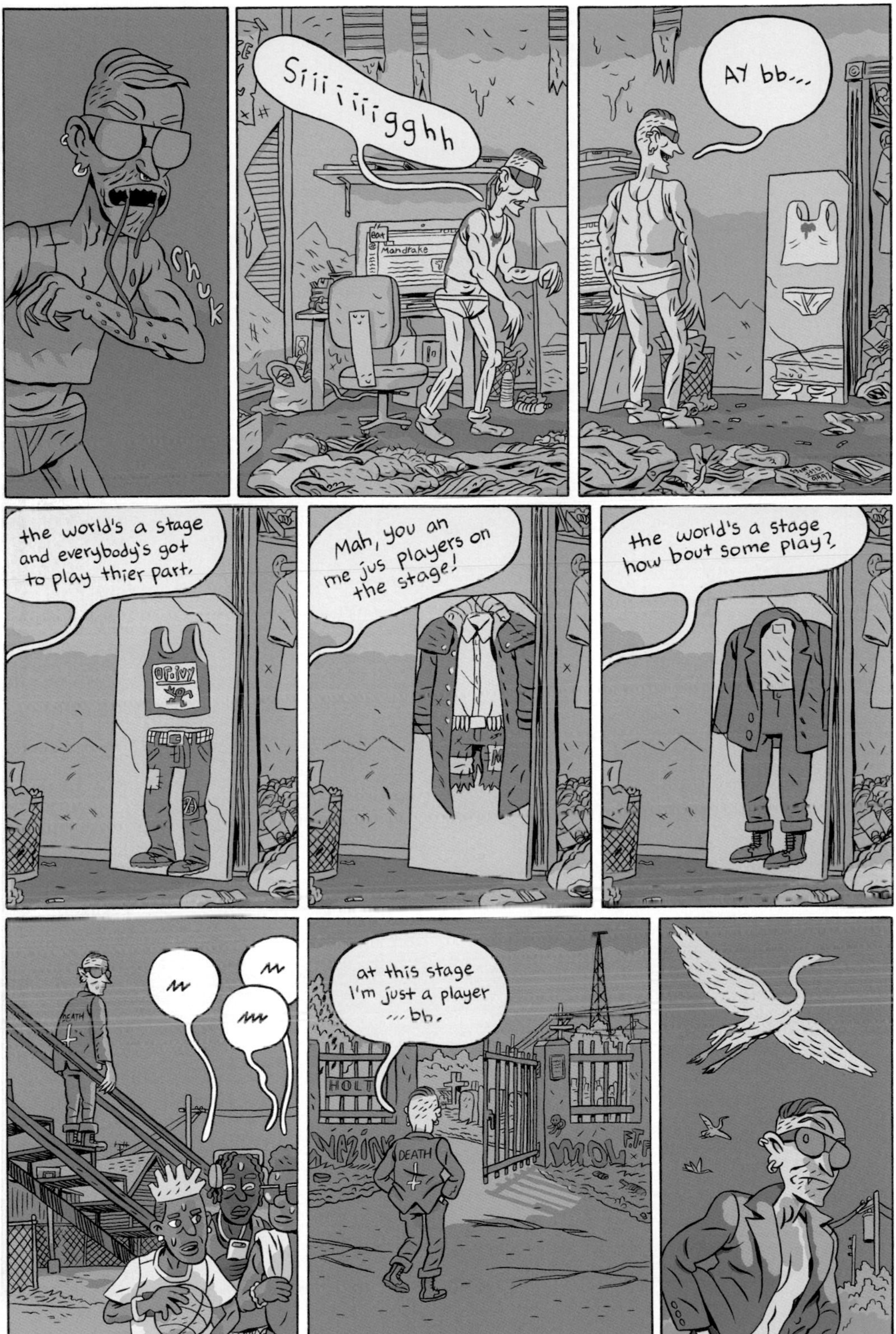
CHUK
Siiiiiiigghh
Mandrake
AY bb...
the world's a stage and everybody's got to play thier part,
Mah, you an me jus players on the stage!
the world's a stage how bout some play?
DEATH
at this stage I'm just a player ...bb.
HOLT
DEATH

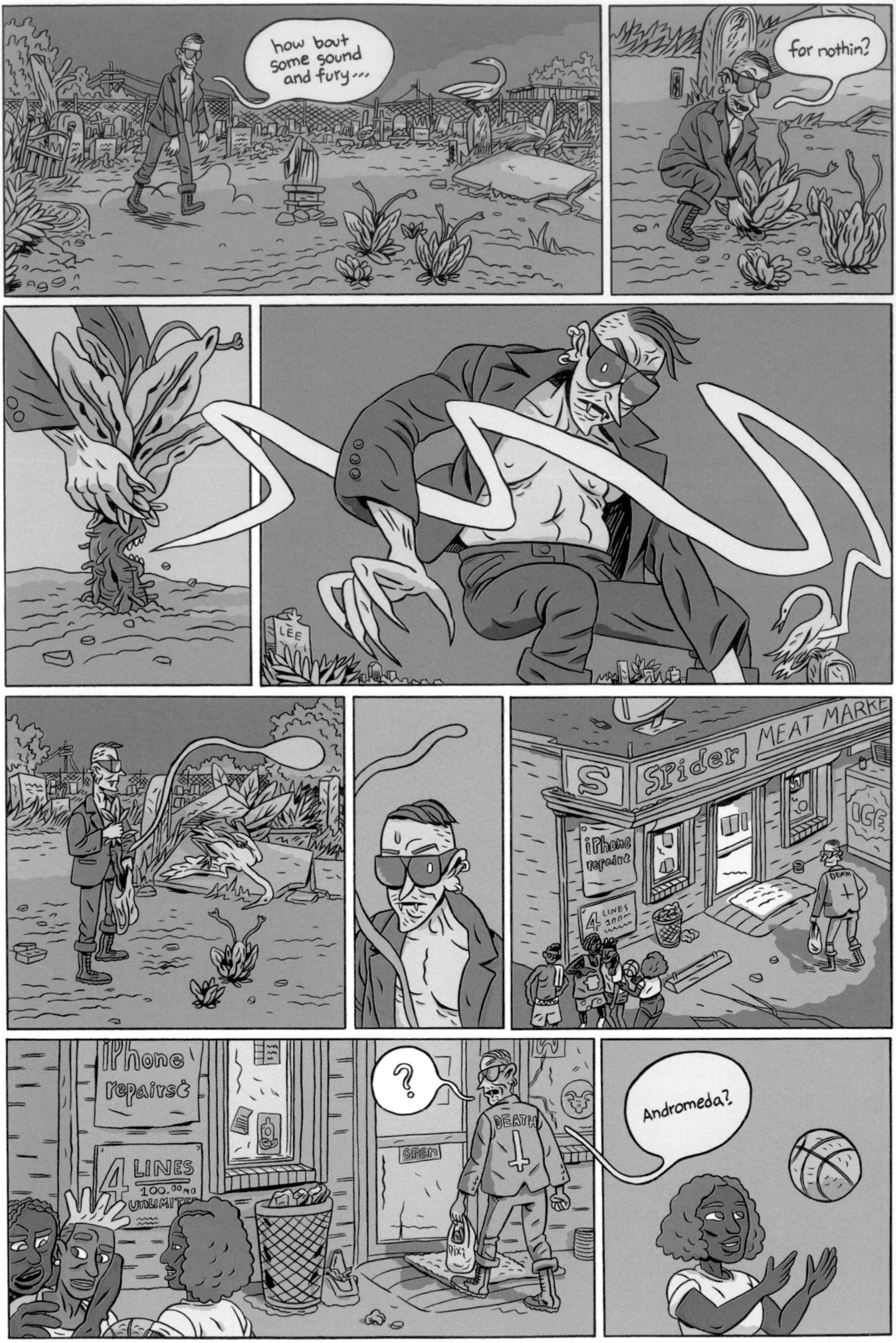
how bout some sound and fury...
for nothin?
LEE
S
Spider
MEAT MARKE
iPhone repairs
4 LINES
ICE
DEATH
iPhone repairs¢
4 LINES
100.00 MO
?
OPEN
DEATH
Andromeda?

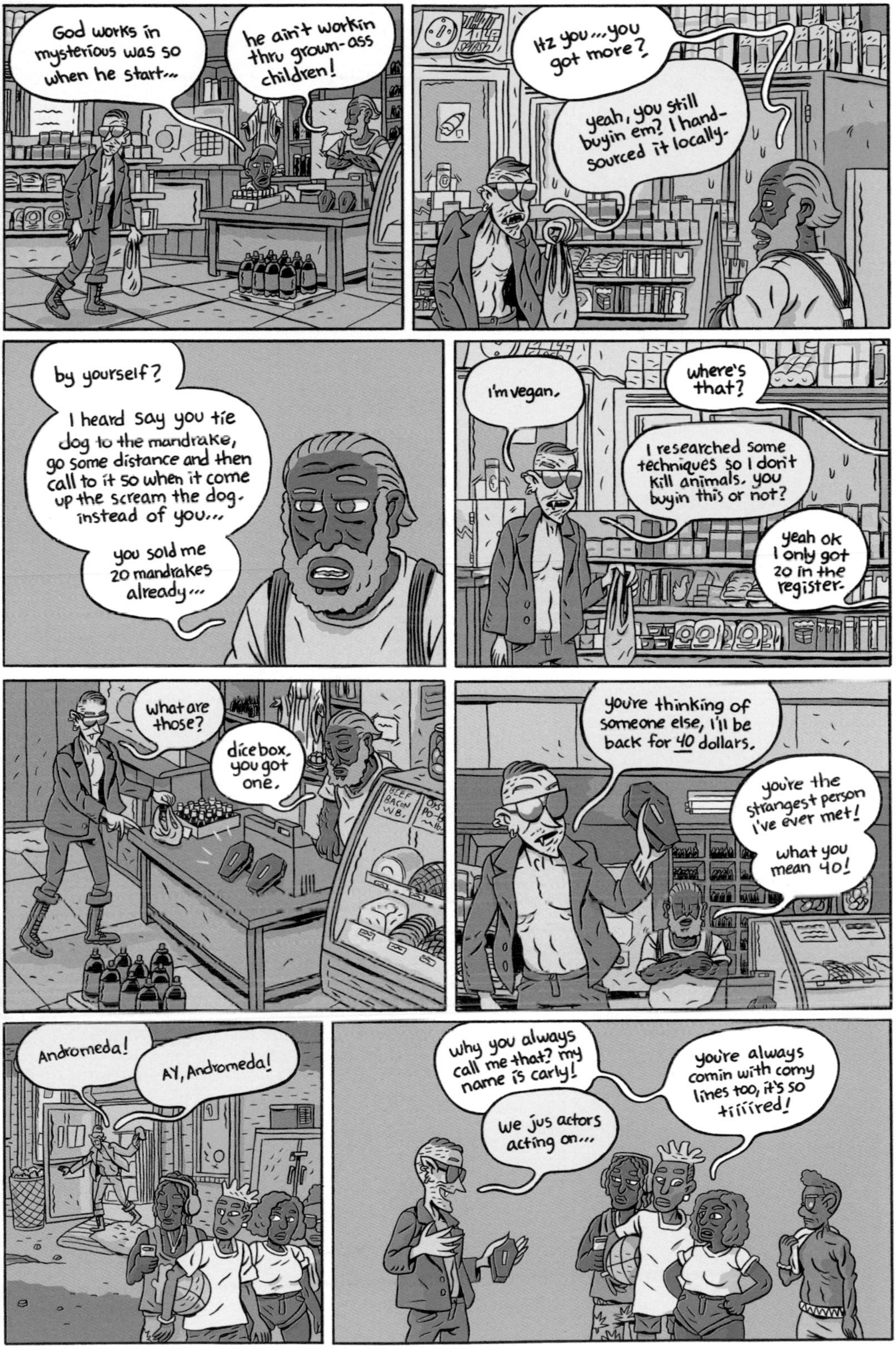
God works in mysterious was so when he start...
he ain't workin thru grown-ass children!
Itz you...you got more?
yeah, you still buyin em? I hand-sourced it locally.
by yourself?
I heard say you tie dog to the mandrake, go some distance and then call to it so when it come up the scream the dog. instead of you...
you sold me 20 mandrakes already...
I'm vegan.
where's that?
I researched some techniques so I don't kill animals. you buyin this or not?
yeah ok I only got 20 in the register.
what are those?
dicebox. you got one.
BEEF BACON
you're thinking of someone else, I'll be back for 40 dollars.
you're the strangest person I've ever met!
what you mean 40!
Andromeda!
AY, Andromeda!
why you always call me that? my name is carly!
we jus actors acting on...
you're always comin with corny lines too, it's so tiiiired!

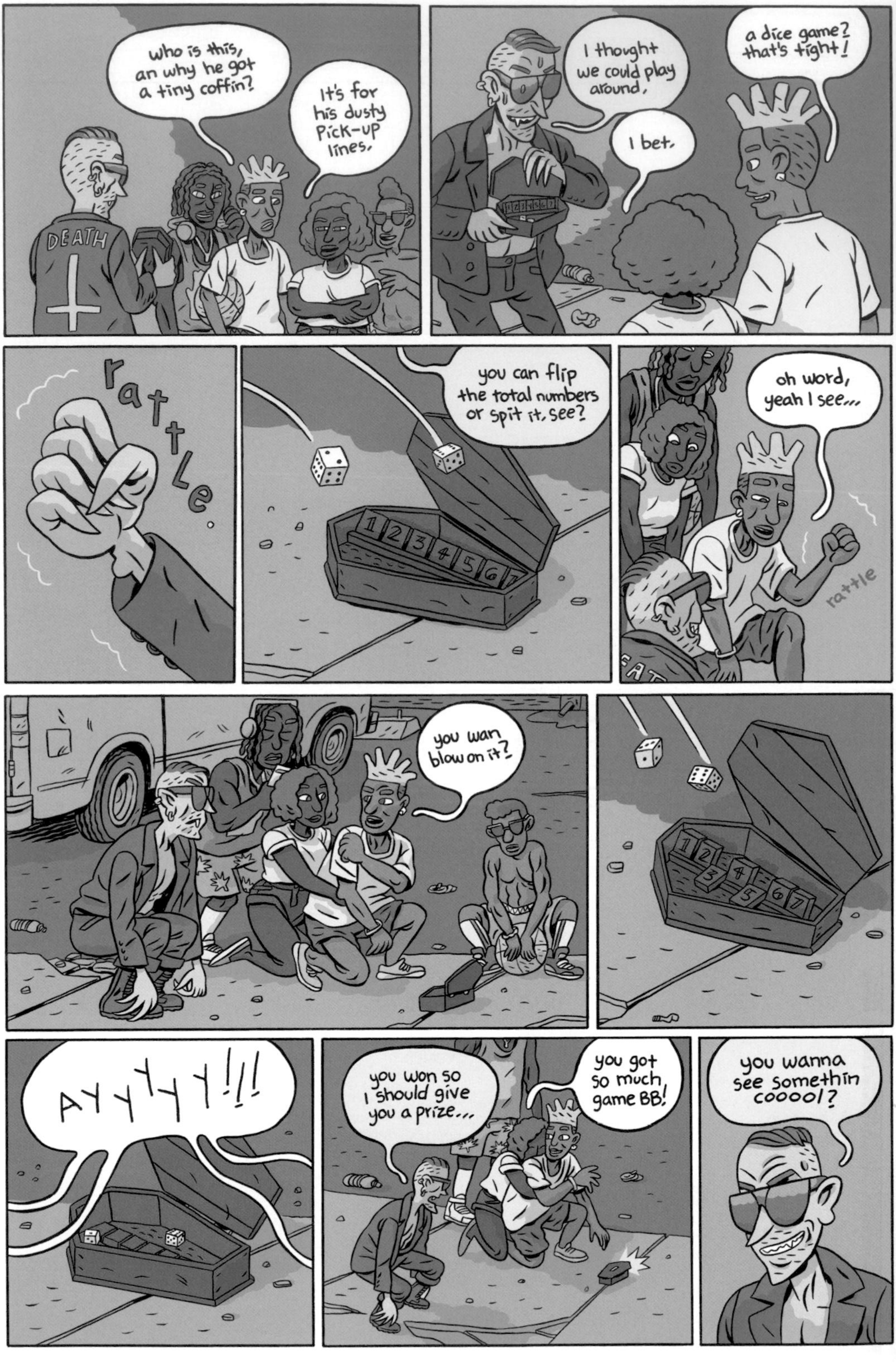
who is this, an why he got a tiny coffin?
It's for his dusty pick-up lines.
DEATH
I thought we could play around,
I bet.
a dice game? that's tight!
rattle.
you can flip the total numbers or spit it, see?
1 2 3 4 5 6 7
oh word, yeah I see...
rattle
you wan blow on it?
AYYYYY!!!
you won so I should give you a prize...
you got so much game BB!
you wanna see somethin cooool?

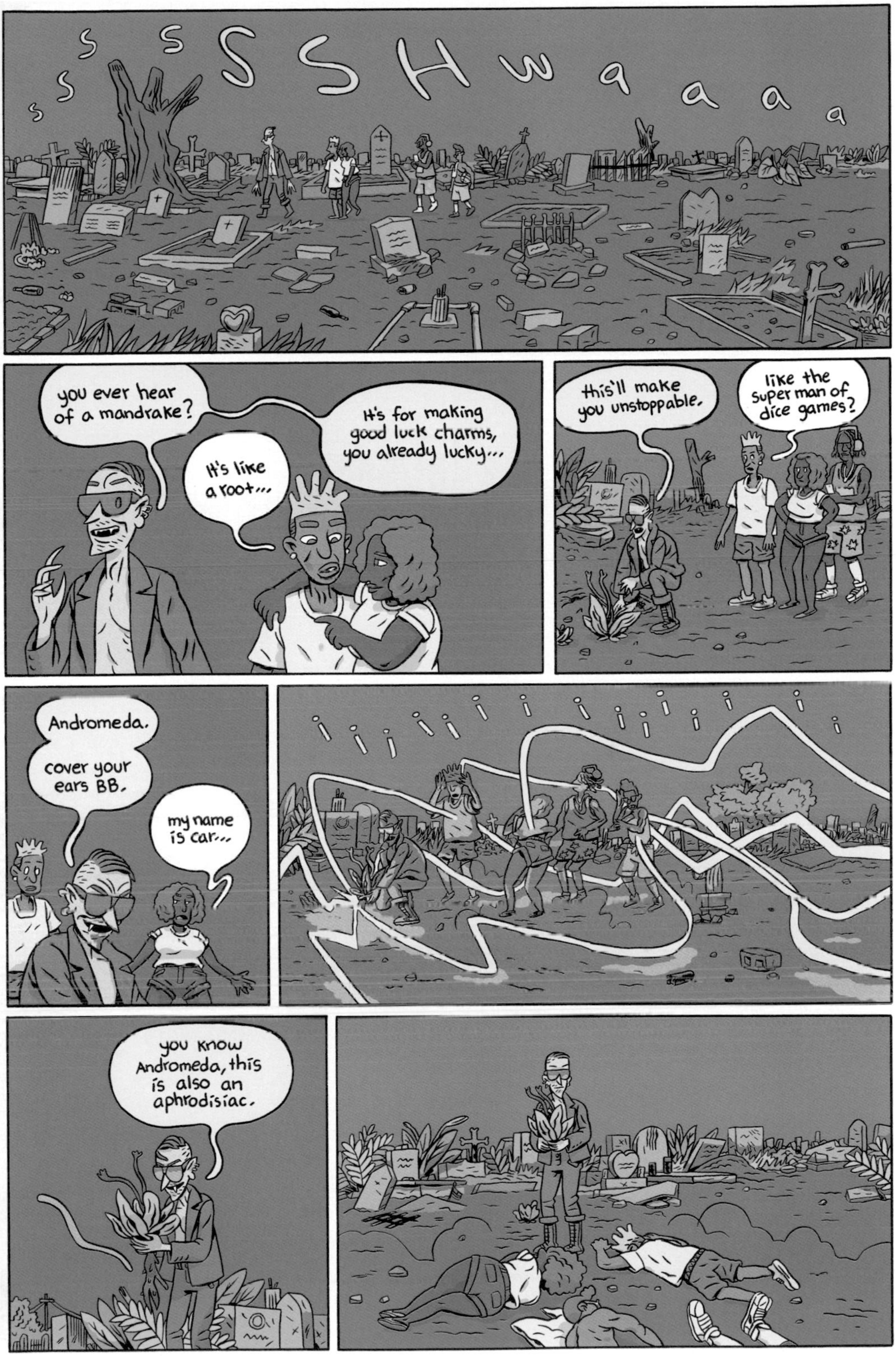
sssSSSHwaaaaa
you ever hear of a mandrake?
it's like a root...
it's for making good luck charms, you already lucky...
this'll make you unstoppable.
like the superman of dice games?
Andromeda.
cover your ears BB.
my name is car...
iiiiiiiiiiiiiiiiiii
you know Andromeda, this is also an aphrodisiac.

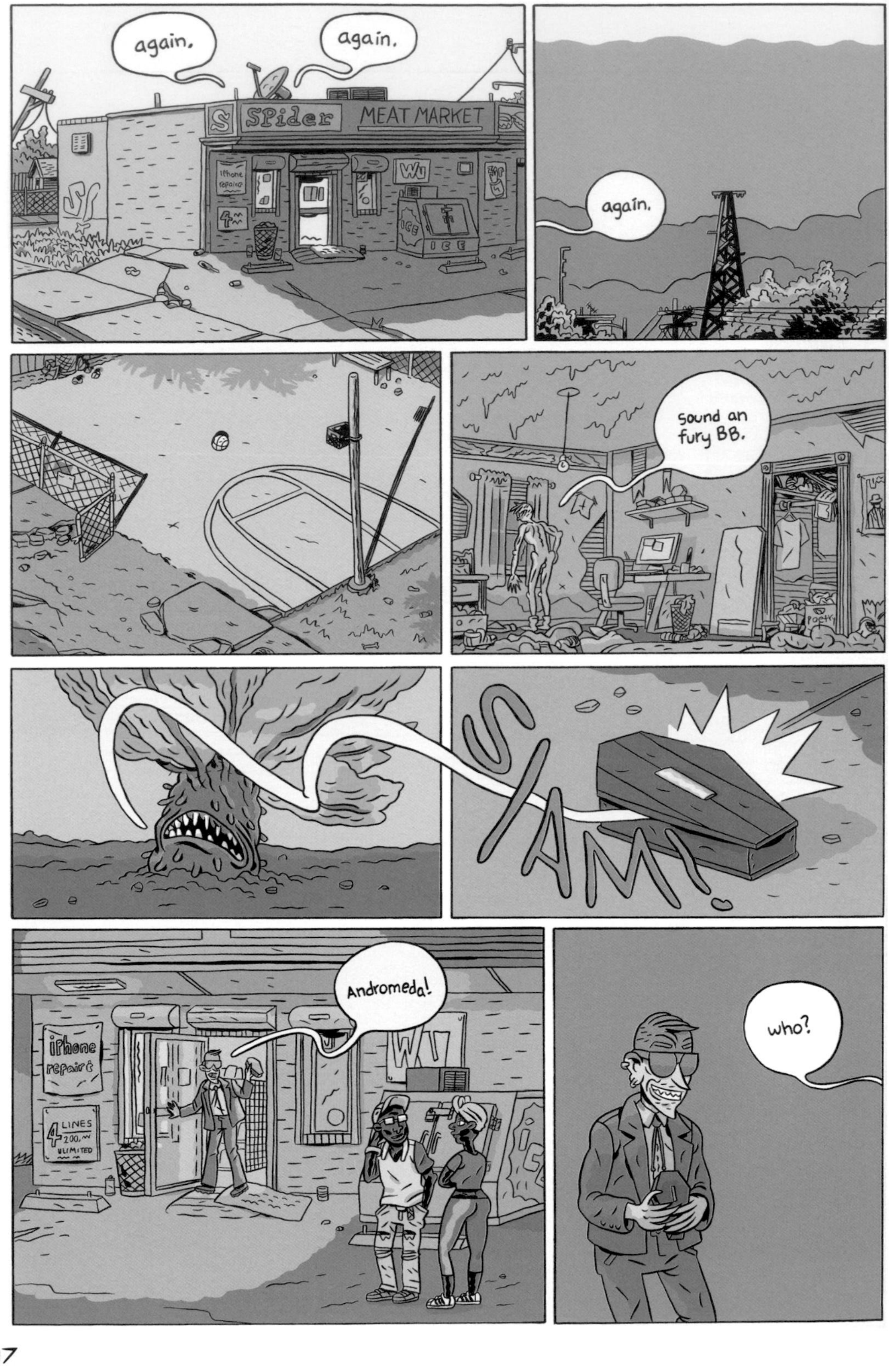
again.
again.
SPider
MEAT MARKET
iPhone repair
again.
sound an fury BB.
SLAM
Andromeda!
iPhone repair
4 LINES 200
who?

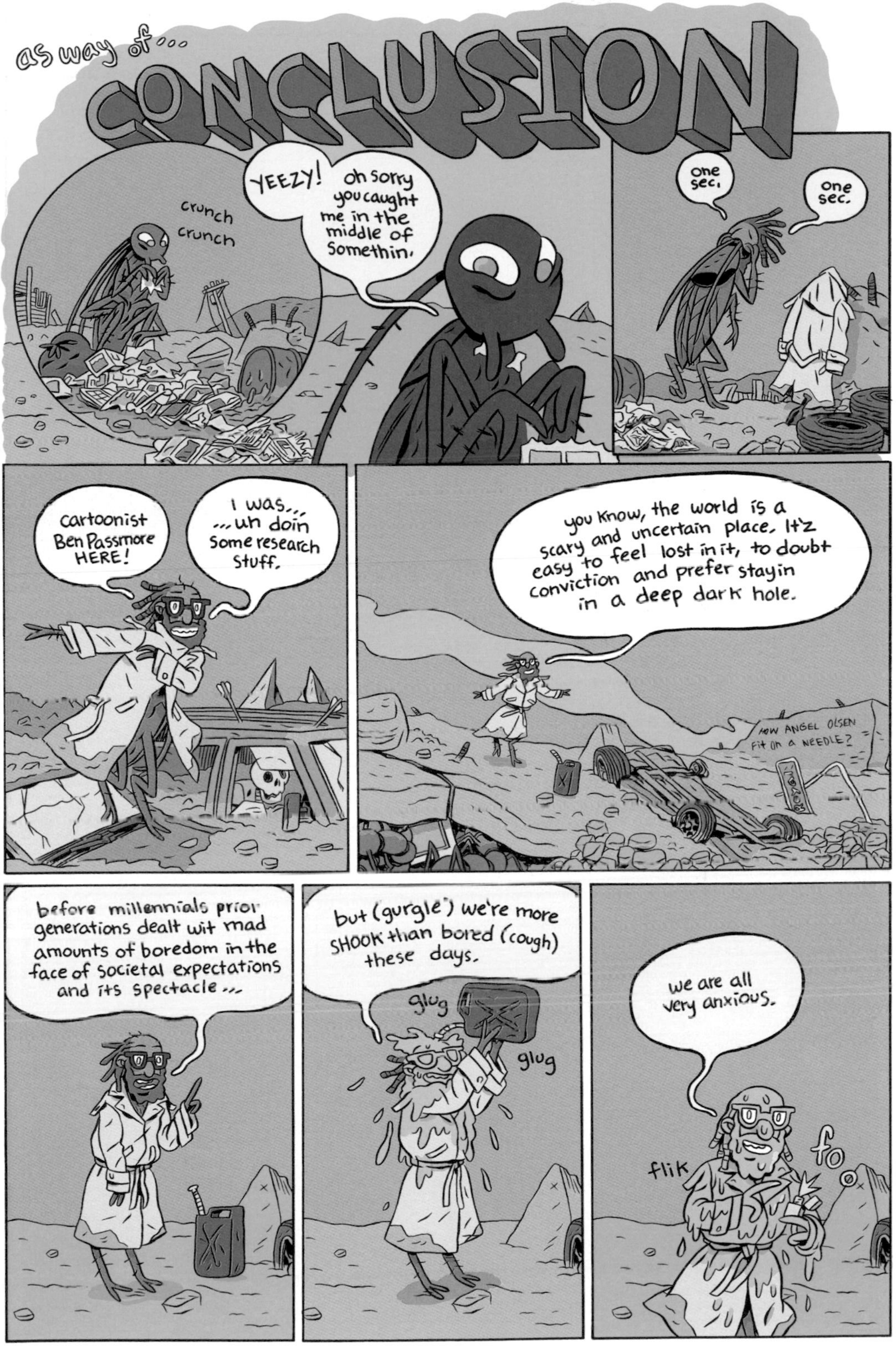
as way of...
CONCLUSION
crunch
crunch
YEEZY!
oh sorry you caught me in the middle of Somethin.
one sec,
one sec.
cartoonist Ben Passmore HERE!
I was... ...uh doin some research stuff.
you know, the world is a scary and uncertain place. It'z easy to feel lost in it, to doubt conviction and prefer stayin in a deep dark hole.
HOW ANGEL OLSEN Fit on A NEEDLE?
before millennials prior generations dealt wit mad amounts of boredom in the face of societal expectations and its spectacle...
but (gurgle) we're more SHOOK than bored (cough) these days.
glug
glug
we are all very anxious.
flik
fo

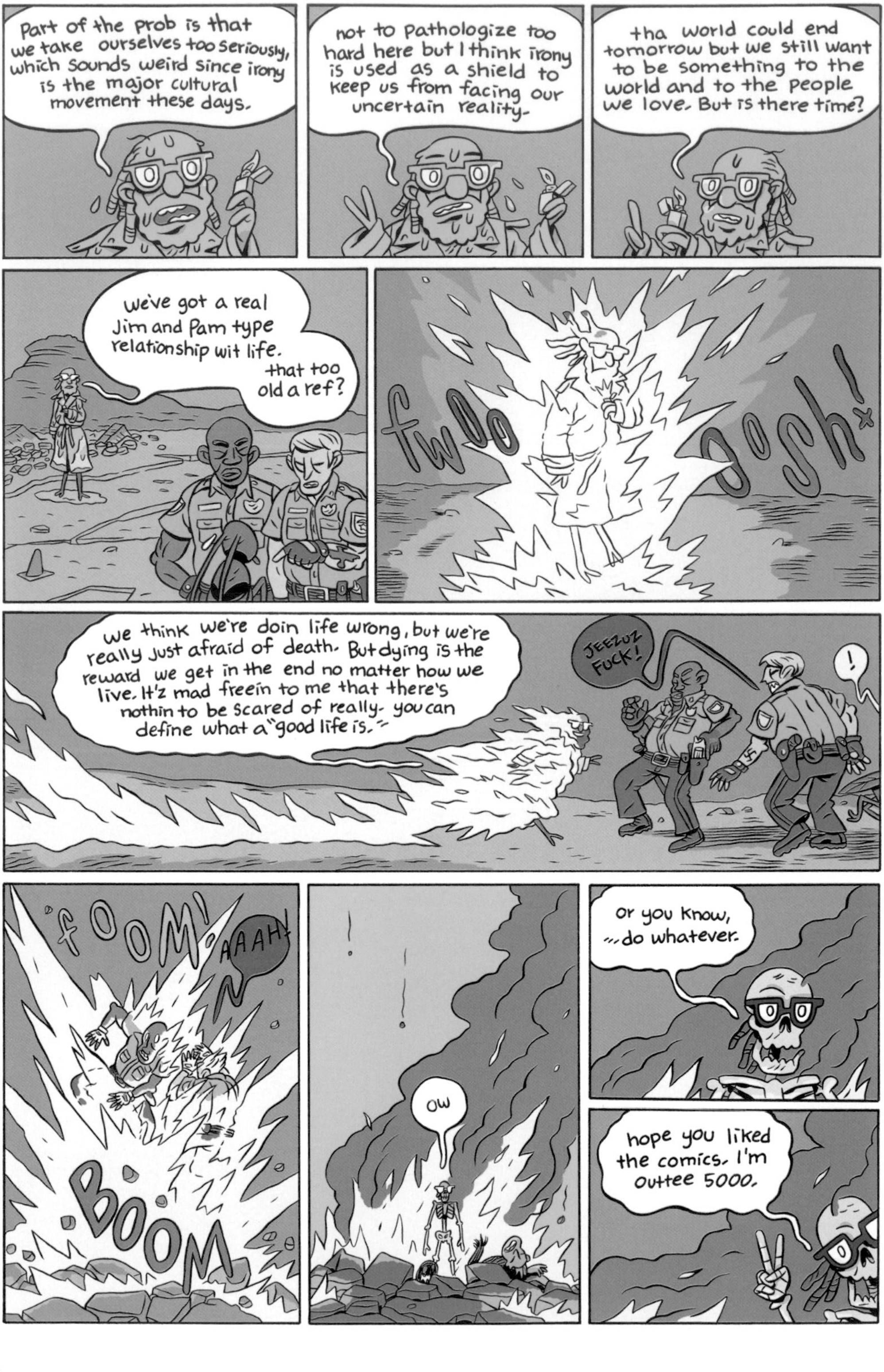
Part of the prob is that we take ourselves too seriously, which sounds weird since irony is the major cultural movement these days.
not to pathologize too hard here but I think irony is used as a shield to keep us from facing our uncertain reality.
tha world could end tomorrow but we still want to be something to the world and to the people we love. But is there time?
we've got a real Jim and Pam type relationship wit life.
that too old a ref?
fwoosh!
we think we're doin life wrong, but we're really just afraid of death. But dying is the reward we get in the end no matter how we live. It'z mad freein to me that there's nothin to be scared of really. you can define what a "good life is."
JEEZUZ FUCK!
!
fOOM!
AAAH!
BOOM
!
!
OW
or you know, ...do whatever.
hope you liked the comics. I'm outtee 5000.

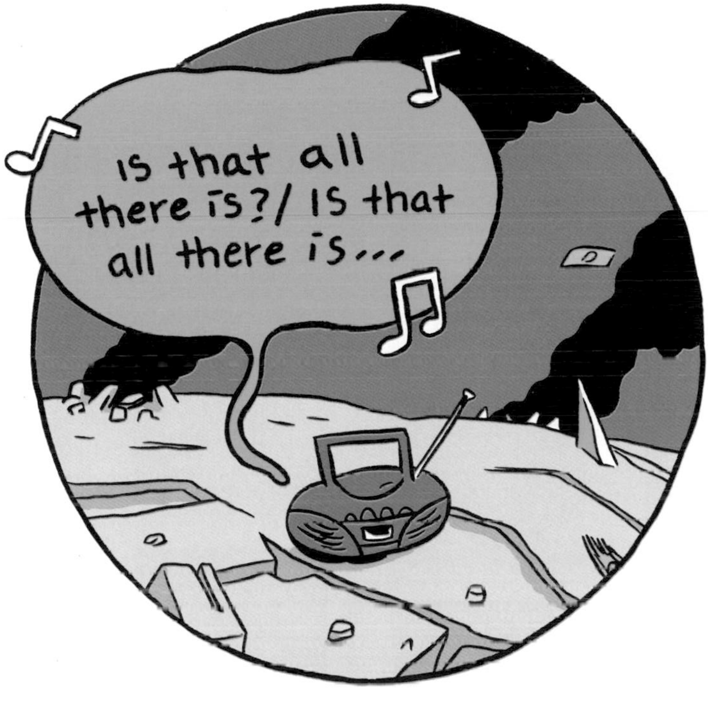
is that all there is?/ is that all there is...

also available from Silver Sprocket

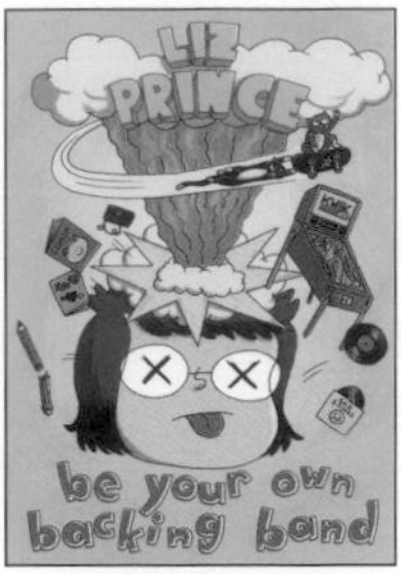
LIZ PRINCE
be your own backing band

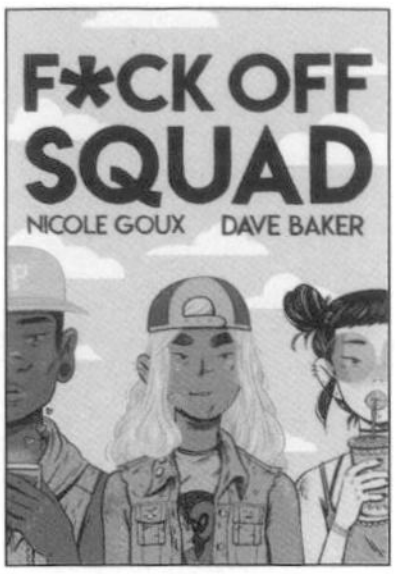
F*CK OFF SQUAD
NICOLE GOUX DAVE BAKER

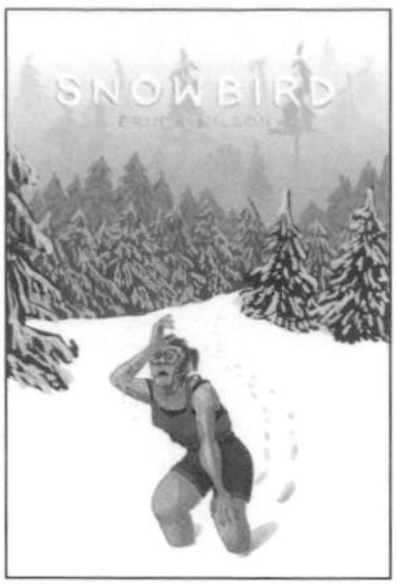
SNOWBIRD

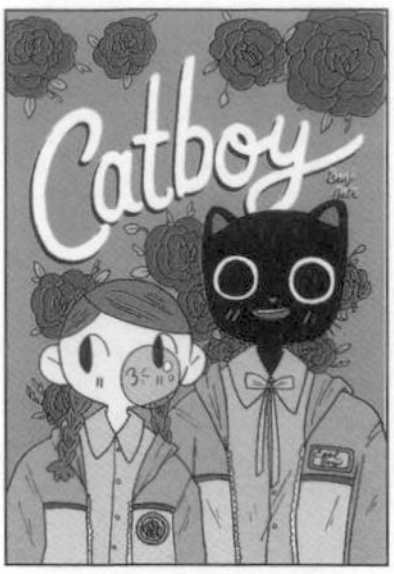
Catboy

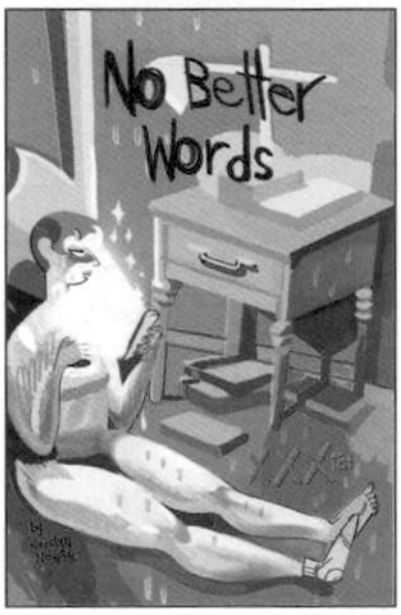
No Better Words

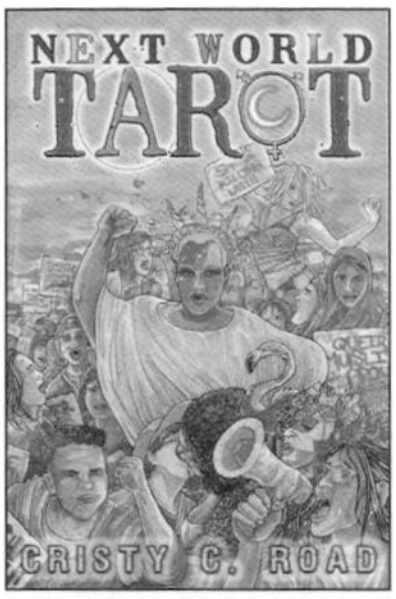
NEXT WORLD TAROT
CRISTY C. ROAD

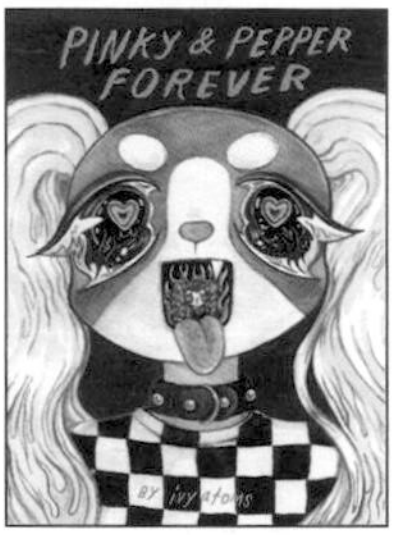
PINKY & PEPPER FOREVER

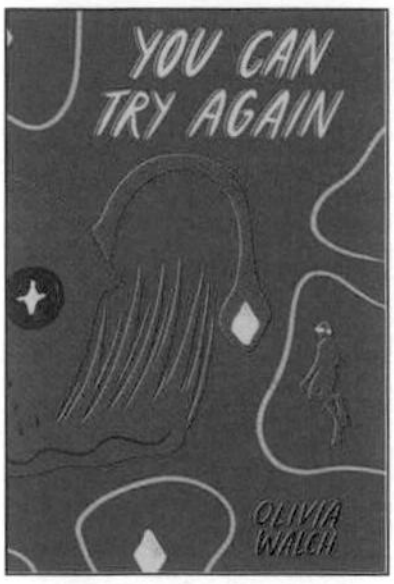
YOU CAN TRY AGAIN
OLIVIA WALCH

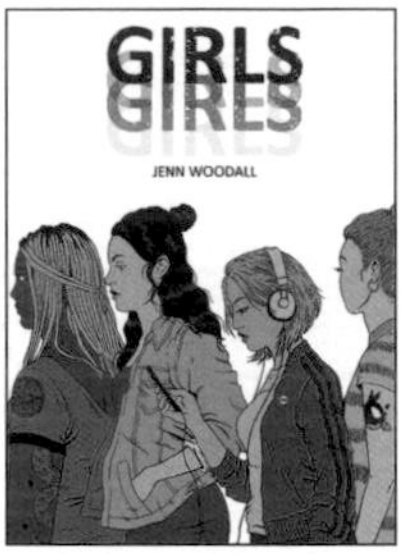
GIRLS
JENN WOODALL

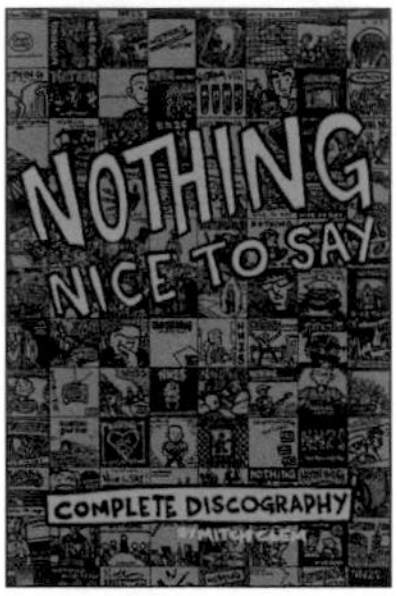
NOTHING NICE TO SAY
COMPLETE DISCOGRAPHY

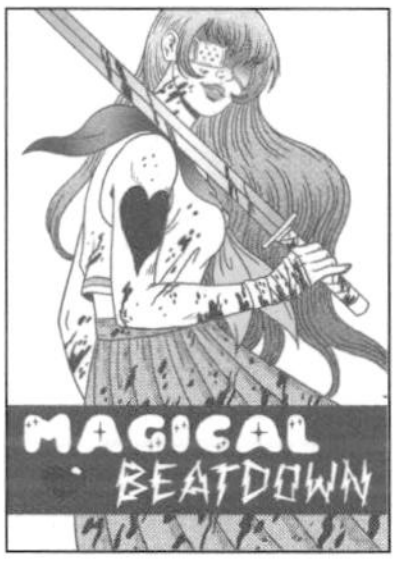
MAGICAL BEATDOWN

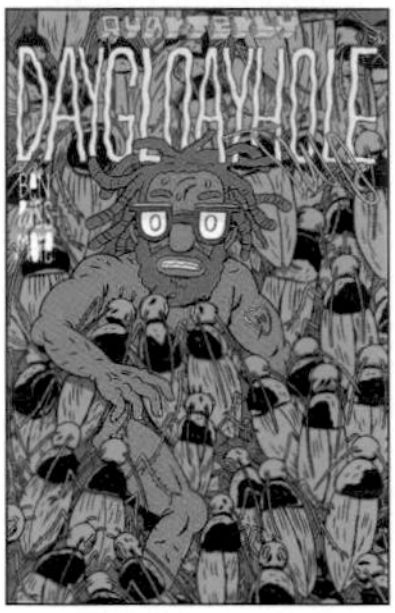

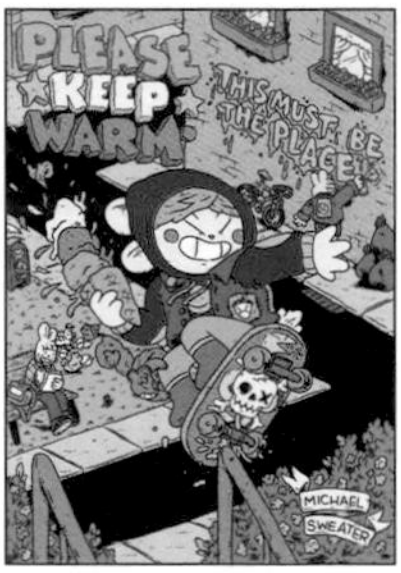
PLEASE KEEP WARM
THIS MUST BE THE PLACE
MICHAEL SWEATER

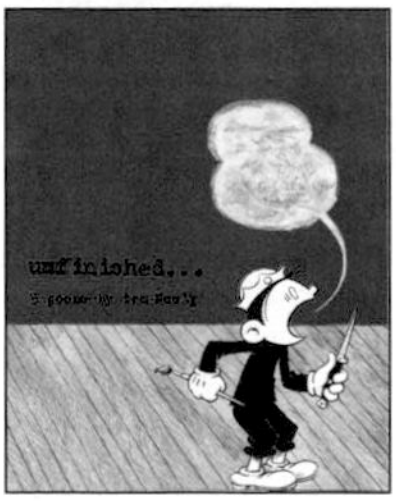
unfinished...

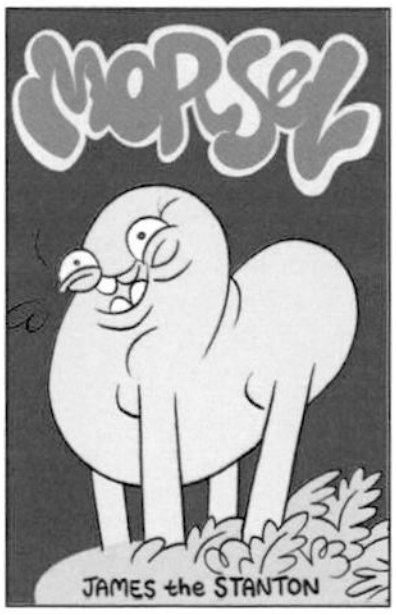
MORSEL
JAMES the STANTON

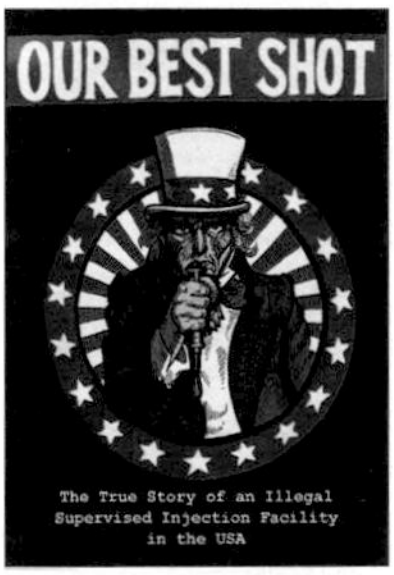
OUR BEST SHOT
The True Story of an Illegal Supervised Injection Facility in the USA

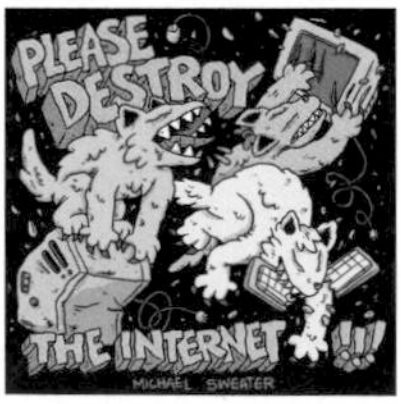
PLEASE DESTROY THE INTERNET
MICHAEL SWEATER

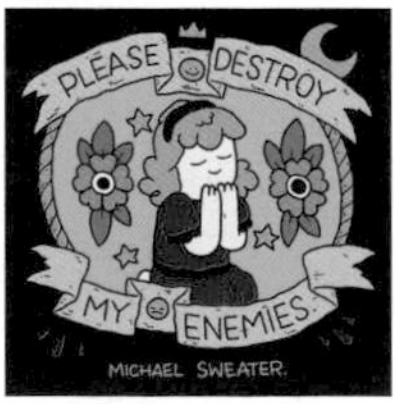
PLEASE DESTROY MY ENEMIES
MICHAEL SWEATER

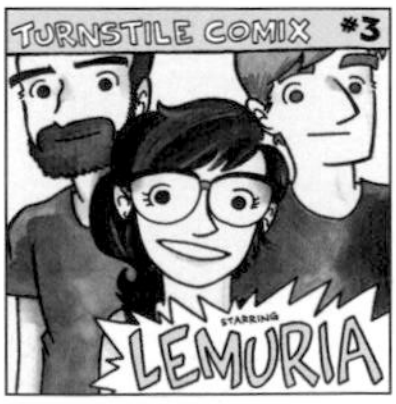
TURNSTILE COMIX #3
STARRING LEMURIA

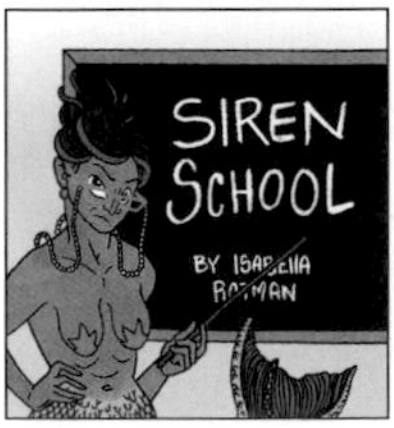
SIREN SCHOOL
BY ISABELLA ROTMAN

www.silversprocket.net

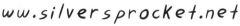

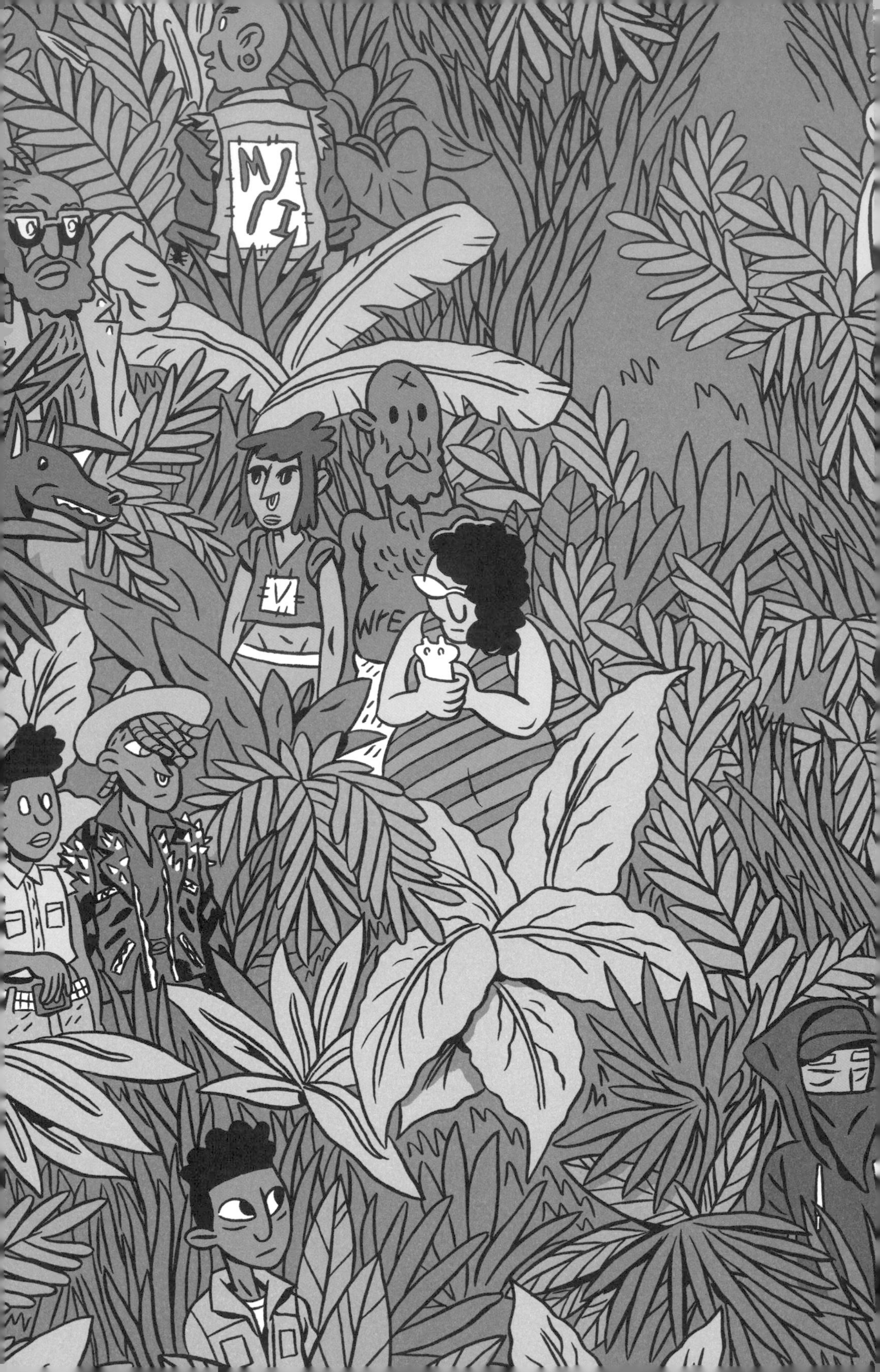
M/I
V
wrE